I HOPE THIS HELPS

I HOPE THIS HELPS

COMICS AND CURES FOR 21ST CENTURY PANIC

BY TOMMY SIEGEL

Andrews McMeel
PUBLISHING®

Andrews McMeel Publishing
a division of Andrews McMeel Universal
1130 Walnut Street, Kansas City, Missouri 64106

www.andrewsmcmeel.com

20 21 22 23 24 SDB 10 9 8 7 6 5 4 3 2 1

ISBN: 978-1-5248-6073-8

Library of Congress Control Number: 2020937000

Editor: Lucas Wetzel
Art Director: Diane Marsh
Production Editor: Amy Strassner
Production Manager: Tamara Haus

ATTENTION: SCHOOLS AND BUSINESSES
Andrews McMeel books are available at quantity discounts
with bulk purchase for educational, business, or sales
promotional use. For information, please e-mail the
Andrews McMeel Publishing Special Sales Department:
specialsales@amuniversal.com.

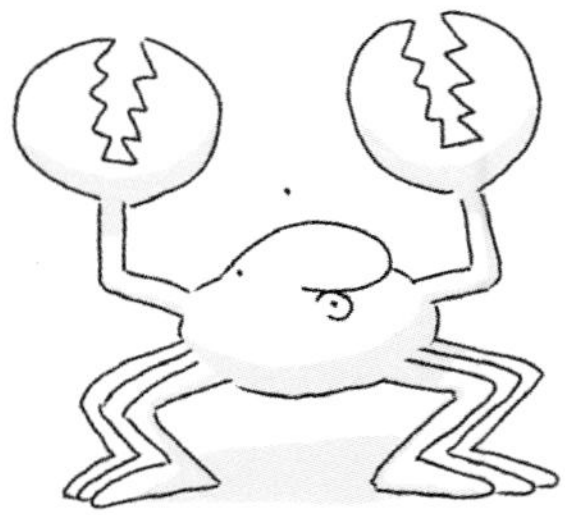

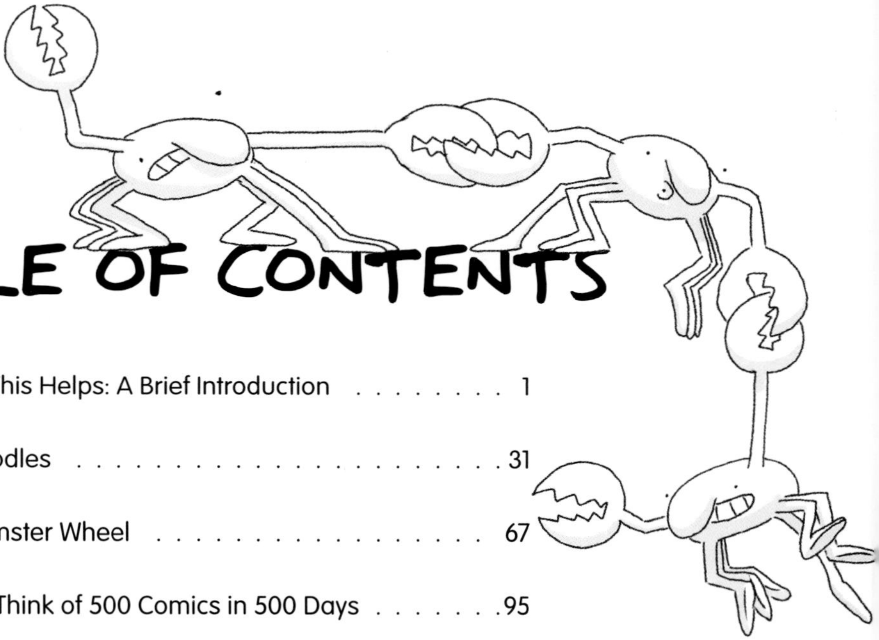

TABLE OF CONTENTS

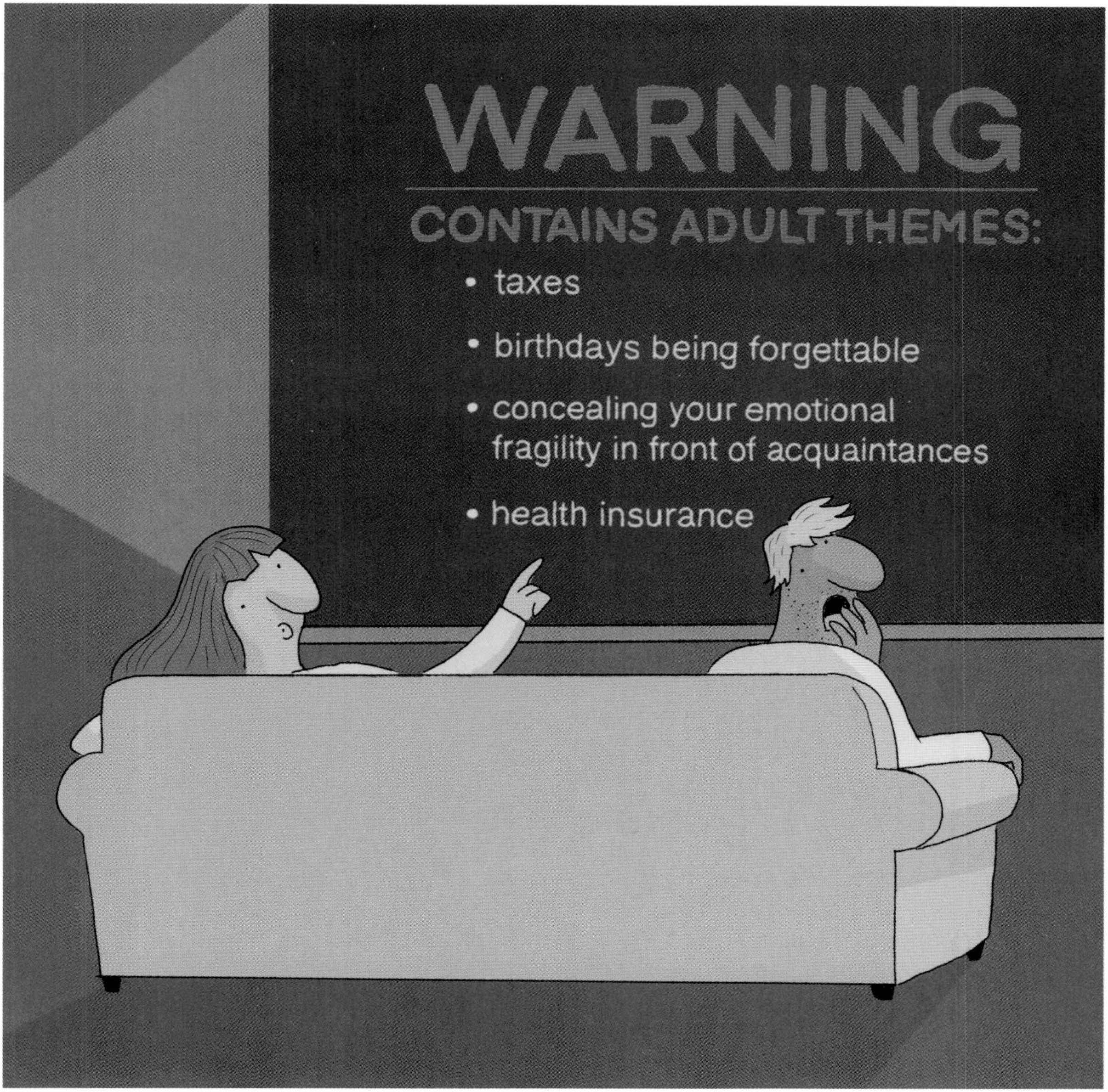
WARNING
CONTAINS ADULT THEMES:
• taxes
• birthdays being forgettable
• concealing your emotional fragility in front of acquaintances
• health insurance

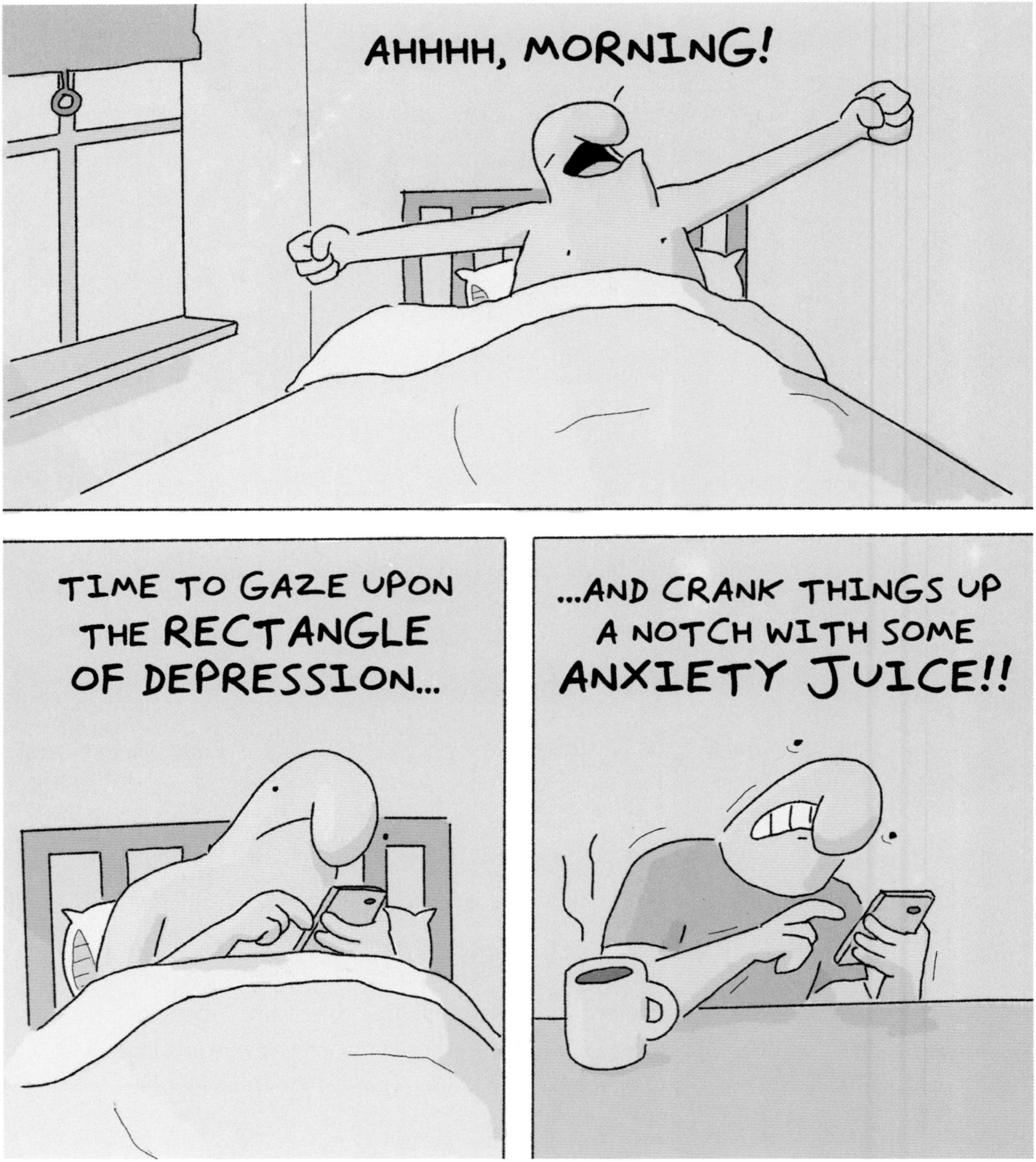
AHHHH, MORNING!
TIME TO GAZE UPON THE RECTANGLE OF DEPRESSION...
...AND CRANK THINGS UP A NOTCH WITH SOME ANXIETY JUICE!!

I HOPE THIS HELPS:
A BRIEF
INTRODUCTION

The sacred morning ritual of the 21st century begins. I wake up and automatically reach for my phone. Before my brain can even register what day of the week it is or whether I'm wearing pants, I've started mindlessly thumbing through social media. A parade of disconnected images flies by. A GIF of a cat in a birthday hat. News about the most recent colossal wildfire. A picture of a distant cousin's soggy-looking brunch. A mix of outrage and defiant support of the latest political tweet, as well as outrage over someone else's defiant support of someone's outrage. An acquaintance from high school got a weird-looking cat but everyone congratulates them anyway. A GoFundMe raising money to pay for a friend of a friend's medical debt. A former prom date posts a multi-paragraph confessional essay about her last breakup and announces a social media hiatus. A video of a bulldog riding a skateboard better than I can. Before I know it, 30 minutes have passed, and my brain is whirring at 500 mph trying to retroactively process and/or suppress a thousand different emotional reactions to a convoluted soup of disconnected images and words.

Like most Americans who aren't Amish, I was addicted. I still am, depending on the day. You probably are too, as the average time Americans spend looking at social media has skyrocketed to *over five hours a day* as of 2019 — a fact that will probably seem obvious to anyone who has looked up from their phone to notice all the other people looking at their phones. I tried everything. Timers on my phone. Deleting apps or hiding them in hard-to-locate folders. And when it worked, it worked! But, I always ended up relapsing. Worst of all, I thought it was a highly personal moral failing that other people were effectively managing. This was a few years ago when the widespread problem wasn't named by academics, with brain science and psychology to back it up. Humans, after all, are highly social animals with a long evolutionary history baked into our perceived needs. Technology companies, recognizing this, have finally found a way to exploit our deep desire for human connection and belonging as a vessel to sell ads.

REDUCING PHONE ADDICTION: A GUIDE

DELETE ALL OF YOUR SOCIAL MEDIA APPS AND RE-DOWNLOAD THEM THE VERY NEXT DAY

GET AN APP THAT TRACKS YOUR PHONE USAGE AND MAKES YOU FEEL GUILTY BUT DOESN'T CHANGE YOUR BEHAVIOR

BUY A FLIP PHONE AND BE LOST ALL THE TIME

IMMERSE YOURSELF IN GARFIELD-THEMED VIRTUAL REALITY SO ENGROSSING THAT YOU FORGET YOU ARE ALIVE

At that time in early 2018, I was still a full-time musician and struggling with how to promote my creative output to the wider world without getting sucked into a vortex of addictive behaviors. With a suspicion that my brain was being casually abused by social media companies and a growing sense of frustration with the mechanics of promoting my band's music online, I started to wonder: If I'm addicted to this thing, is there any way to use social media to my advantage? As in: If I'm gonna smoke cigarettes, shouldn't I at least be *enjoying* it? And if I'm not even enjoying it, shouldn't it at least be furthering my career? Shouldn't it, at minimum, be . . . you know, *useful*?

Over the course of 2017, I had watched one of my favorite comic artists, Branson Reese, draw 365 comics in 365 days. I loved the outlandish ambition of it, and I couldn't help but notice that his joke writing and drawing style got sharper and sharper with each comic. As a lifelong doodler from a young age, I wondered if I could make similar strides by taking on the same challenge. *Maybe,* I thought, I could make this social media hellscape work to my advantage. But before I embarked on this journey, I sent him a message asking if I should give it a try. His answer was succinct and prophetic: "It's horrible, and you should do it."

Armed in the beginning with only a scanner, pens, and paper, I set off on a drawing gauntlet that eventually produced 500 consecutive daily comics and 500 consecutive days of no free time at all. The book that follows is a self-curated assortment of my favorite comics from the project, along with some context and commentary on the experience of doing this half-ambitious, half-idiotic undertaking.

Some of the comics have been spruced up from their original state; one of the strangest difficulties about assembling this project was that I sucked less and less as an artist over its duration, which rendered hundreds of these comics unpublishable by my current standards. Rather than waste valuable Dead Trees™ on comics I can't bear to look at, I figured I'd special-edition[1] a handful of them to honor the project in its totality without putting out a book containing drawings that filled me with shame.

And though you are currently reading these comics in the relaxing confines of a book, the project as it unfolded was primarily a social media venture. So, if you'd like to see the project in its terrifying warts-and-all wholeness, you can scroll endlessly through my feeds on:

Twitter: @tommysiegel
Facebook: @tommysiegel
Instagram: @tommysiegel

Anyway, here are some dumb drawings I made. I hope you find them helpful. I think they helped me.

---

1. And yes, like George Lucas, I used modern computer software to spruce up my old comics. And not coincidentally, Jar Jar Binks is featured in this book. Yousa welcome.

CHOOSE YOUR METHOD OF SELF-CARE

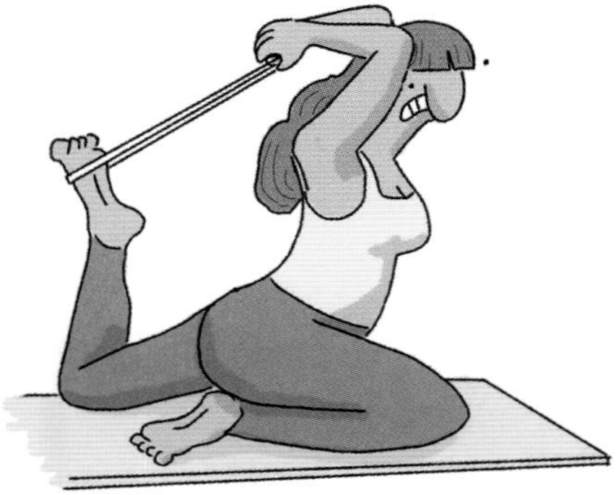

CONTORT YOUR BODY
INTO PAINFUL SHAPES

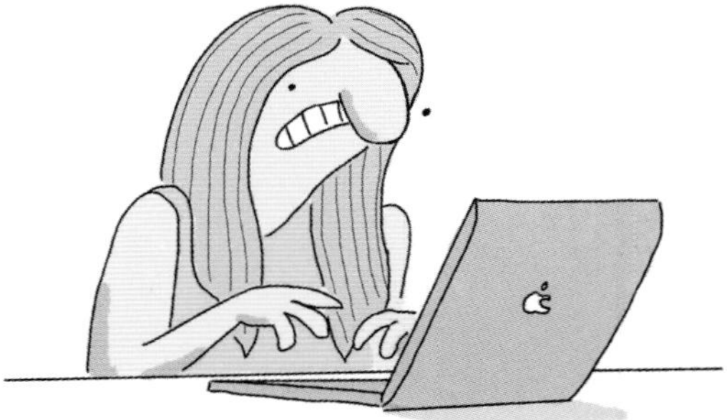

SPEND A WEEK'S SALARY ON
DUBIOUS ETSY PRODUCTS

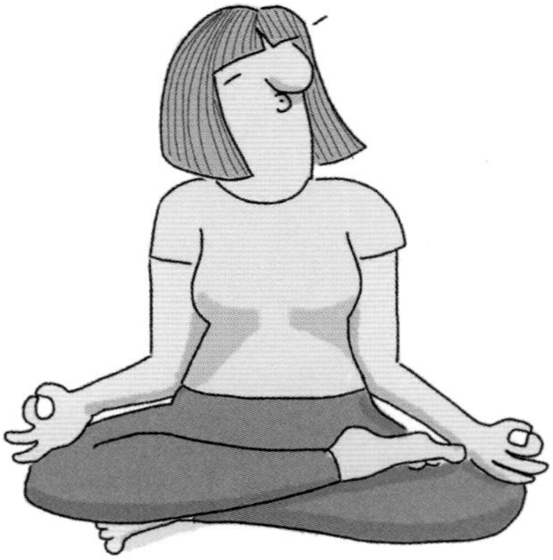

SIT SILENTLY AND PRETEND
YOU HAVE NO BRAIN

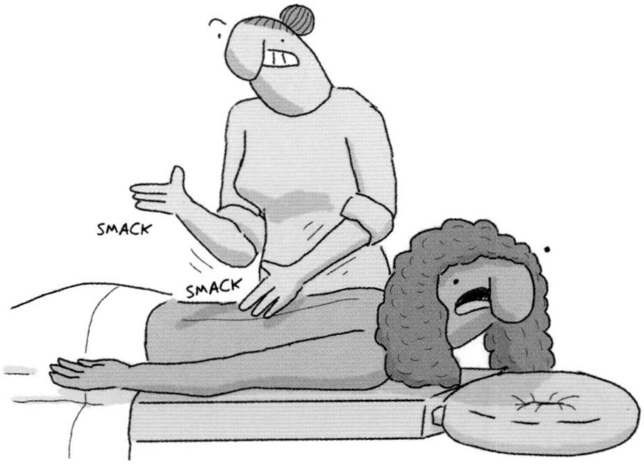
SMACK
SMACK

PAY A STRANGER
TO HIT YOU

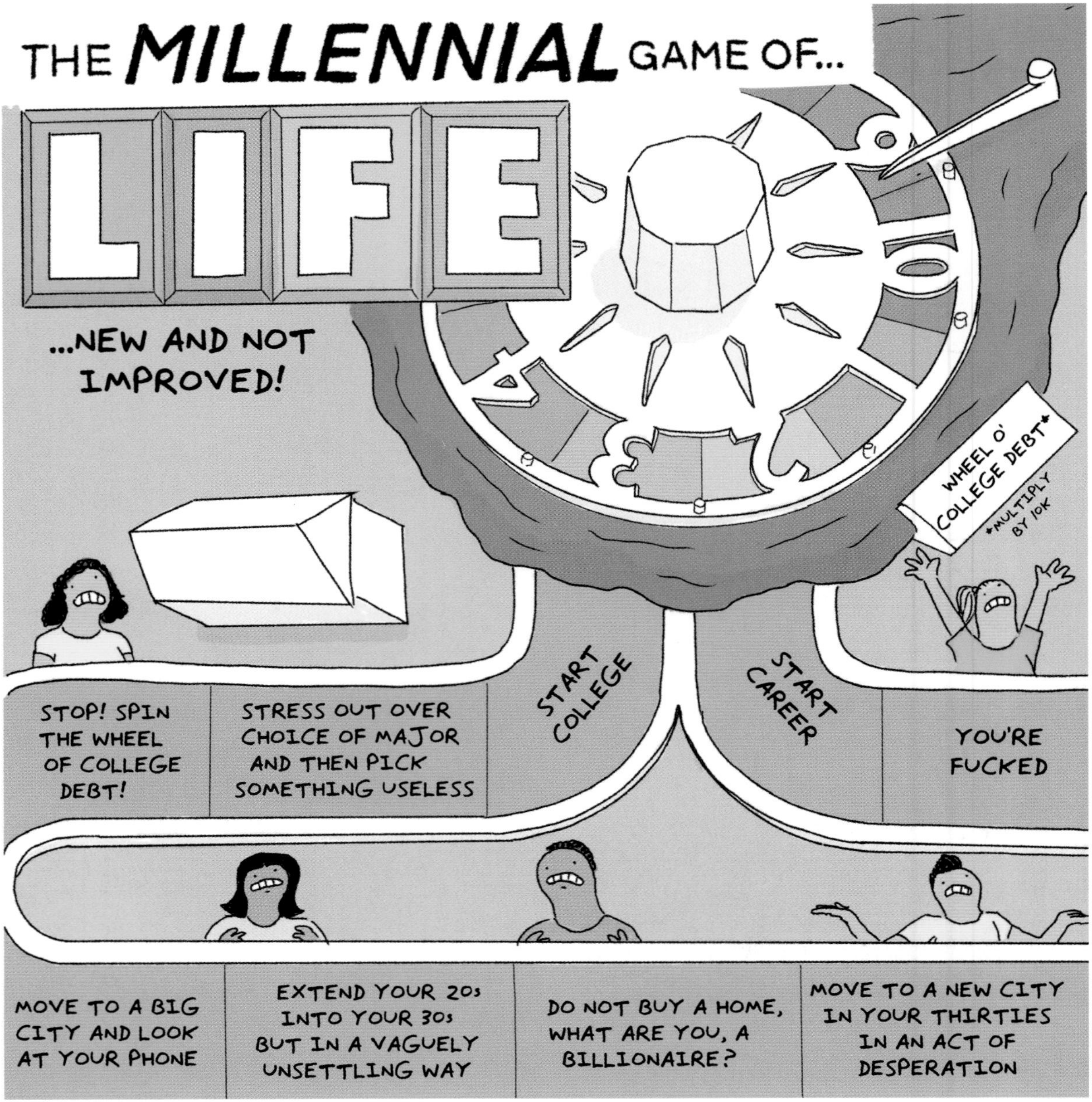
THE MILLENNIAL GAME OF...
LIFE
...NEW AND NOT IMPROVED!
WHEEL O' COLLEGE DEBT*
*MULTIPLY BY 10K
STOP! SPIN THE WHEEL OF COLLEGE DEBT!
STRESS OUT OVER CHOICE OF MAJOR AND THEN PICK SOMETHING USELESS
START COLLEGE
START CAREER
YOU'RE FUCKED
MOVE TO A BIG CITY AND LOOK AT YOUR PHONE
EXTEND YOUR 20s INTO YOUR 30s BUT IN A VAGUELY UNSETTLING WAY
DO NOT BUY A HOME, WHAT ARE YOU, A BILLIONAIRE?
MOVE TO A NEW CITY IN YOUR THIRTIES IN AN ACT OF DESPERATION

IT'S THAT EASY!

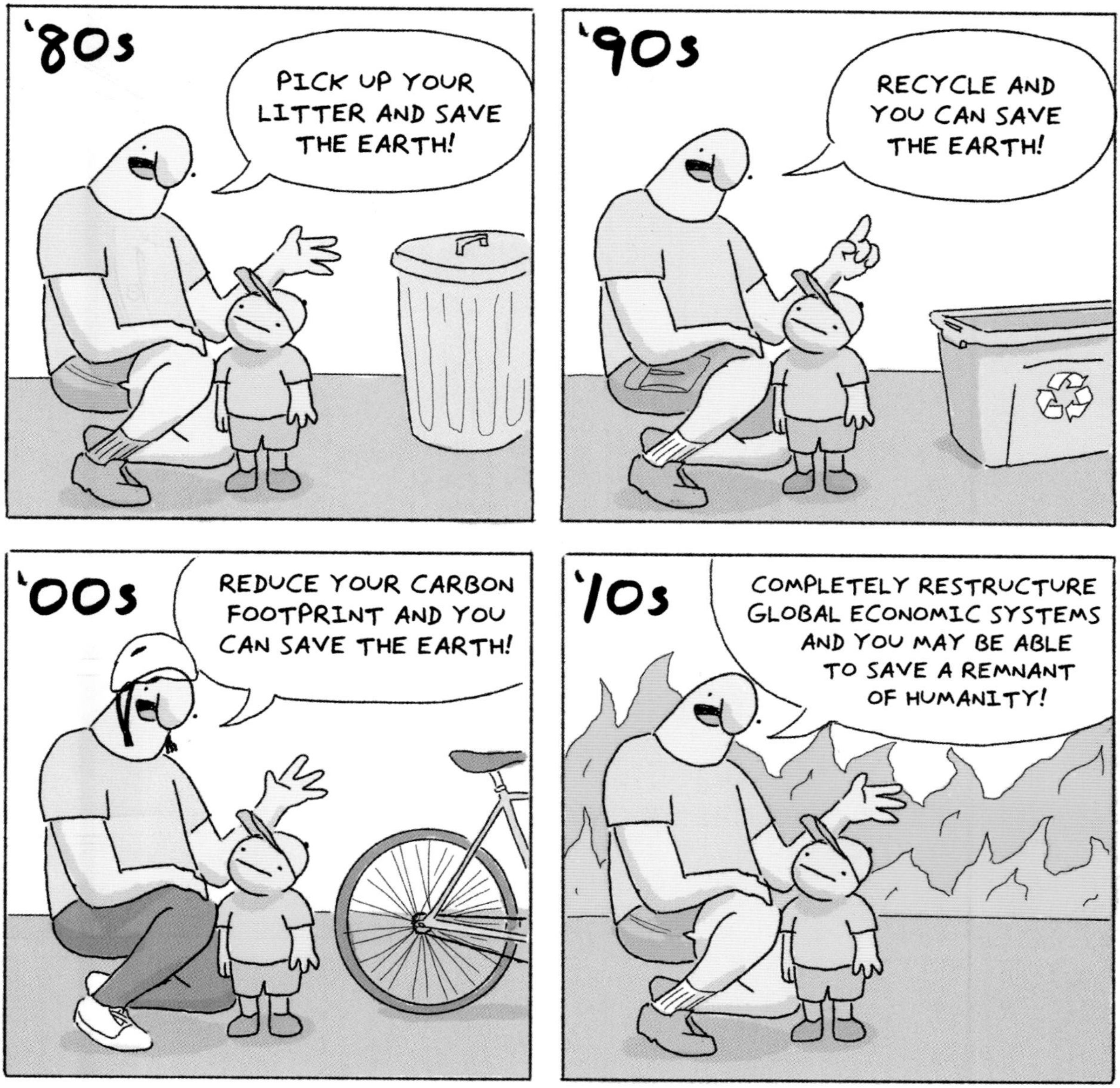
'80s
PICK UP YOUR LITTER AND SAVE THE EARTH!
'90s
RECYCLE AND YOU CAN SAVE THE EARTH!
'00s
REDUCE YOUR CARBON FOOTPRINT AND YOU CAN SAVE THE EARTH!
'10s
COMPLETELY RESTRUCTURE GLOBAL ECONOMIC SYSTEMS AND YOU MAY BE ABLE TO SAVE A REMNANT OF HUMANITY!

WHAT YOUR COFFEE PREPARATION METHOD SAYS ABOUT YOU

NOT REALLY INTO
ABSTRACT ART

HAS A NEW YORKER
SUBSCRIPTION BUT
HAS NEVER READ IT

FACE THE FACTS:
YOU'RE FAKING
FANCY

HAS A NEW YORKER
SUBSCRIPTION AND
SOMEHOW READS IT

BELIEVES VINYL IS
ALWAYS HIGHER
QUALITY DESPITE
CONFLICTING
EVIDENCE

UNBEARABLE
YOUNG SNOB
OR GERIATRIC
ITALIAN

WHO HURT YOU

TYPES OF ONLINE-ING

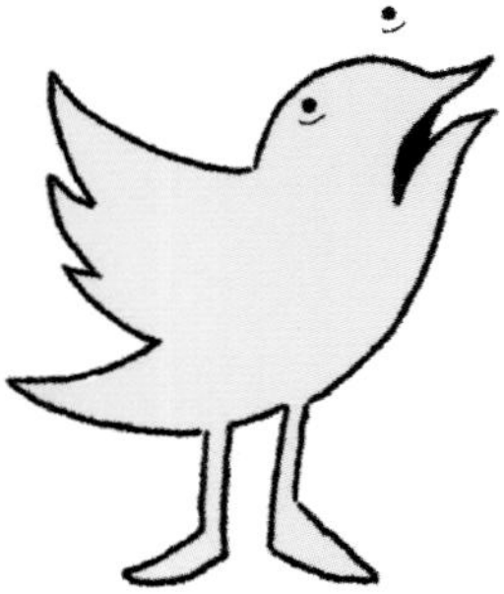

PERFORMATIVE
ANXIETY/DEPRESSION

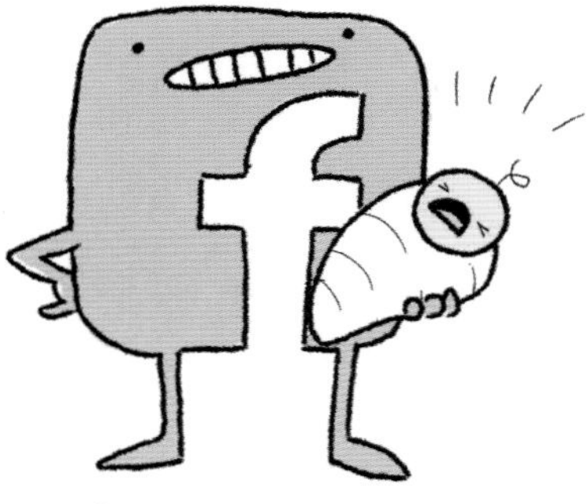

PERFORMATIVE
LIFE MILESTONE

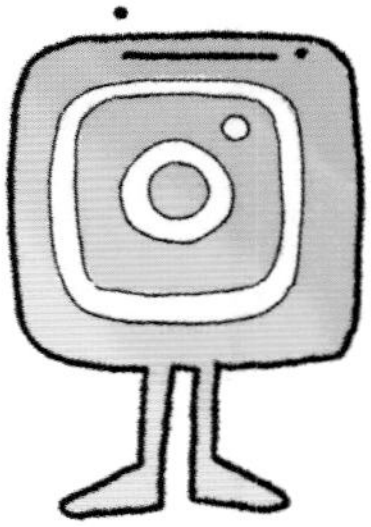

PERFORMATIVE
LEISURE

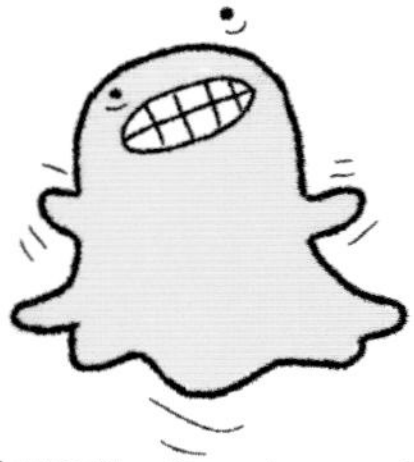

PERFORMATIVE
ATTENTION DEFICIT
DISORDER

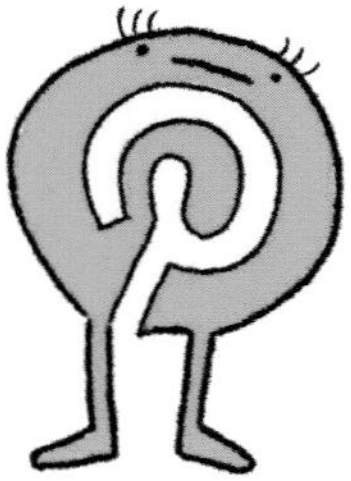

PERFORMATIVE
PREEMPTIVE
WEDDING REGISTRY

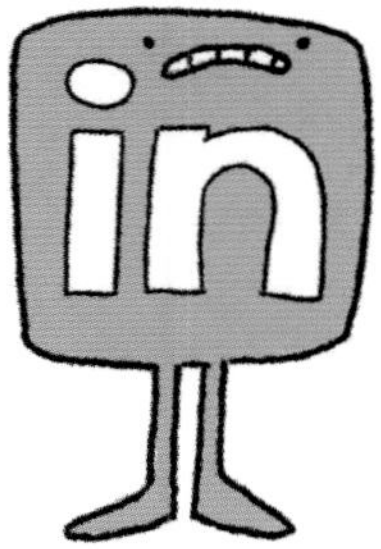

PERFORMATIVE
UNEMPLOYMENT

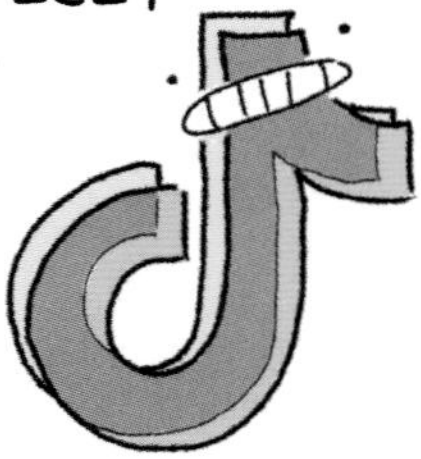

ACTUALLY PERFORMING, BUT
FOR A CHINESE DATA FIRM

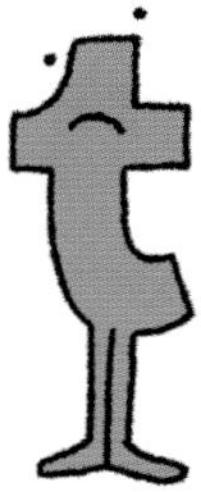

PERFORMING
FOR NO ONE AT ALL

NEW TO SELFIES? PICK A STYLE!

PRETEND YOU ARE A DUCK

PRETEND YOU ARE A FISH

ACCIDENTALLY PRETEND YOU ARE A WALRUS

USE INVASIVE FACIAL RECOGNITION SOFTWARE TO PRETEND YOU ARE A CAT

PRETEND THAT BEING ALONE ON YOUR PHONE IS FUN

THE STAGES OF GENTRIFICATION: A GUIDE

PUNKS AND
WEIRDO ARTISTS

GRAPHIC DESIGNERS AND
SYNTH-POP BANDS WHO
MAKE AD MUSIC

CREATIVES WHO WORK
FOR PFIZER BUT DON'T
HAVE AN OFFICE

TECH BROS WHO LIKE
LCD SOUNDSYSTEM

FINANCE BROS WHO
HAVEN'T HEARD OF
LCD SOUNDSYSTEM

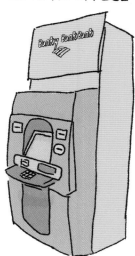

NO PEOPLE, JUST
ATMs AND PROPERTY
SPECULATION

MINDFULNESS MEDITATION vs MINDLESS SCROLLING

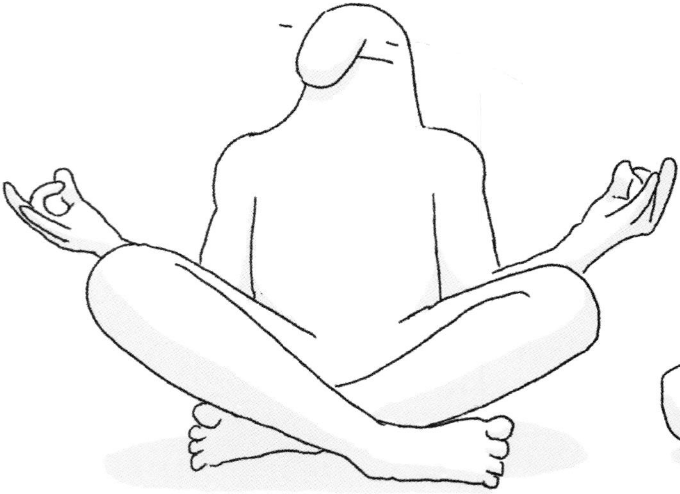

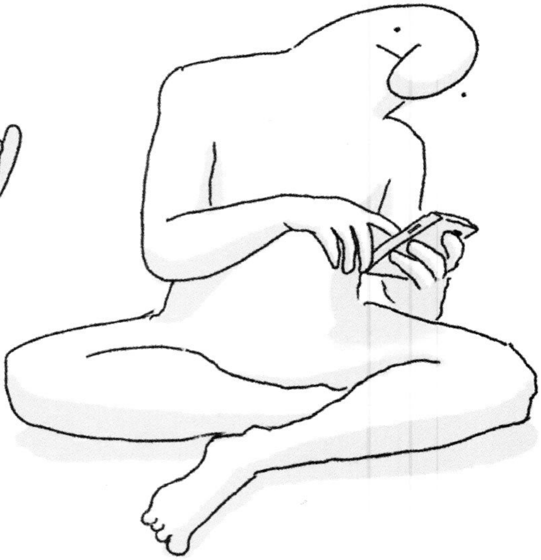

MINDFULNESS MEDITATION

- OH NO, FEELINGS
- WAIT AM I ALLOWED TO FEEL OR SHOULD I NOT
- 1 MINUTE FEELS LIKE 30 MINUTES
- SO BORING THAT IT'S STIMULATING

MINDLESS SCROLLING

- AHH, NO FEELINGS
- EXCEPT THE VAGUE UNDERCURRENT OF DREAD
- 30 MINUTES FEELS LIKE 1 MINUTE
- SO STIMULATING THAT IT'S BORING

THE POWER OF POSITIVE SELF-IMAGE

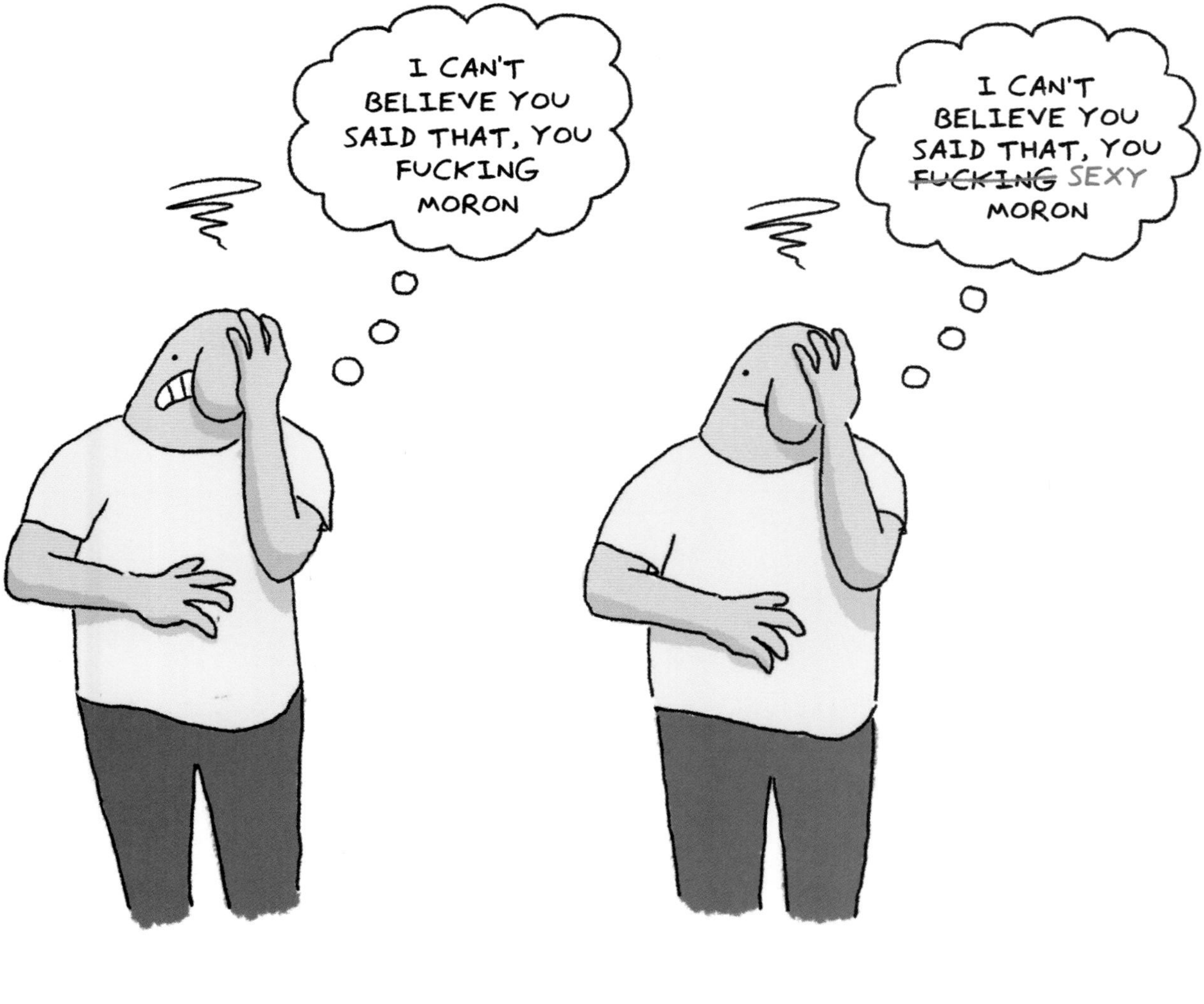
I CAN'T BELIEVE YOU SAID THAT, YOU FUCKING MORON
I CAN'T BELIEVE YOU SAID THAT, YOU ~~FUCKING~~ SEXY MORON

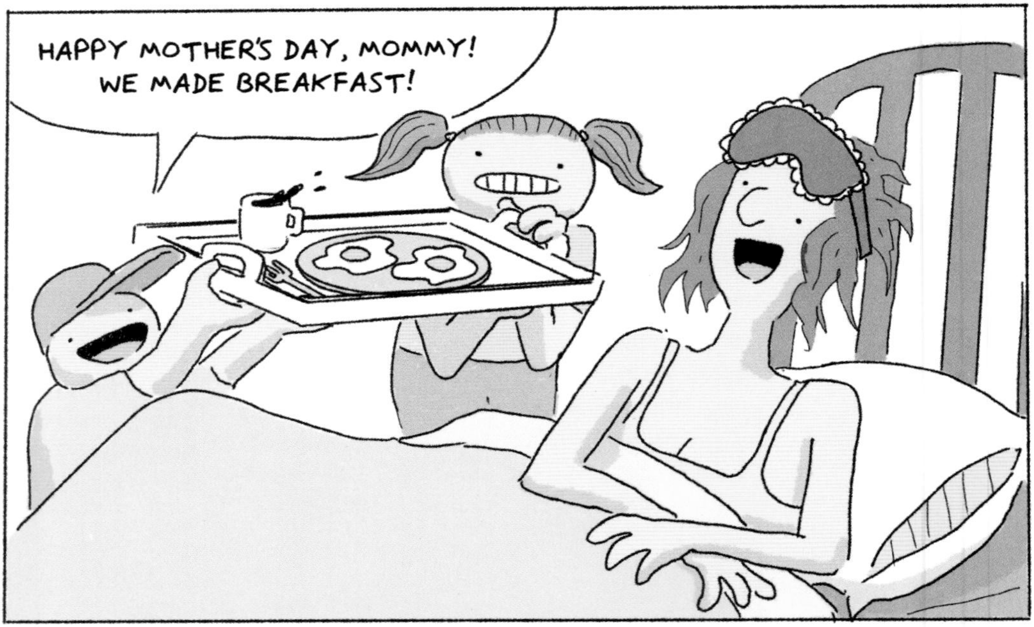
HAPPY MOTHER'S DAY, MOMMY!
WE MADE BREAKFAST!

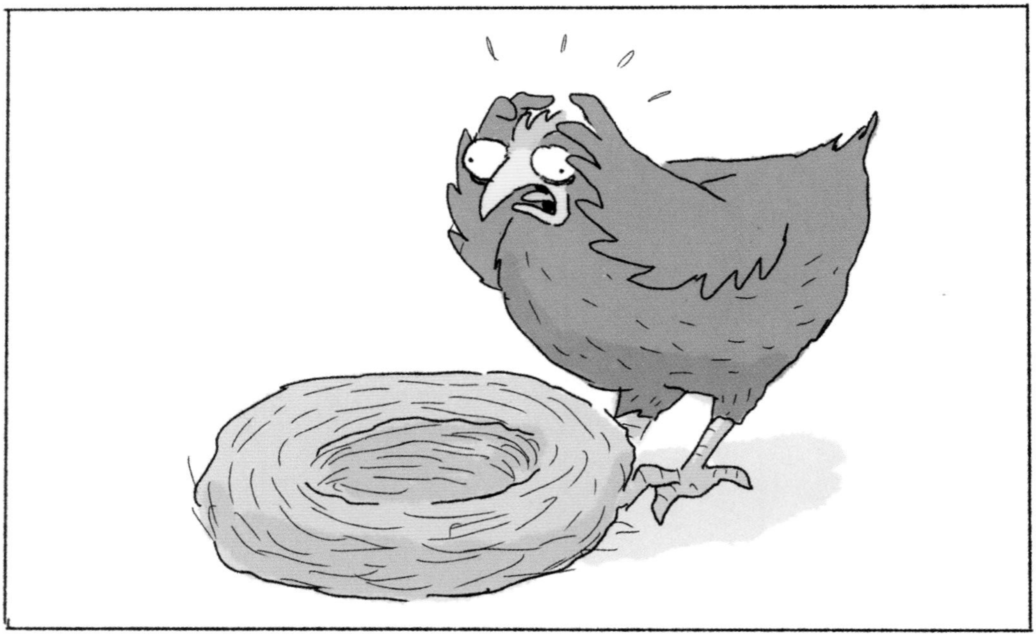

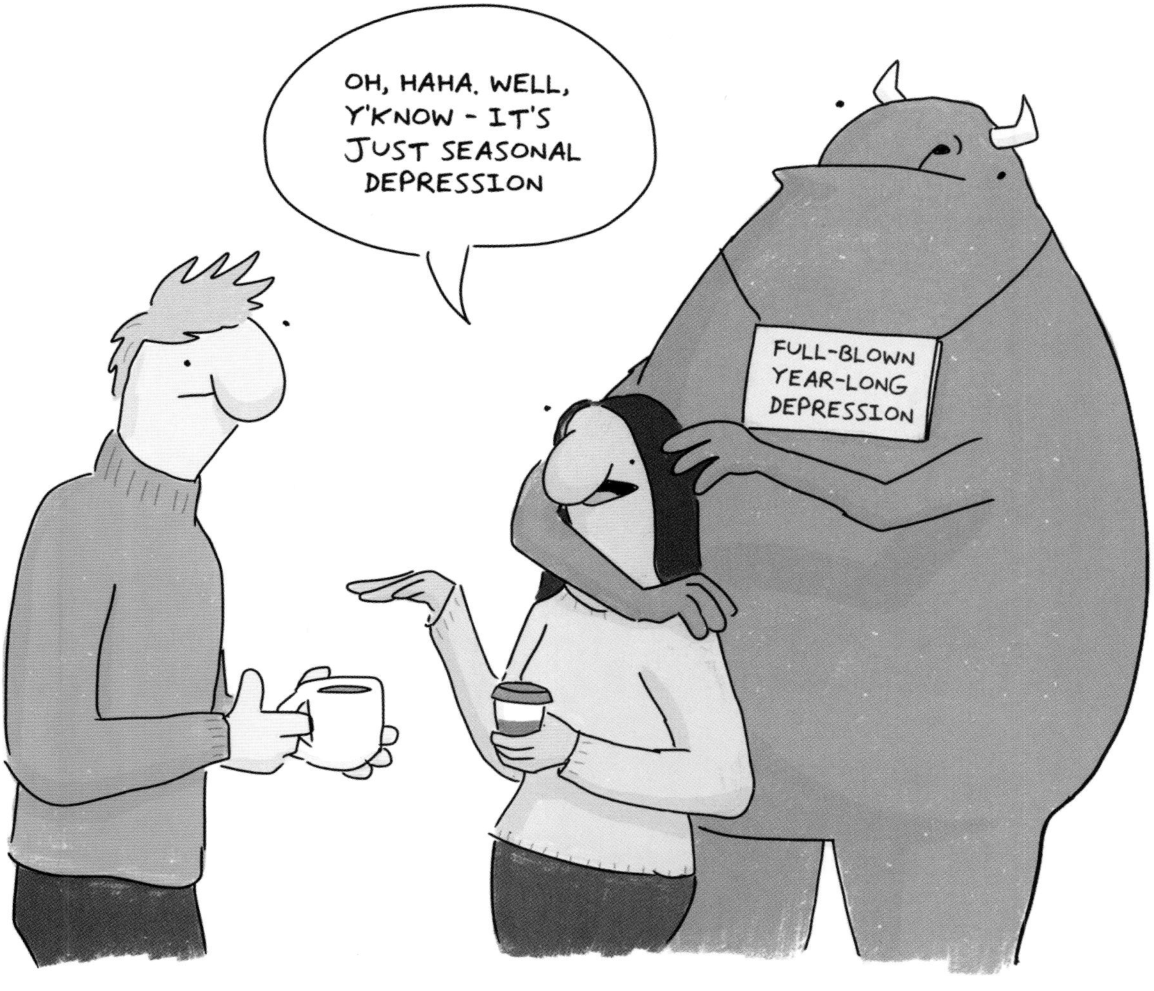
OH, HAHA. WELL, Y'KNOW - IT'S JUST SEASONAL DEPRESSION
FULL-BLOWN YEAR-LONG DEPRESSION

LIGHT BEER vs IPAs

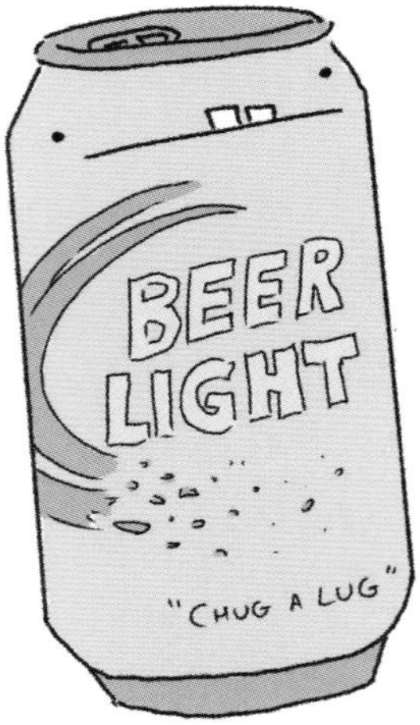
BEER LIGHT
"CHUG A LUG"

- DRINK IT WITH A FRIGGIN' HAMBURGER
- PAIRS WELL WITH GOIN' HOG WILD AND RASSLIN' THE BOYS
- PRETTY TASTY FOR HORSE PISS

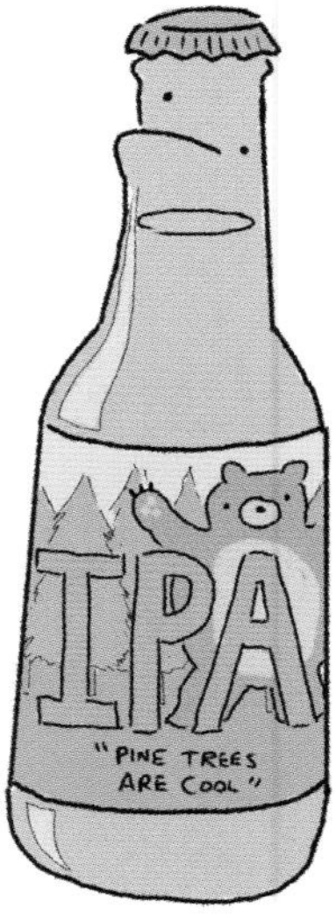
IPA
"PINE TREES ARE COOL"

- FEELS LIKE YOU DRANK A FRIGGIN' HAMBURGER
- PAIRS WELL WITH MICROGREENS AND RADIOLAB
- PRETTY TASTY FOR BUG SPRAY

THESE YOUNG PEOPLE ARE LOOKING AT
THEIR PHONES SO MUCH THEY CAN BARELY
APPRECIATE THE GRADUAL ONSET OF
CATACLYSMIC CLIMATE CHANGE!

CURES FOR THE VOID

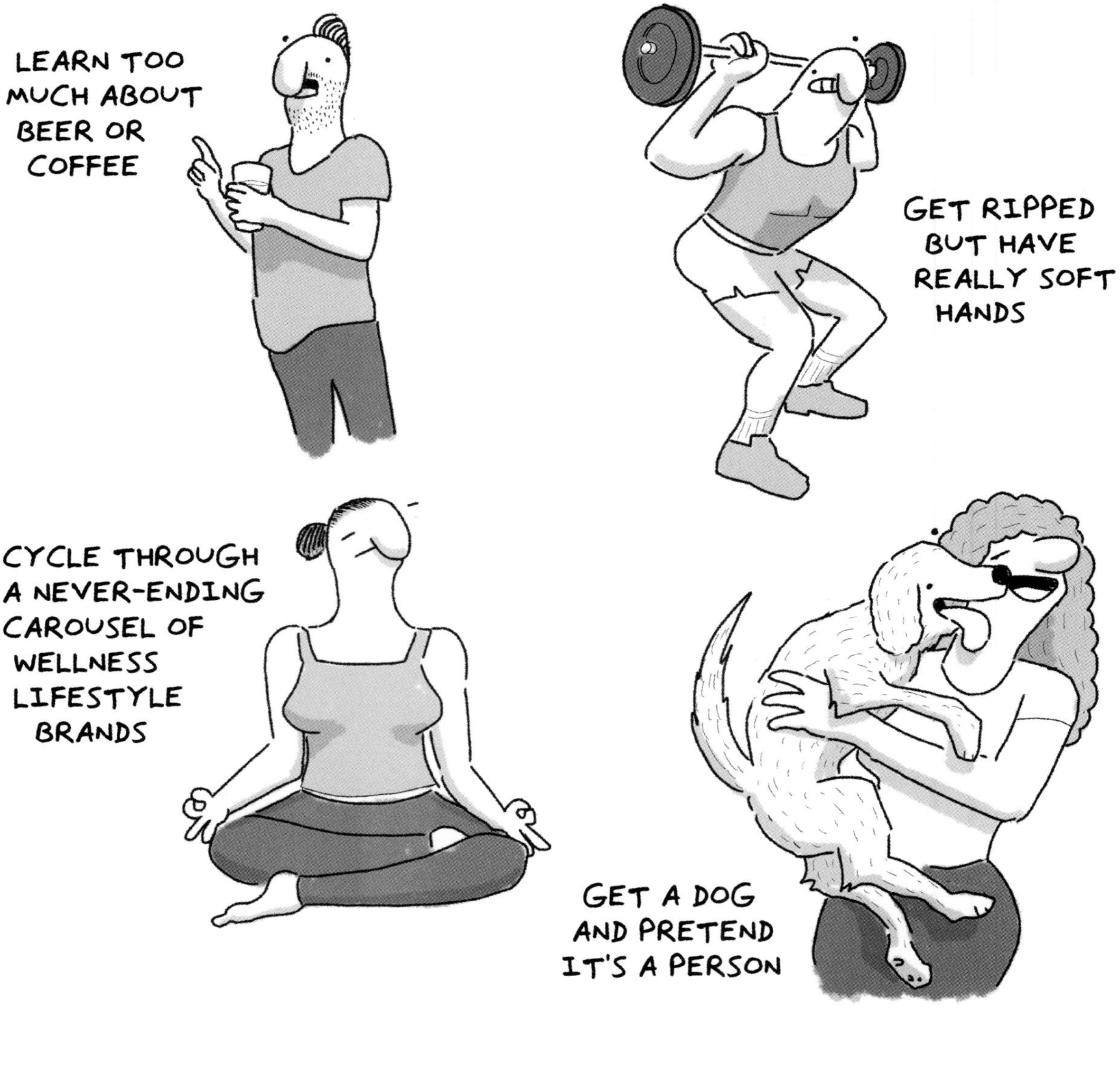
LEARN TOO MUCH ABOUT BEER OR COFFEE
GET RIPPED BUT HAVE REALLY SOFT HANDS
CYCLE THROUGH A NEVER-ENDING CAROUSEL OF WELLNESS LIFESTYLE BRANDS
GET A DOG AND PRETEND IT'S A PERSON

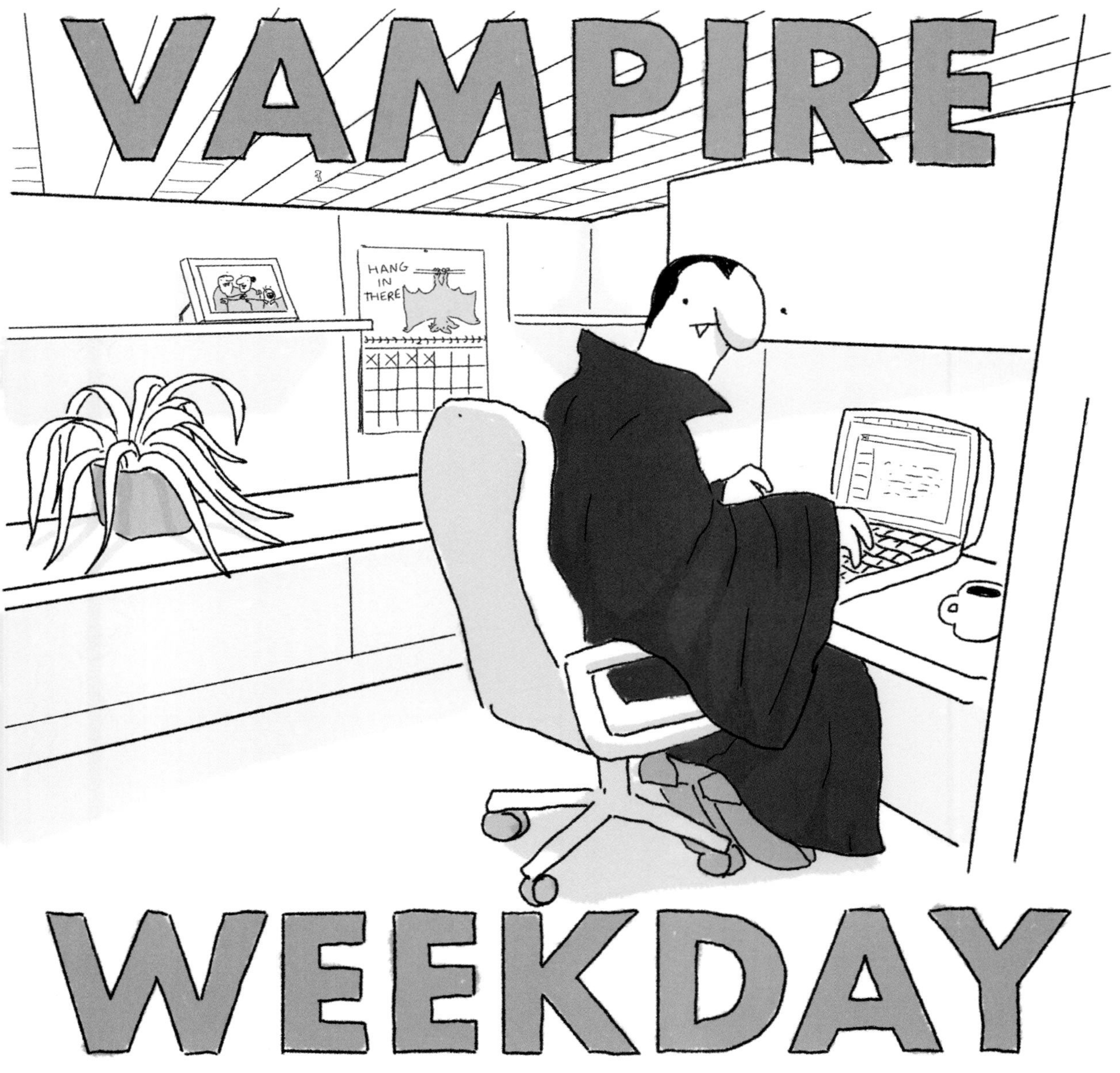
VAMPIRE
HANG IN THERE
WEEKDAY

A GUIDE TO BEARDS

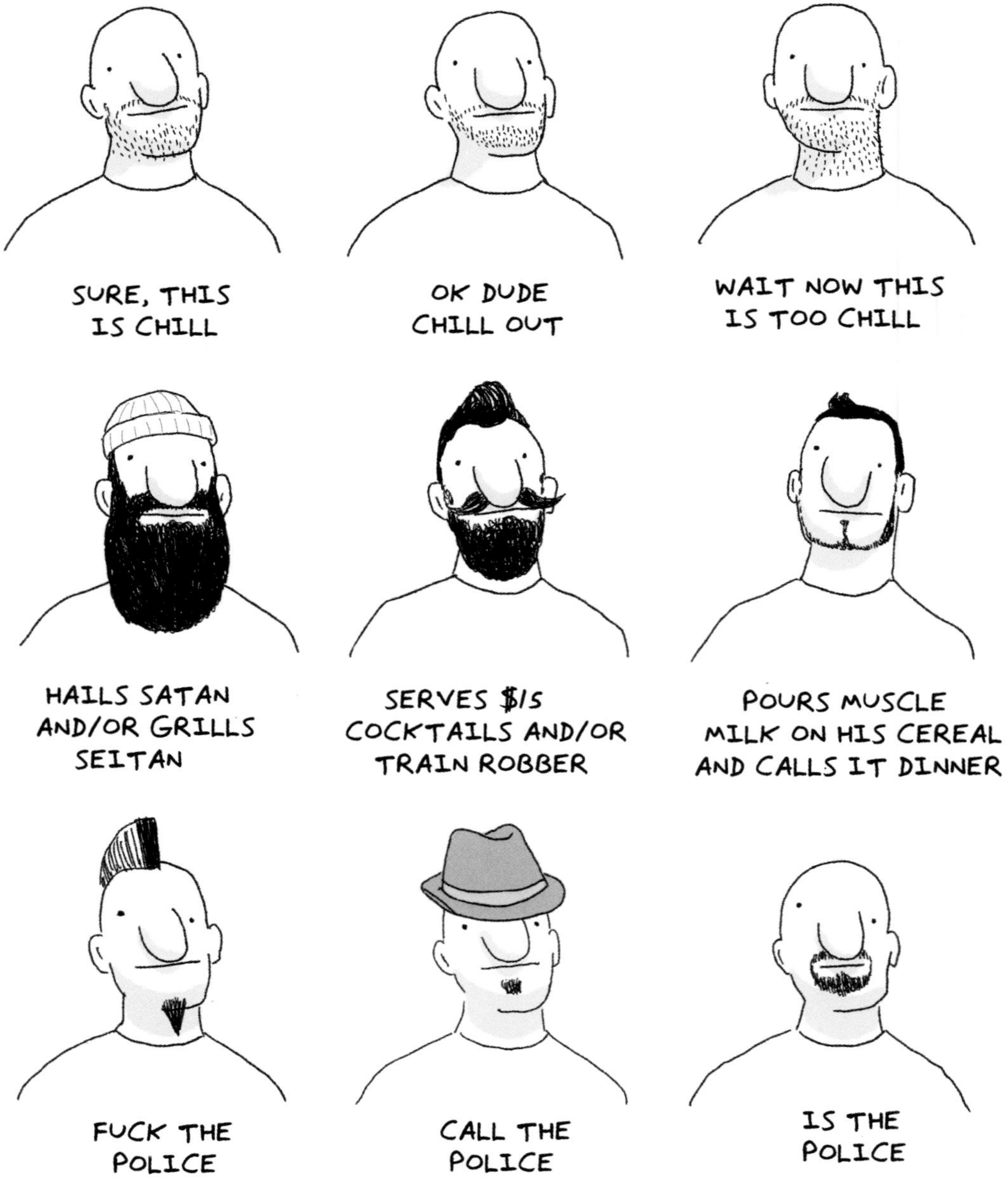
SURE, THIS IS CHILL
OK DUDE CHILL OUT
WAIT NOW THIS IS TOO CHILL
HAILS SATAN AND/OR GRILLS SEITAN
SERVES $15 COCKTAILS AND/OR TRAIN ROBBER
POURS MUSCLE MILK ON HIS CEREAL AND CALLS IT DINNER
FUCK THE POLICE
CALL THE POLICE
IS THE POLICE

A QUIET NIGHT IN

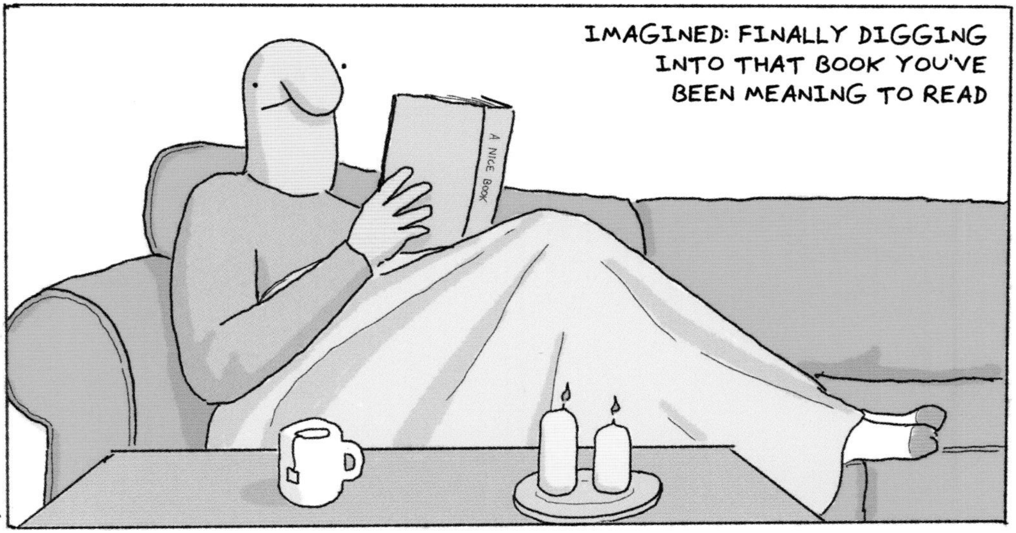
IMAGINED: FINALLY DIGGING INTO THAT BOOK YOU'VE BEEN MEANING TO READ
A NICE BOOK

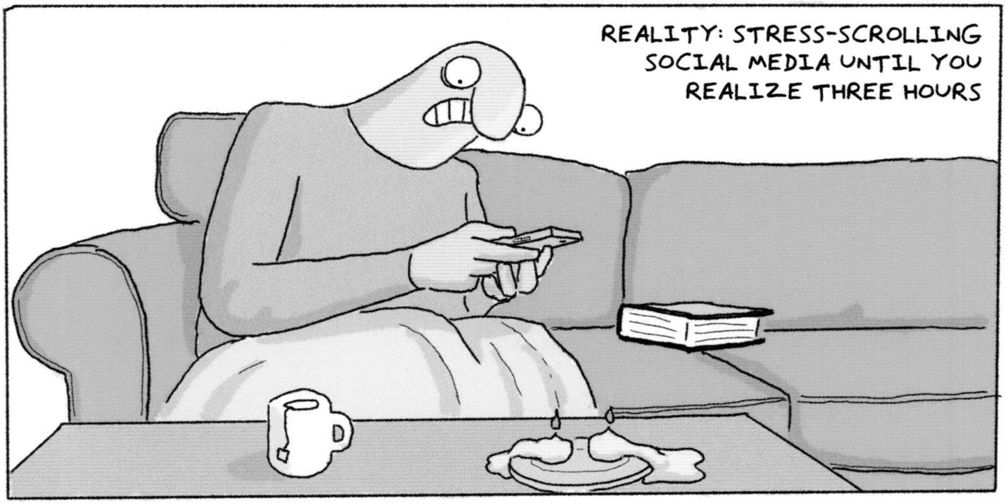
REALITY: STRESS-SCROLLING SOCIAL MEDIA UNTIL YOU REALIZE THREE HOURS

This comic, among many in this book, was a collaboration with my best friend, Dan, who is a wilderness guide in Alaska for a living. It gives me great solace to know that he also struggles with phone addiction, even with natural predators around to keep him on his toes.

BATHROOM PRIVACY OPTIONS: A GUIDE

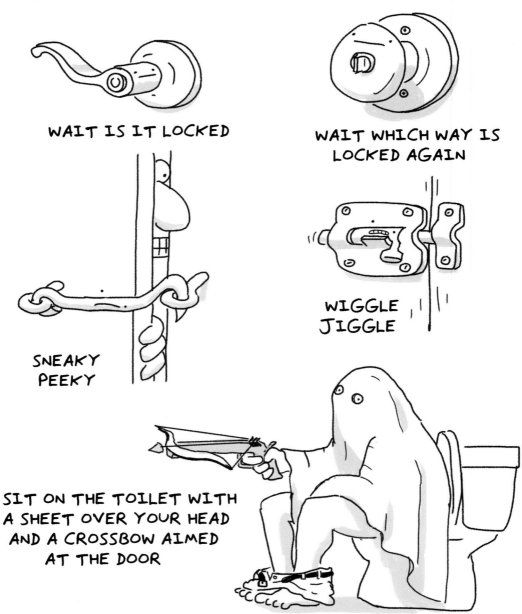

WAIT IS IT LOCKED

WAIT WHICH WAY IS LOCKED AGAIN

SNEAKY PEEKY

WIGGLE JIGGLE

SIT ON THE TOILET WITH A SHEET OVER YOUR HEAD AND A CROSSBOW AIMED AT THE DOOR

...OOH, I WANNA KNOW MORE
ABOUT YOUR **DARK** SIDE!

AND WHAT DO *YOU* WANT TO BE WHEN YOU GROW UP
IN THE CLIMATE-INDUCED FAMINE WARS?

NEW TO INSTAGRAM? CHOOSE YOUR PERSONAL BRAND!

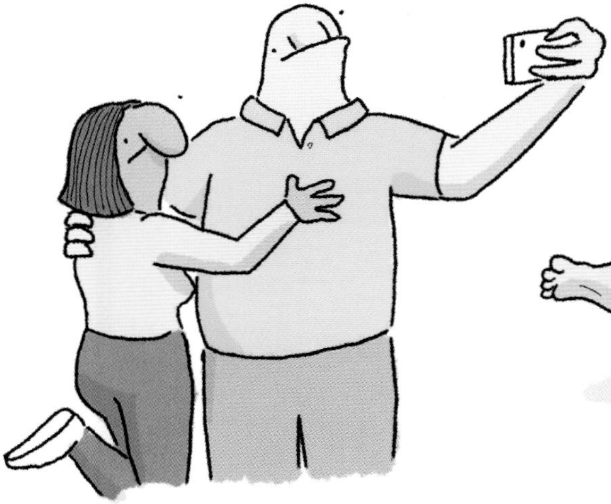

AN ELABORATE PR CAMPAIGN TO SALVAGE YOUR ROCKY RELATIONSHIP

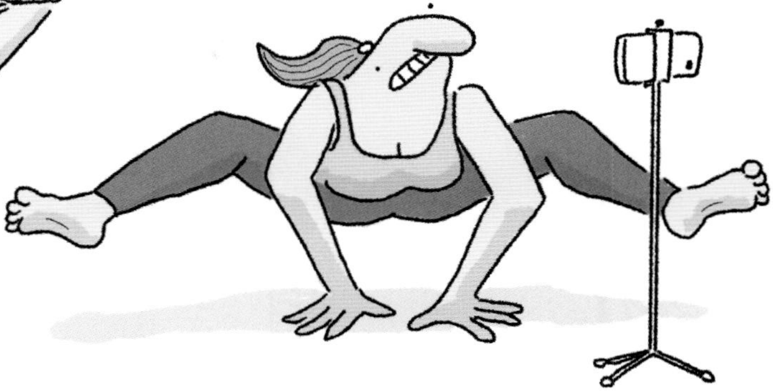

NEW AGE AND WELLNESS LIFESTYLE EVANGELISM AS A COPING MECHANISM

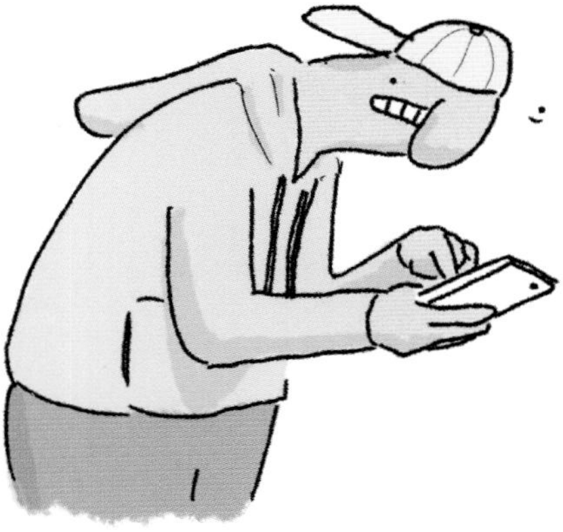

USE NICHE, INCOMPREHENSIBLE MEMES TO SHOW OFF HOW MUCH TIME YOU SPEND ON YOUR PHONE

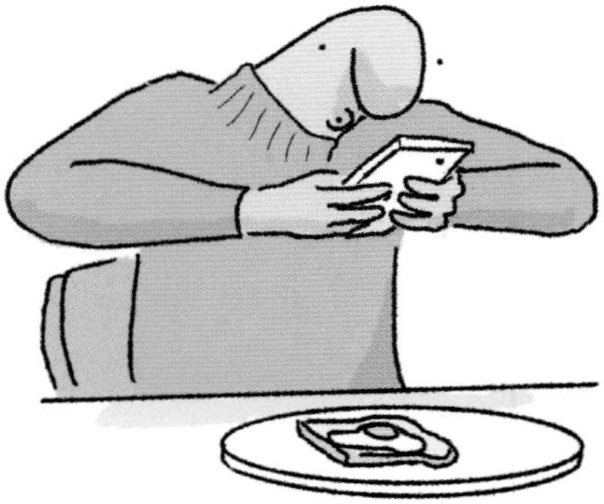

AN ENDLESS PHOTO DIARY OF EVERYTHING YOU PUT IN YOUR MOUTH AND POOP OUT YOUR ASS

"YOU TOO"

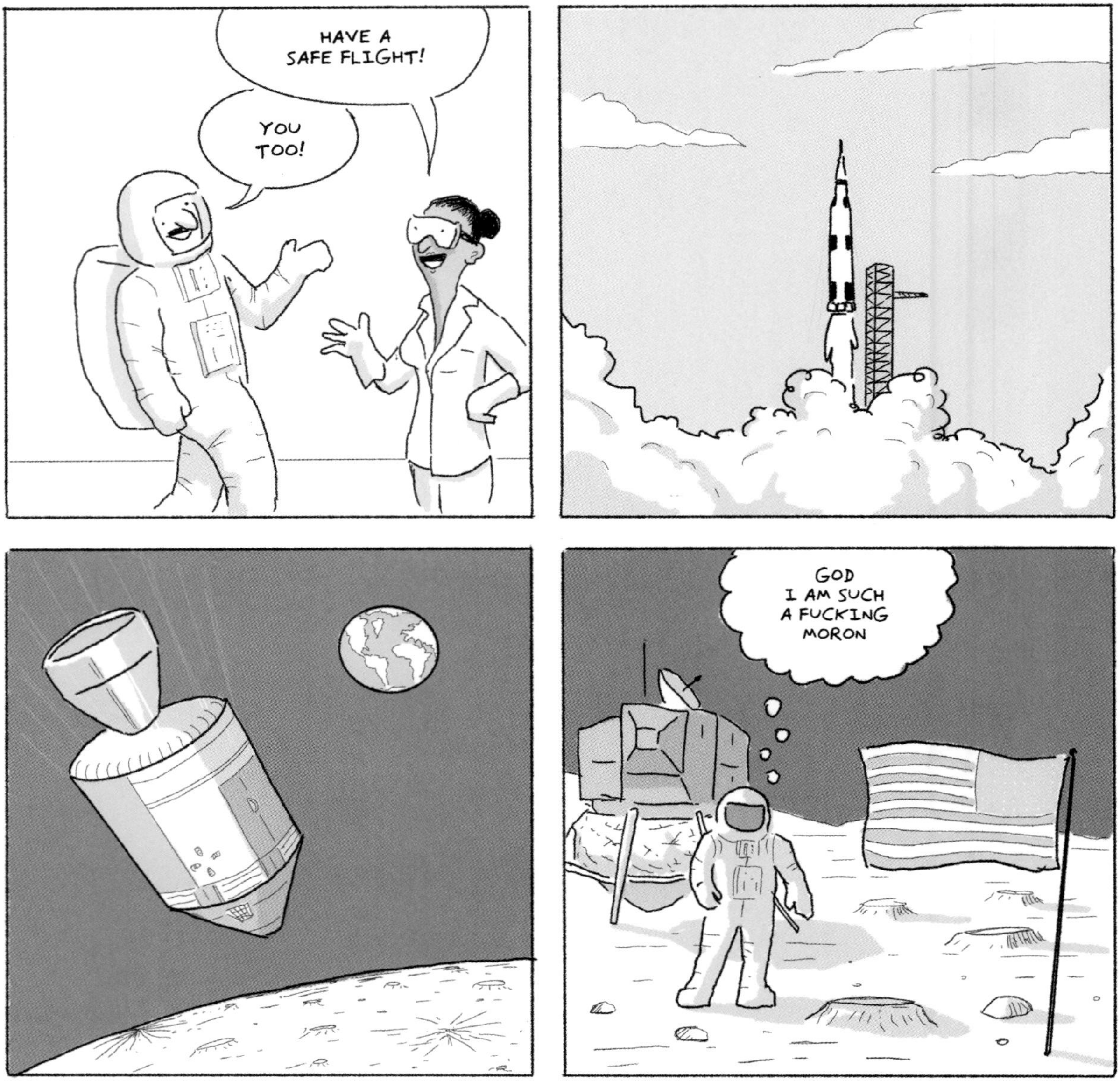
HAVE A SAFE FLIGHT!
YOU TOO!
GOD I AM SUCH A FUCKING MORON

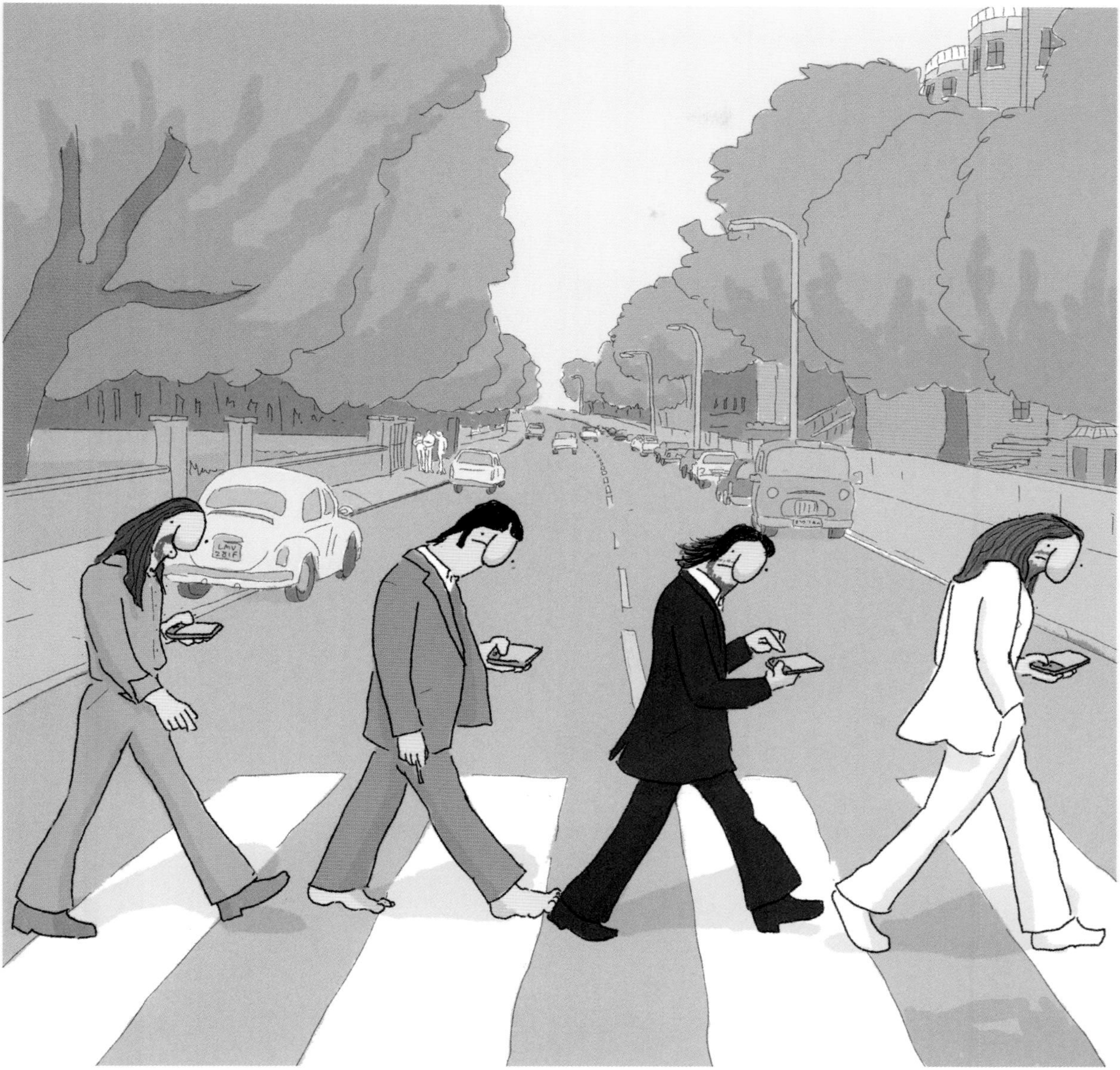

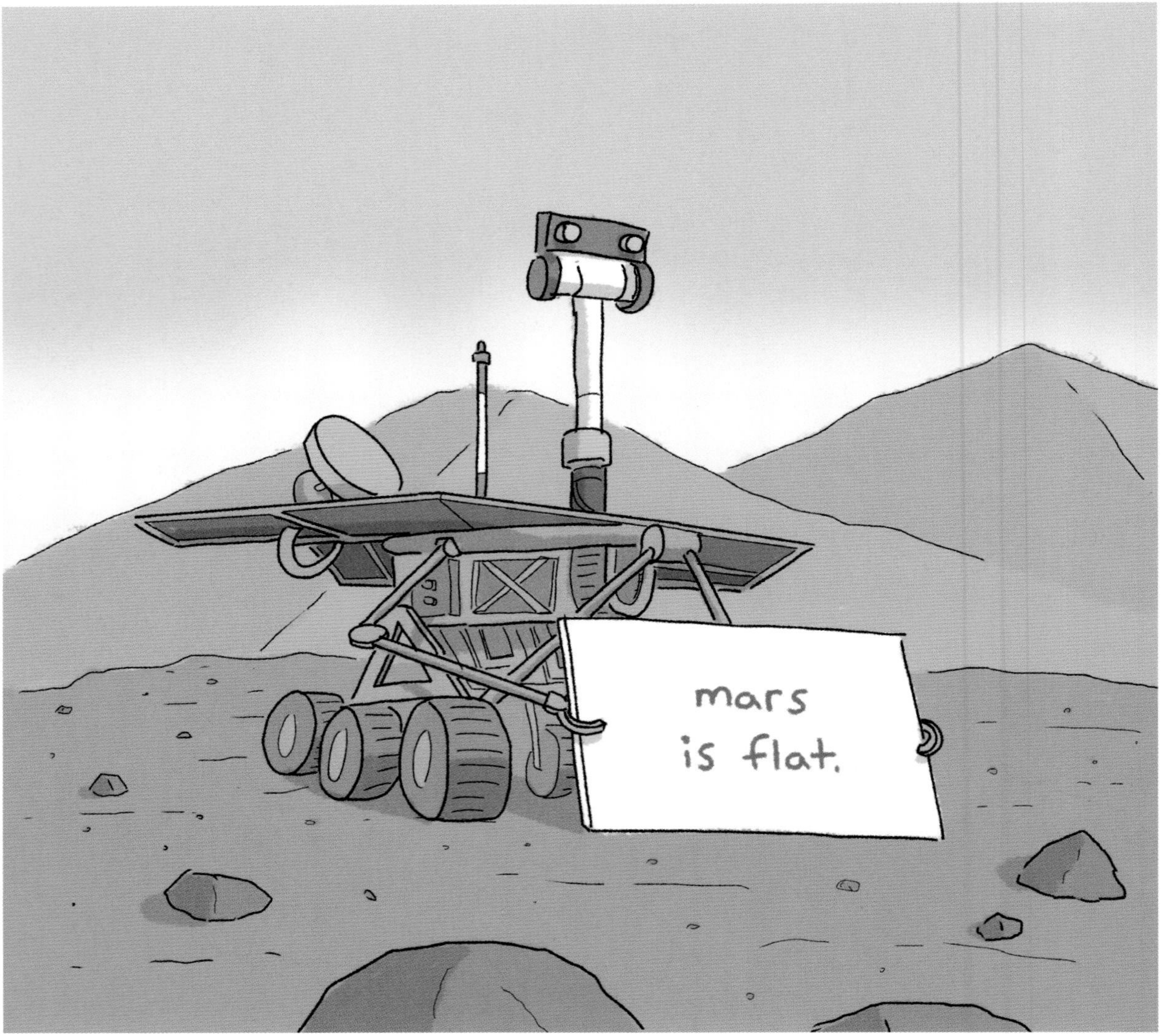
mars
is flat.

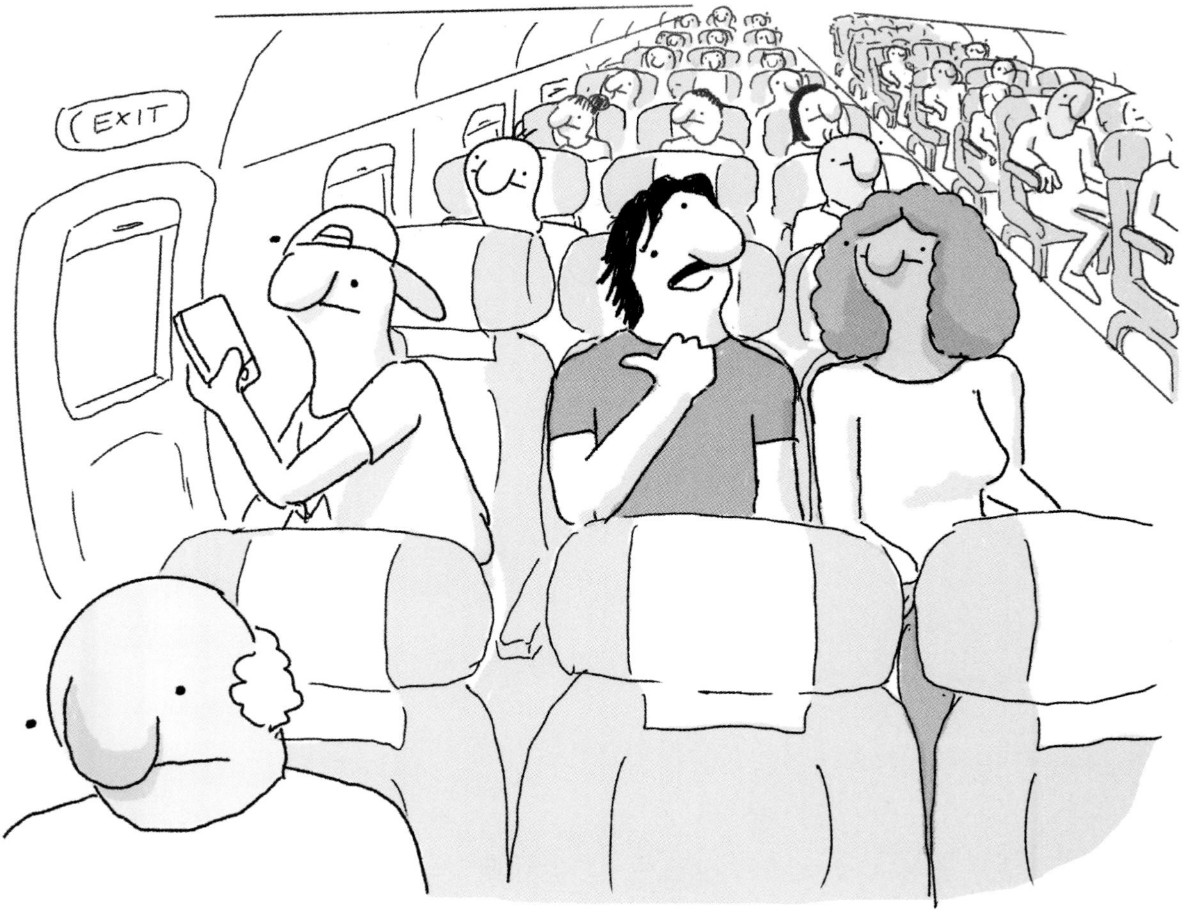
EXIT

HAH! LOOK AT THIS YOUNG MILLENNIAL SNAPCHATTING THE SUNSET! IT IS I, AGING MILLENNIAL, WHO WILL HAVE THE LAST LAUGH WHEN I TWEET ABOUT HOW DUMB THAT IS!

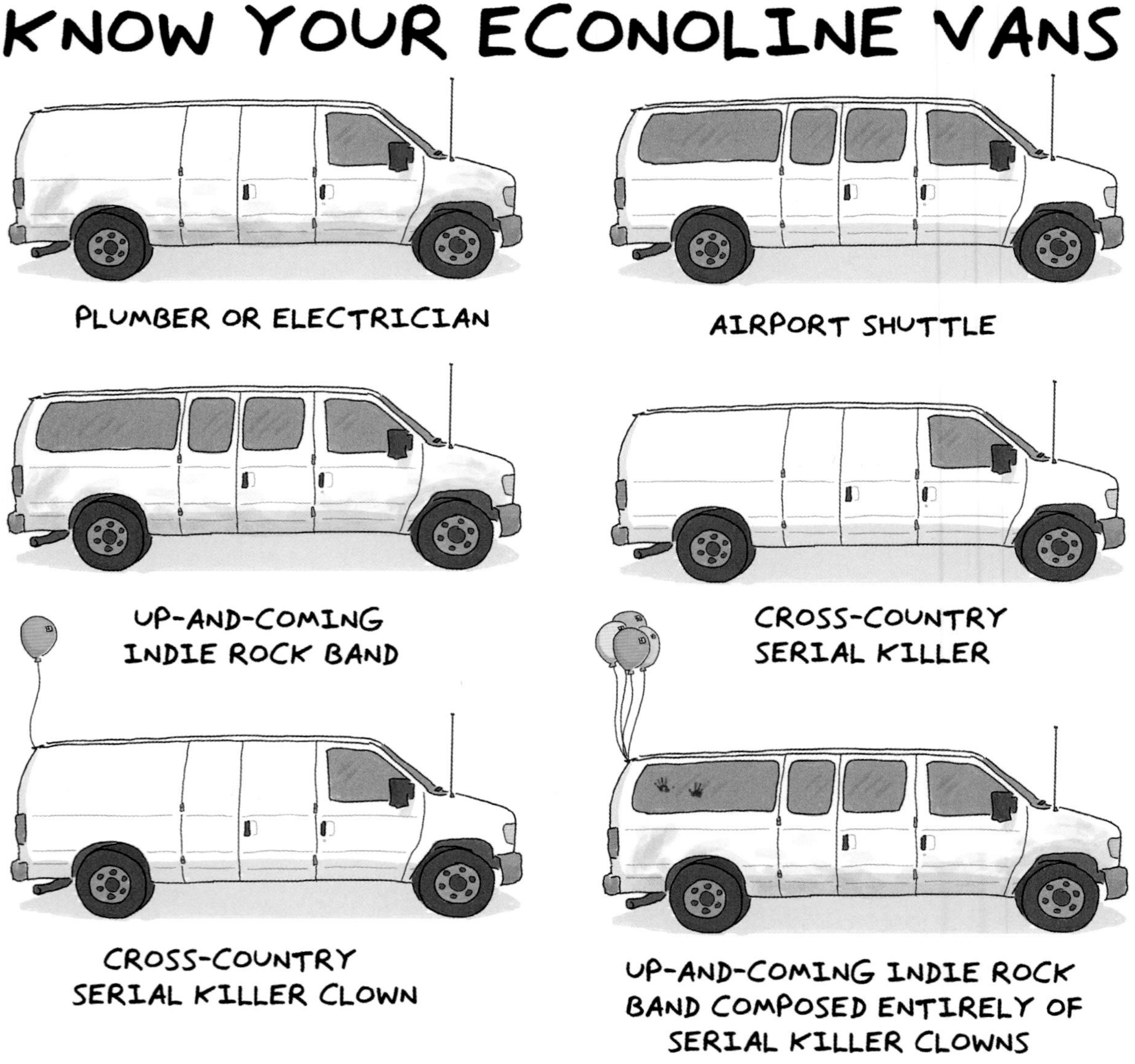

KNOW YOUR ECONOLINE VANS

PLUMBER OR ELECTRICIAN

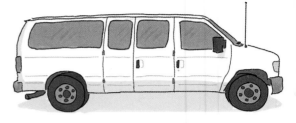

AIRPORT SHUTTLE

UP-AND-COMING
INDIE ROCK BAND

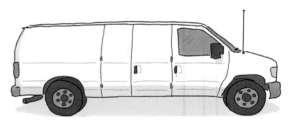

CROSS-COUNTRY
SERIAL KILLER

CROSS-COUNTRY
SERIAL KILLER CLOWN

UP-AND-COMING INDIE ROCK
BAND COMPOSED ENTIRELY OF
SERIAL KILLER CLOWNS

VAN DOODLES

I realize I should probably interject at this point to explain why I know so much about Econoline vans. And simultaneously, why I started taking cartooning seriously. This is my Batman origin story. But instead of wealthy murdered parents and a black leather fetish, it's the tale of a bored musician in a dark Econoline van who has never solved a crime of any kind.[1]

The truth is this: I'm not *really* a cartoonist. I'm starting to become one, I think. But for most of my adult life, I've been a full-time touring musician as a guitarist and singer in my own band, which means that my comics were often drawn in the back of a tour van hurtling down the highway at 65 mph or frantically scribbled between obligations at a music venue.

Throughout the project, I was often asked: "How do you have the *time* to draw so many comics on tour?"

The truth is, there's an enormous gulf between other people's perception of your daily life in a touring rock band and the actual grinding machinations that make up a day on the road. Sure, the shows are action-packed and an absolute thrill. I can't deny that. But generally, most of your time on tour before 5 p.m. is spent

---

1. I swear this is all connected and is not a long con to advertise my band, but also, you can check out my band if you want — we are called Jukebox the Ghost. See if I care.

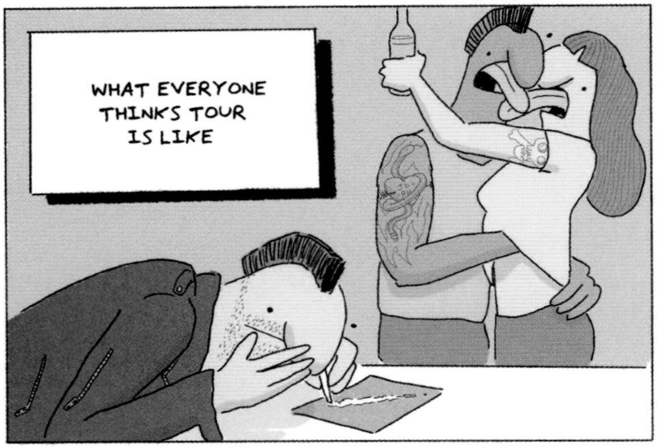
WHAT EVERYONE THINKS TOUR IS LIKE

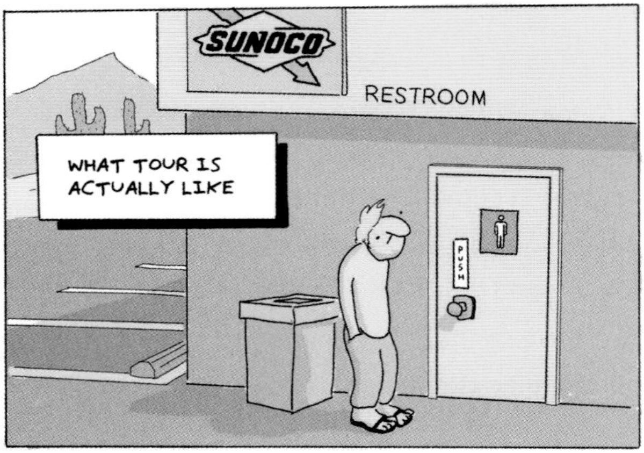
SUNOCO
RESTROOM
WHAT TOUR IS ACTUALLY LIKE
PUSH

traveling from city to city in a cramped van, gazing at wilting median grass and blurs of roadkill whizzing by, and aimlessly wandering around truck stops. You could be in Ohio, and likely are.[2] The typical travel day on tour is one in which a machine that makes commemorative pennies at a state-sponsored rest stop becomes a heart-racing thrill, and a successful round at a claw machine at a gas station borders on sexual pleasure.

For years, I tried to stay intellectually stimulated on long drives. But, I always found it was difficult to ingest a great American novel with a podcast about murder scene forensics blasting from the front. And on tour, I tend to get extremely sick of music after being pummeled with it for hours every night. I tried getting into podcasts, but it always felt synaptically challenging to listen to a podcast in my earbuds when there was

2. Ohio is a state, but it is also a state of mind. If you unfocus your mind while behind the wheel and use your mental willpower, you could be in Ohio in any moment that you desire to be. And you might as well be. Namaste.

already a podcast playing on the van speakers. Two Ira Glasses[3] in an enclosed space is a violation of Newton's law.

The typical diet of a touring musician isn't particularly conducive to productive thinking either. Most days, the struggle to get a good night's sleep means that the drives from venue to venue are always so down to the wire that a side trek to a Whole Foods isn't in the cards. The choices for breakfast can be particularly dire. Choose your weapon, if you dare:

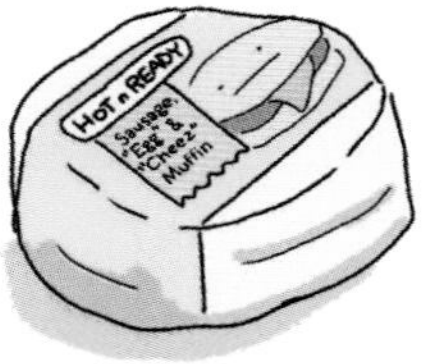
HOT n READY

A SIX-MONTH-OLD EGG SANDWICH

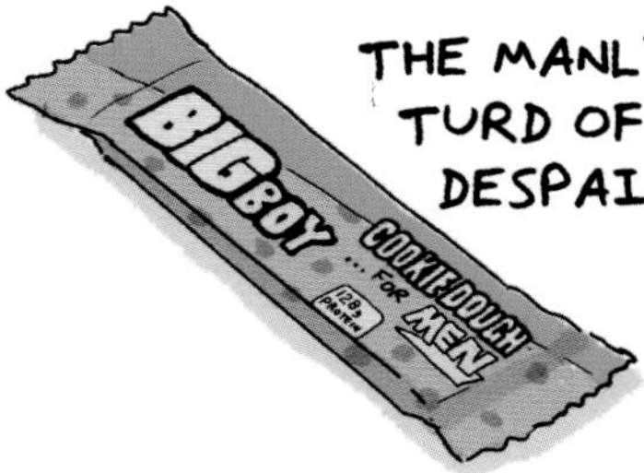
BIGBOY
NEW
COOKIE DOUGH
...FOR MEN

THE MANLY TURD OF DESPAIR

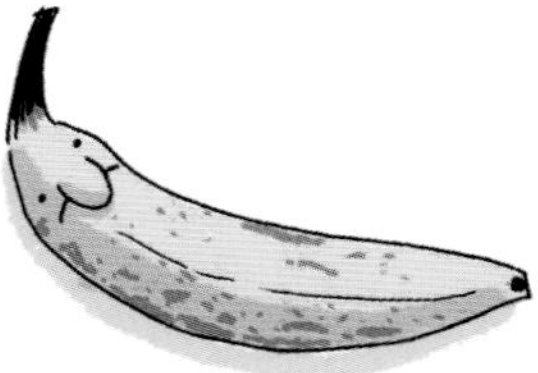

THE WORLD'S SADDEST BANANA

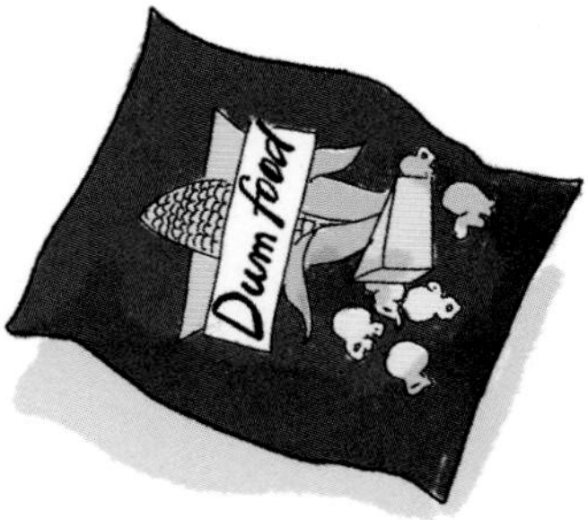
Dum food

FUCK IT, IT'S POPCORN O'CLOCK SOMEWHERE

3. I will continue to use this as his plural form unless he personally tells me to stop.

HI, I'M A ROCK MUSICIAN!

I KNOW A LOT ABOUT:

- ~~MUSIC THEORY~~

- ~~SCALES~~

- ~~HOW TO SUCCEED IN MY FIELD~~

- WHICH FAST-FOOD PLACES WON'T MAKE YOU POOP TOO BAD

I could go on, but I'm going to stop going into too much gritty detail to make my central point: Tour is a lot more boring than you'd expect, and for most of the day, you're essentially a trucker in skinny jeans. A trucker in skinny jeans who has a lot of time on his hands.

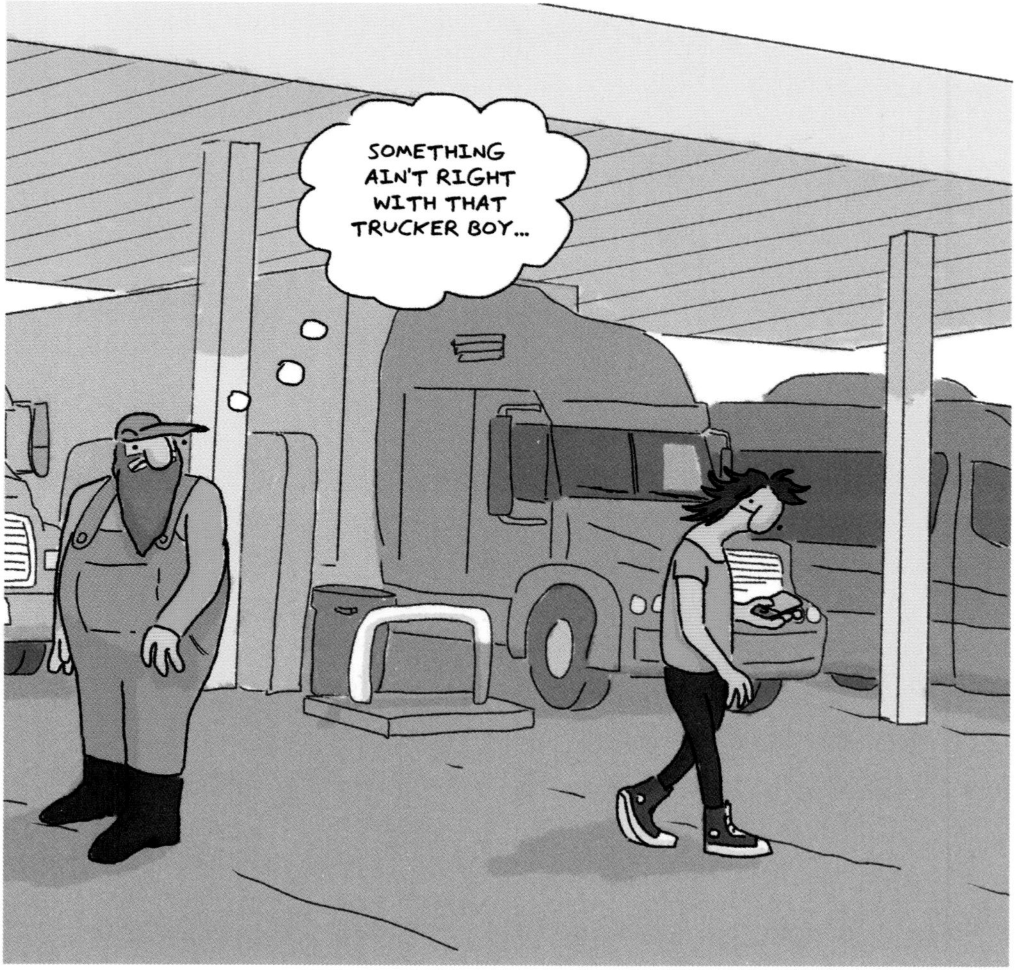
SOMETHING AIN'T RIGHT WITH THAT TRUCKER BOY...

Many years ago on a long drive, as I mindlessly doodled the same thing I always ended up drawing[4] in the van, our band's keyboardist, Ben, interrupted to make a request from behind the wheel. "Tommy, can you draw me . . . shrimp . . . having a party . . . on the belly of a goat," he said, not knowing the unsettlingly prolific hobby he had just unlocked. Sitting in shotgun, I obliged.

Somehow, I still possess this drawing:

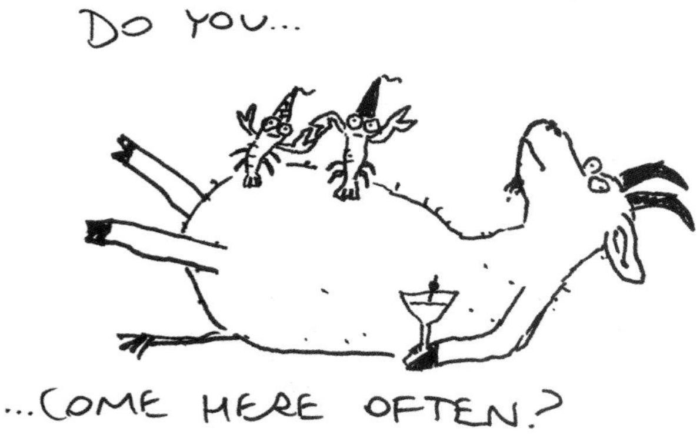
DO YOU...
...COME HERE OFTEN?

Next, he requested an octopus carrying a bucket filled with [redacted].[5]

Soon everyone wanted a turn. And by everyone, I mean strangers on Twitter, after we tweeted some of the early results onto the band's feed and our fans started requesting their own cartoons in response. The requests came in by the dozens and, suddenly, by the hundreds.

---

4. Dinosaurs with human noses.
5. I have decided not to put this image in this book. This is theoretically supposed to be, at worst, a PG-13-rated-ish sort of a book. But since you've read all the way to the bottom of a footnote, I suppose I should just spill the beans and tell you that he wanted me to draw an octopus carrying a bucket full of dicks, and that I did as he asked, and everyone agreed that it was very good. But you'll just have to imagine it, and shame on you for doing so.

Eventually, it spiraled into an endless back-and-forth via our band's social media. Fans would ask for things like "Broccula," and they would receive a "Broccula," direct to their phones.

BROCCULA

Plus, it served a use: beating the social media algorithms, which generally prioritize quick blasts of dopamine-triggering visual ephemera. Though advertised as a tool to eradicate email lists, running a band's social media page to raise awareness about our new album or tour dates had started to feel more like trying to start the wave at a baseball game by flailing wildly and hoping the masses of people took pity.

The problem, of course, is much larger than Facebook: Music doesn't compete in its own lane like it used to. We used to only go up against other bands. We competed with them in *Rolling Stone*, *Spin*, *Pitchfork*, record store shelves — it was a simpler game and we knew the rules. But in the last 10 years, you name the media gatekeeper, they've been largely replaced by algorithms and payola playlists on streaming services. Music, like all information, has been swallowed into the all-consuming beast we call the *social internet*. We're no longer competing with other piano-led pop/rock acts for your attention. We're competing with the latest celebrity feud. We're competing with

PLEASE CHECK OUT MY BAND

cat memes. And in an era of immediate visual stimulation, the 40-minute album is an unadapted dinosaur. An album requires intimacy. It requires headphones. It requires possessing an attention span longer than a gerbil's.[6]

We think of social media as a vehicle for just about anything, but the nature of the medium does advantage certain kinds of content. Brief flurries of text. Shocking headlines. Pictures. Any kind of visual ephemera that can be digested in under five seconds. Music, which requires some degree of space and patience to process, just can't compete. We're no longer jockeying for attention against other bands — we're competing against the Kardashians. And we can't win, though we've tried.

And though the "van doodles" had become a fun mainstay of our touring career, something felt like it was missing. I had drawn hundreds and hundreds of fan requests, but I still wasn't sure what *I* wanted to draw on my own volition. I had gotten bored of honoring requests to draw our band as Lego figurines, Harry Potter characters, potatoes, Beyoncé's backup dancers, and even as a single multiheaded cactus. Like songwriting, I figured there was probably a creative well waiting to be tapped, but I didn't know how to turn on the faucet myself. So I figured it might make sense to force myself to draw something every day just to see what might happen. And thankfully, I had a career with a lot of downtime to reawaken a dormant childhood hobby.

Fast forward, and here we are enjoying the fruits of my labor. Including my masterpiece on the following page, which I revealed to the world on the 467th day of daily comics, when my mind had finally completely unraveled from overworking myself amid a steady diet of gas station snacks. Probably while driving through Ohio. You're welcome.

------

6. I had a gerbil as a preteen, so trust me: Gerbils don't give a shit about music. Sometimes I suspected Sparky didn't even know or care that John Lennon was dead.

I'M COMING OUT OF MY CAN

AND I'VE BEEN DOING JUST FINE

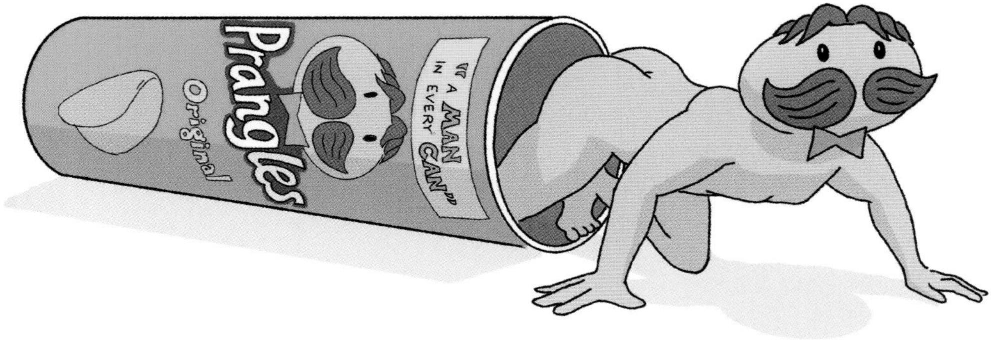
Prangles
Original
"A MAN IN EVERY CAN"

Let's move on. It's all we can do.

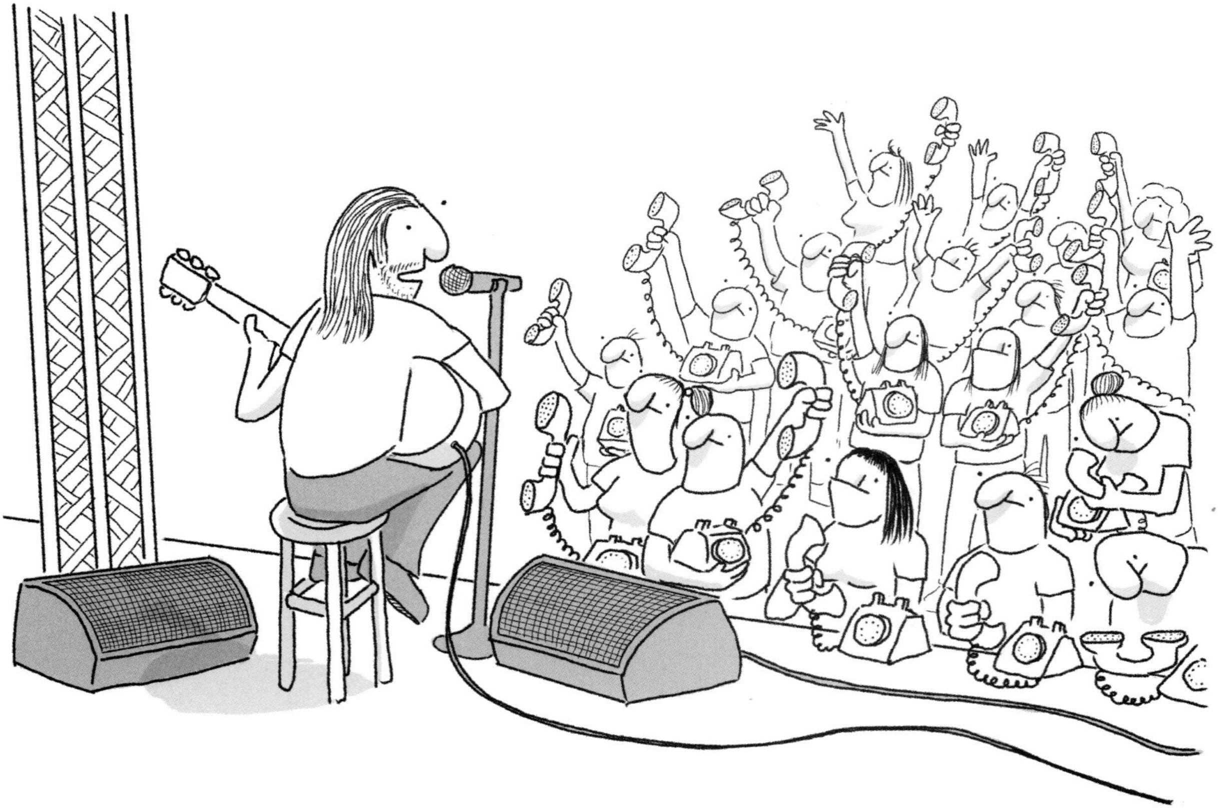

(CONCERTS BACK IN THE GOOD OLD DAYS)

BUDGETING AND ACCOUNTING AS A MUSICIAN

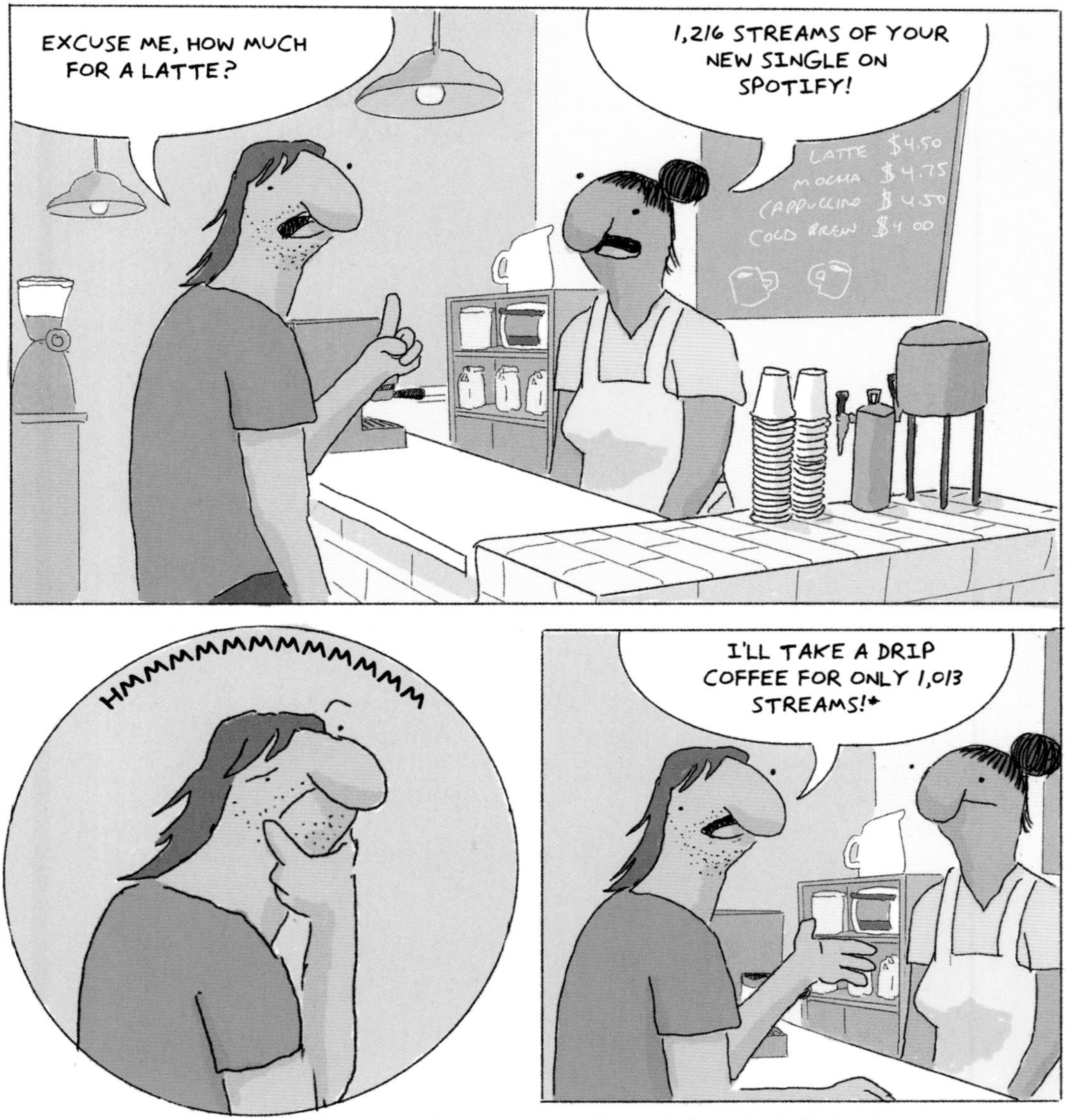

EXCUSE ME, HOW MUCH FOR A LATTE?
1,216 STREAMS OF YOUR NEW SINGLE ON SPOTIFY!
LATTE $4.50
MOCHA $4.75
CAPPUCCINO $4.50
COLD BREW $4.00
HMMMMMMMMMMMM
I'LL TAKE A DRIP COFFEE FOR ONLY 1,013 STREAMS!*

*THESE NUMBERS BASED ON SPOTIFY'S 2019 REPORTED ROYALTY RATE OF $0.0037 PER STREAM

BAND PHOTOS: A GUIDE

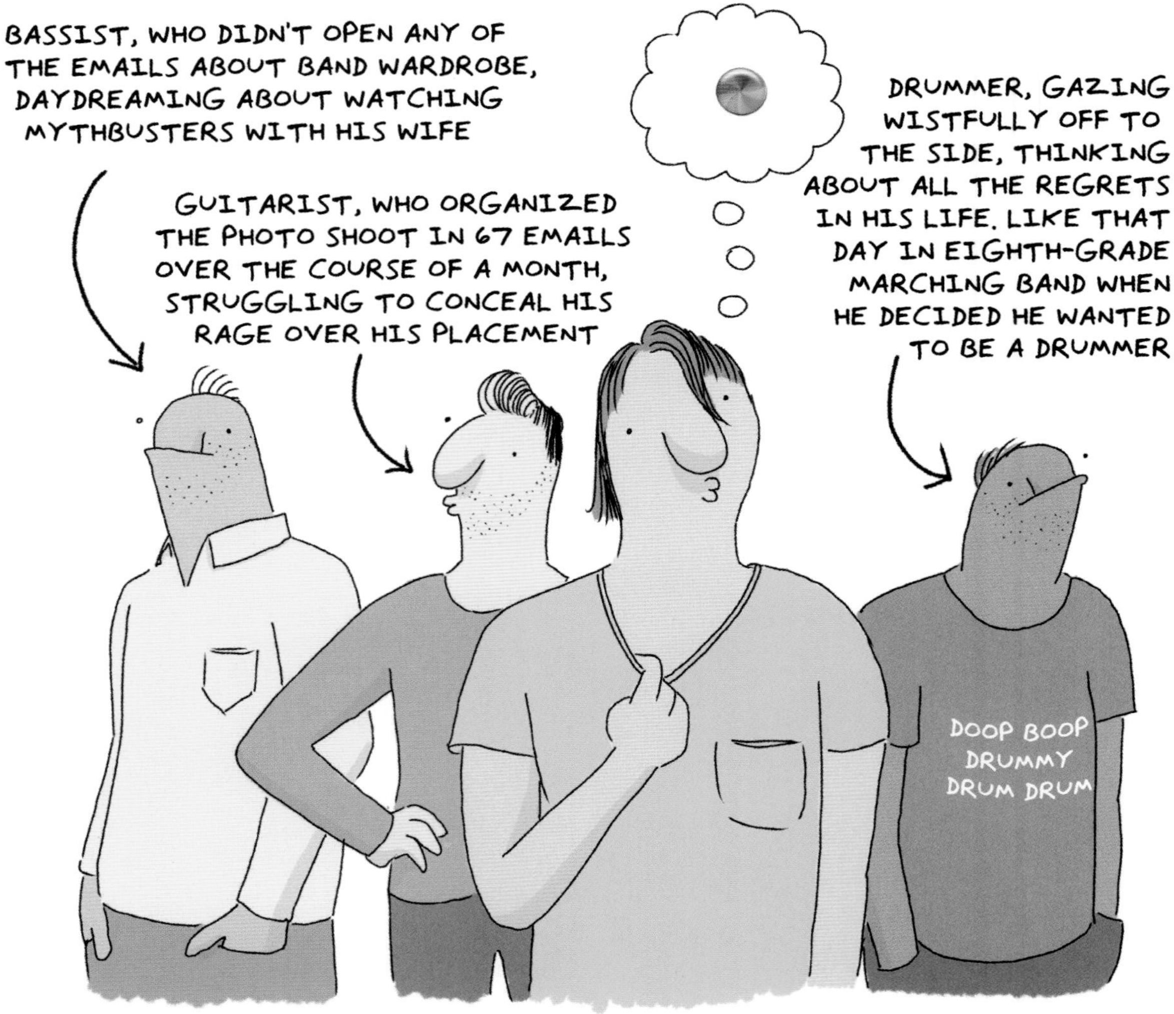
BASSIST, WHO DIDN'T OPEN ANY OF THE EMAILS ABOUT BAND WARDROBE, DAYDREAMING ABOUT WATCHING MYTHBUSTERS WITH HIS WIFE
GUITARIST, WHO ORGANIZED THE PHOTO SHOOT IN 67 EMAILS OVER THE COURSE OF A MONTH, STRUGGLING TO CONCEAL HIS RAGE OVER HIS PLACEMENT
DRUMMER, GAZING WISTFULLY OFF TO THE SIDE, THINKING ABOUT ALL THE REGRETS IN HIS LIFE. LIKE THAT DAY IN EIGHTH-GRADE MARCHING BAND WHEN HE DECIDED HE WANTED TO BE A DRUMMER
DOOP BOOP DRUMMY DRUM DRUM

I just want to make it known that Jesse, the drummer of my band, came up with the text on the drummer's shirt, so you know it's authentic.

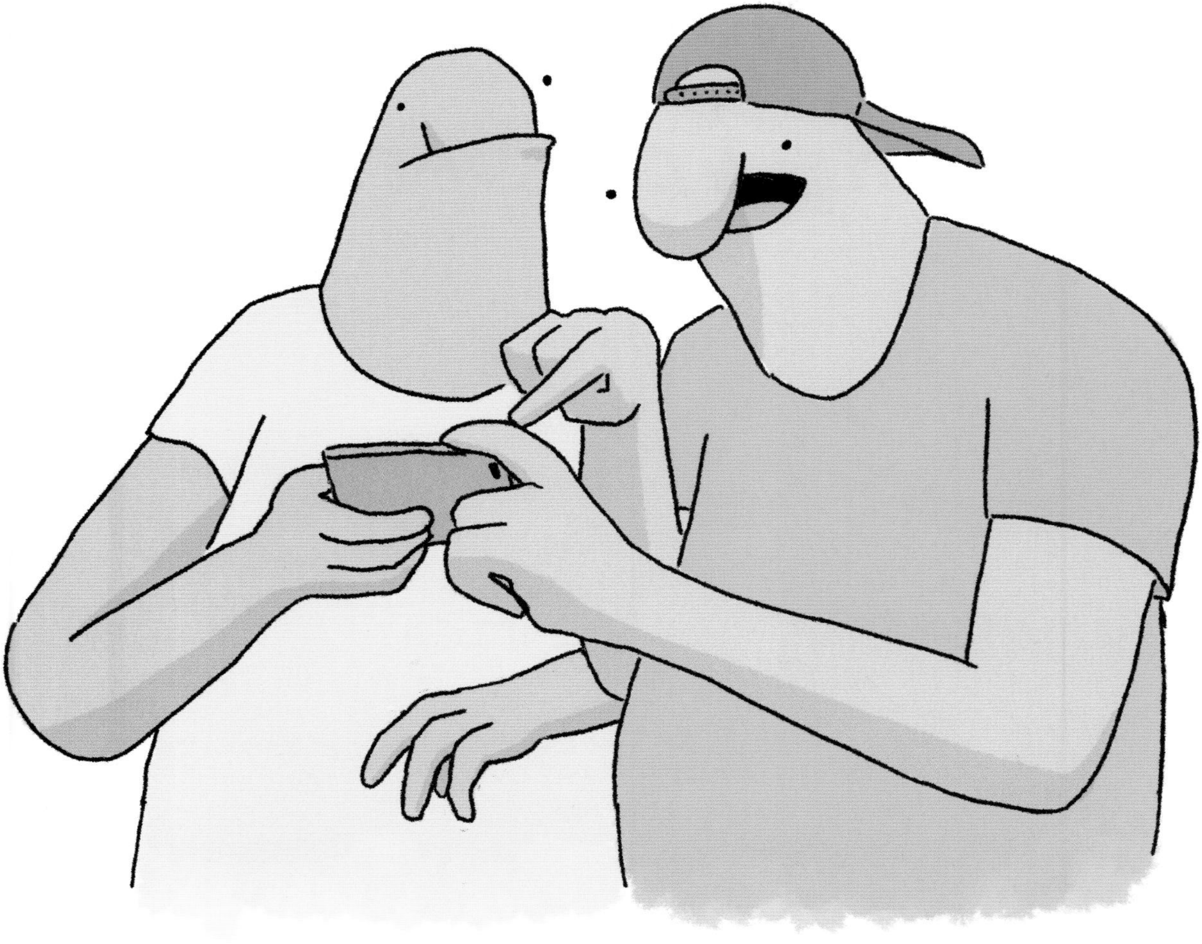

HAHA! LOOK AT THIS FUNNY THING
ON THE SMALL COMPUTER I NEVER WASH
BUT USE ALL THE TIME WHILE I'M POOPING

CANNABIS: A CONSUMER GUIDE

SATIVA

IF YOU FREAK
OUT, IT WAS CUZ
OF HER

INDICA

IF YOU CONK
OUT, IT WAS CUZ
OF HER

CBD

IF ANYTHING
GOOD HAPPENS TO
YOU FOR THE REST
OF YOUR LIFE, SHE
CLAIMS IT WAS HER

METAMORPHOSIS:
NATURE'S MAGNIFICENT REVEAL

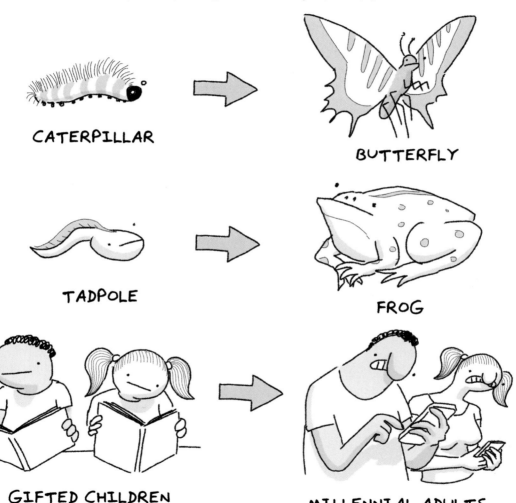

CATERPILLAR

BUTTERFLY

TADPOLE

FROG

GIFTED CHILDREN

MILLENNIAL ADULTS
WITH SEVERE SOCIAL
MEDIA ADDICTION
AND ANXIETY

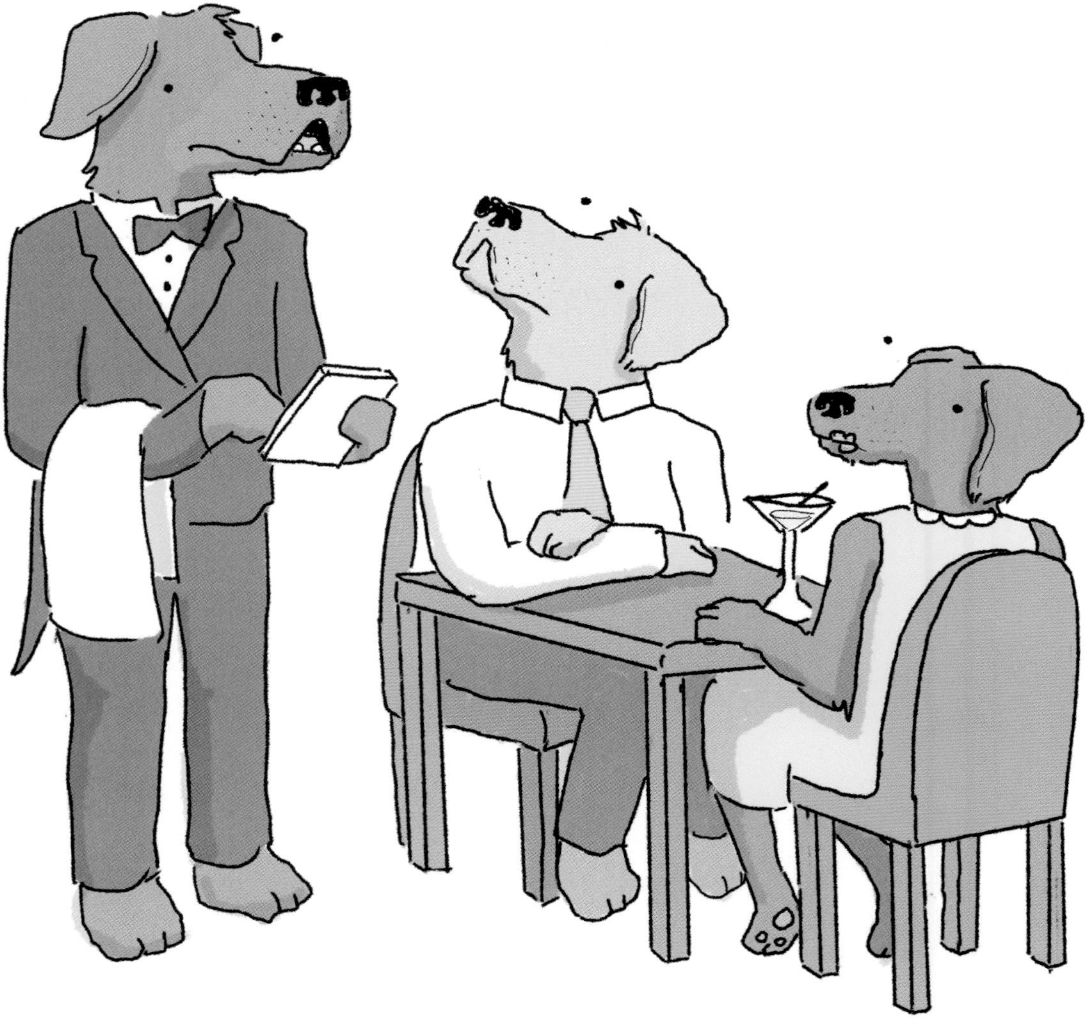

...AND CAT SHIT FOR THE MISSUS?

TYPES OF MODERN MUSICAL ARTISTS

LA-BASED SYNTH-POP DUO FORMED
TO PERFORM SONG WRITTEN FOR
A LIFE INSURANCE COMMERCIAL

SOUNDCLOUD RAPPER WHO SAMPLES
SPONGEBOB SQUAREPANTS AND
GUARDS A TERRIBLE SECRET

MOSTLY FEMALE, PHILLY-BASED
PUNK BAND WITH HULKING, WILDLY
OUT-OF-PLACE DUDE DRUMMER

THIRTEEN-YEAR-OLD
EDM ARTIST WITH HIS
OWN FESTIVAL

STAR WARS vs STAR TREK

- NO NO DON'T START WITH THE "FIRST" MOVIE, LET ME TELL YOU WHICH ONES ARE GOOD

- '70s FARM EQUIPMENT IN OUTER SPACE

- A LONG TIME AGO, THINGS WERE VERY BAD

- J.J. ABRAMS FUCKING RUINED IT

- NO NO DON'T START WITH ANY OF THE FIRST SEASONS, LET ME TELL YOU WHICH ONES ARE GOOD

- '90s CARNIVAL CRUISE IN OUTER SPACE

- IN THE FUTURE, EVERYTHING WILL BE AWESOME

- J.J. ABRAMS FUCKING RUINED IT

WHAT YOUR GUITAR SAYS ABOUT YOU

- YOU SAY YOUR HANDS ARE "TOO SMALL" TO PLAY BARRE CHORDS

- BUT DEEP DOWN YOU KNOW IT'S BECAUSE YOU'RE A WIMP WITH COMMITMENT ISSUES

- YOU DERIVE PLEASURE FROM POST-1998 DAVE MATTHEWS BAND

- AND THE SOUND OF RUBBER BANDS SMACKING AGAINST A PLASTIC BUCKET

- YOU ARE A DENTIST

- OH WOW YOU KNOW SCALES

- I WISH YOU DIDN'T KNOW SCALES

- "ALT" COUNTRY IS "IMPORTANT"

- IPA PUNDIT

- NOT GREAT AT GUITAR

- BUT A GREAT DAD

WAFFLE HOUSE
INTERNATIONAL HOUSE OF PANCAKES
HALFWAY HOUSE FOR WAYWARD TOAST

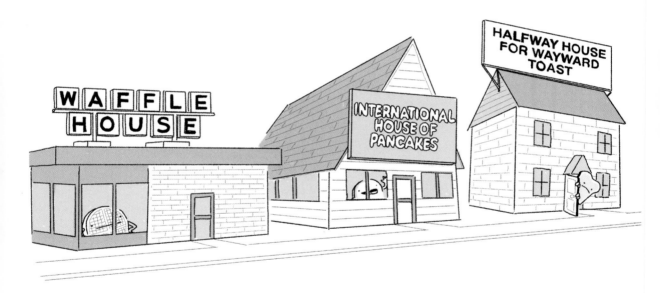

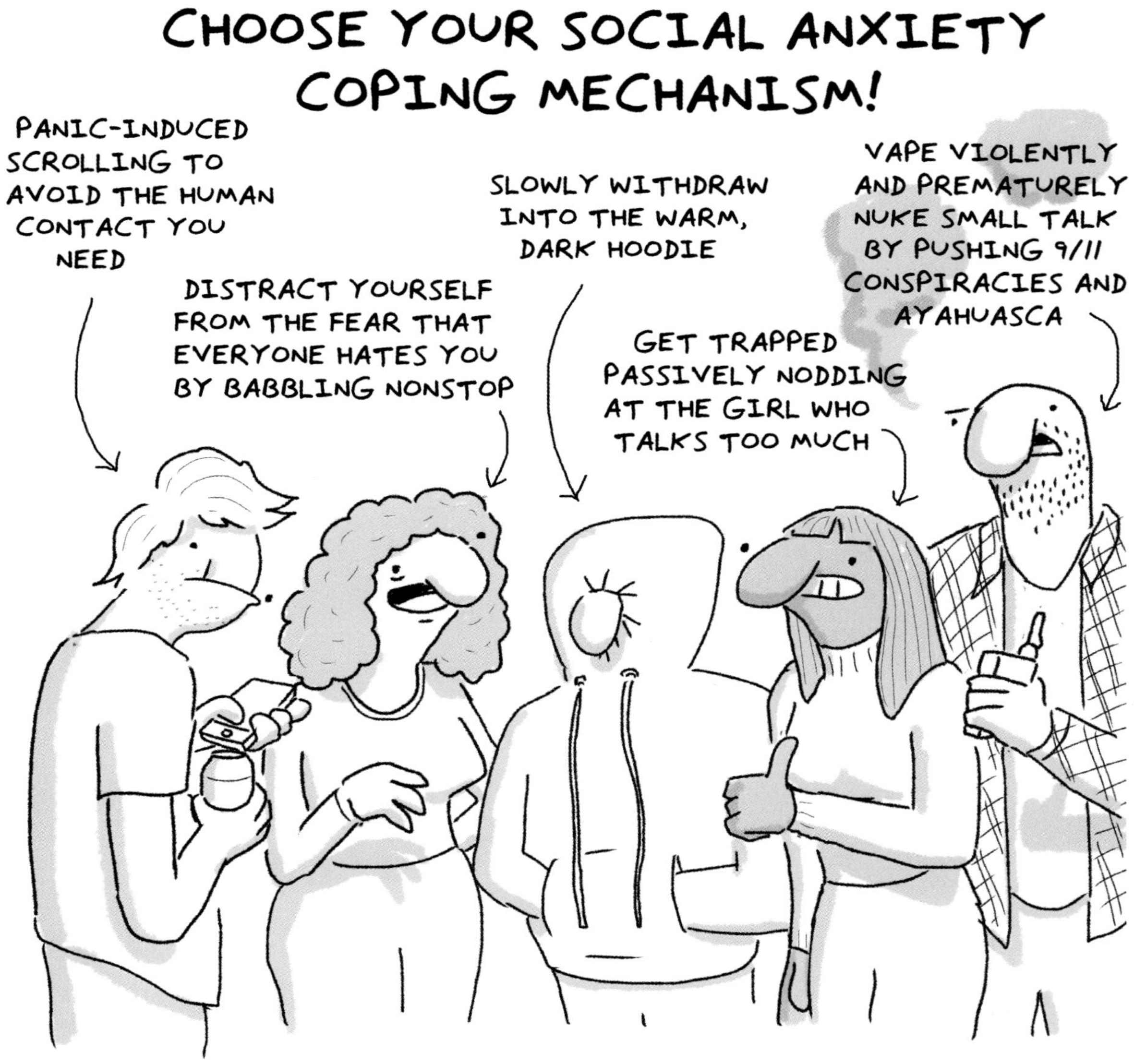
CHOOSE YOUR SOCIAL ANXIETY COPING MECHANISM!
PANIC-INDUCED SCROLLING TO AVOID THE HUMAN CONTACT YOU NEED
DISTRACT YOURSELF FROM THE FEAR THAT EVERYONE HATES YOU BY BABBLING NONSTOP
SLOWLY WITHDRAW INTO THE WARM, DARK HOODIE
GET TRAPPED PASSIVELY NODDING AT THE GIRL WHO TALKS TOO MUCH
VAPE VIOLENTLY AND PREMATURELY NUKE SMALL TALK BY PUSHING 9/11 CONSPIRACIES AND AYAHUASCA

In case you were curious, I'm the one on the left.

LEARN HOW TO IDENTIFY THE PARTS OF A DRUM KIT

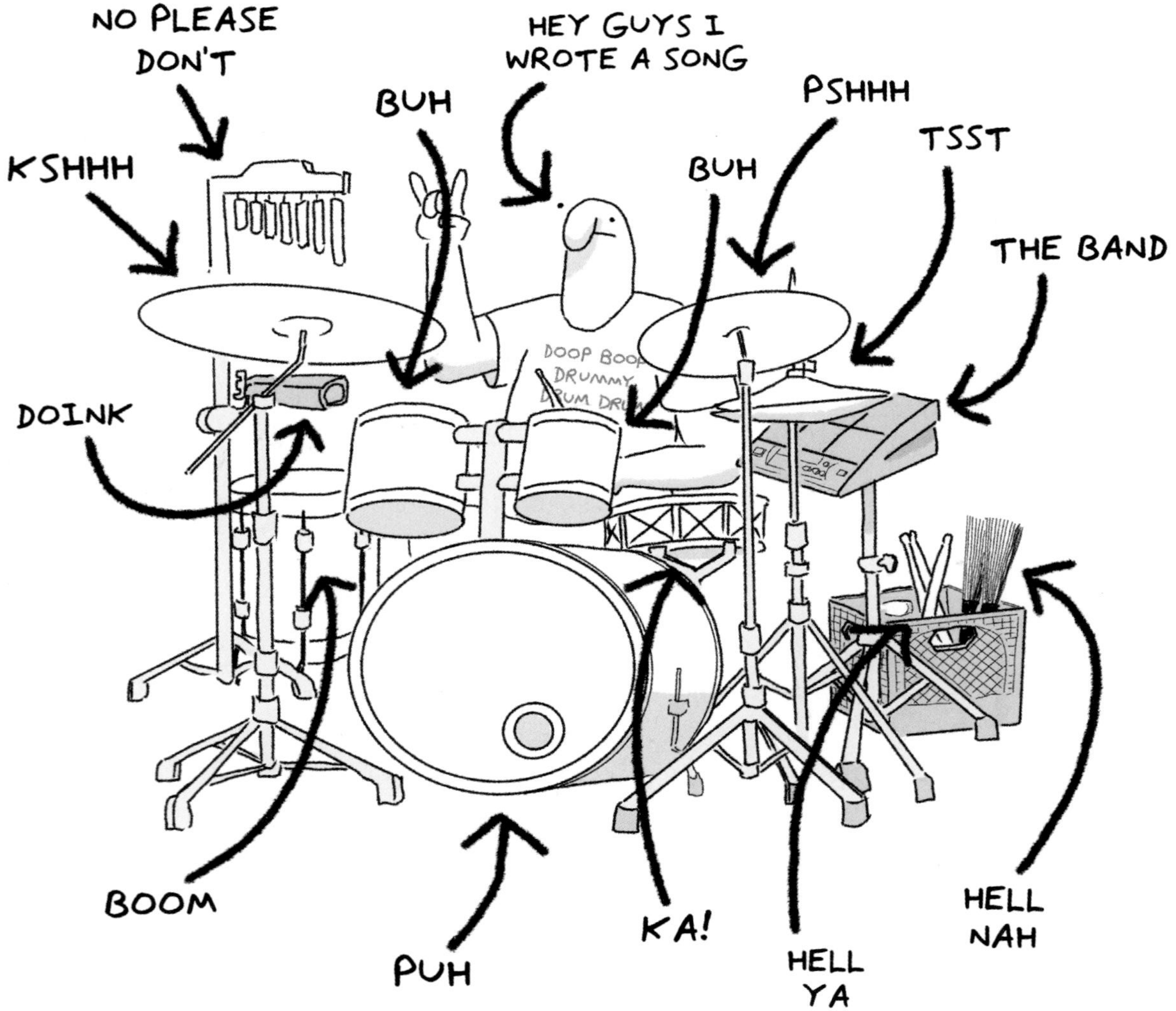
NO PLEASE DON'T
HEY GUYS I WROTE A SONG
BUH
PSHHH
TSST
KSHHH
BUH
THE BAND
DOOP BOOP DRUMMY DRUM DRUM
DOINK
BOOM
PUH
KA!
HELL YA
HELL NAH

A GUIDE TO KOMBUCHA

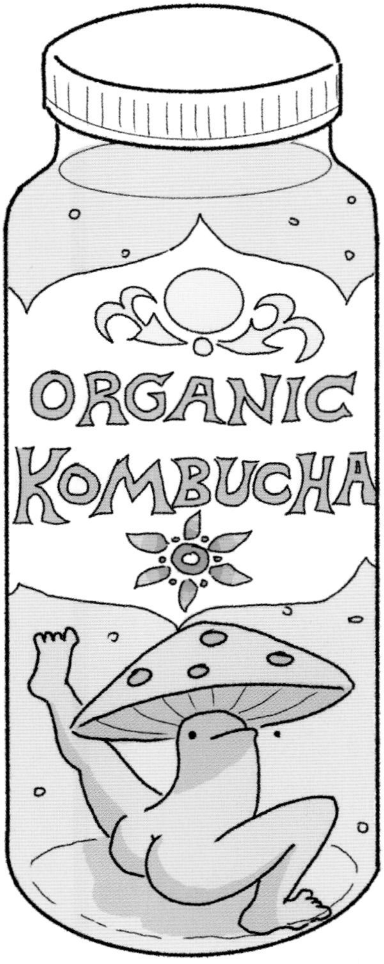
ORGANIC
KOMBUCHA

- PROBIOTIC, CARBONATED TEA WITH POSSIBLE HEALTH BENEFITS
- THERE IS A LIVING MUSHROOM INSIDE EACH BOTTLE
- HIS NAME IS BERT STUMPKINS
- BERT MAKES MAGICAL HEALING JUICE IF YOU BRING HIM SNACKS AND SACRIFICES
- THIS IS GOOD FOR YOUR HEALTH, BUT AT A TERRIBLE COST: AN ANCIENT CURSE ON YOUR FRIENDS AND FAMILY
- EACH BOTTLE COSTS $70 OR SOMETHING

A GUIDE TO MUSTACHES

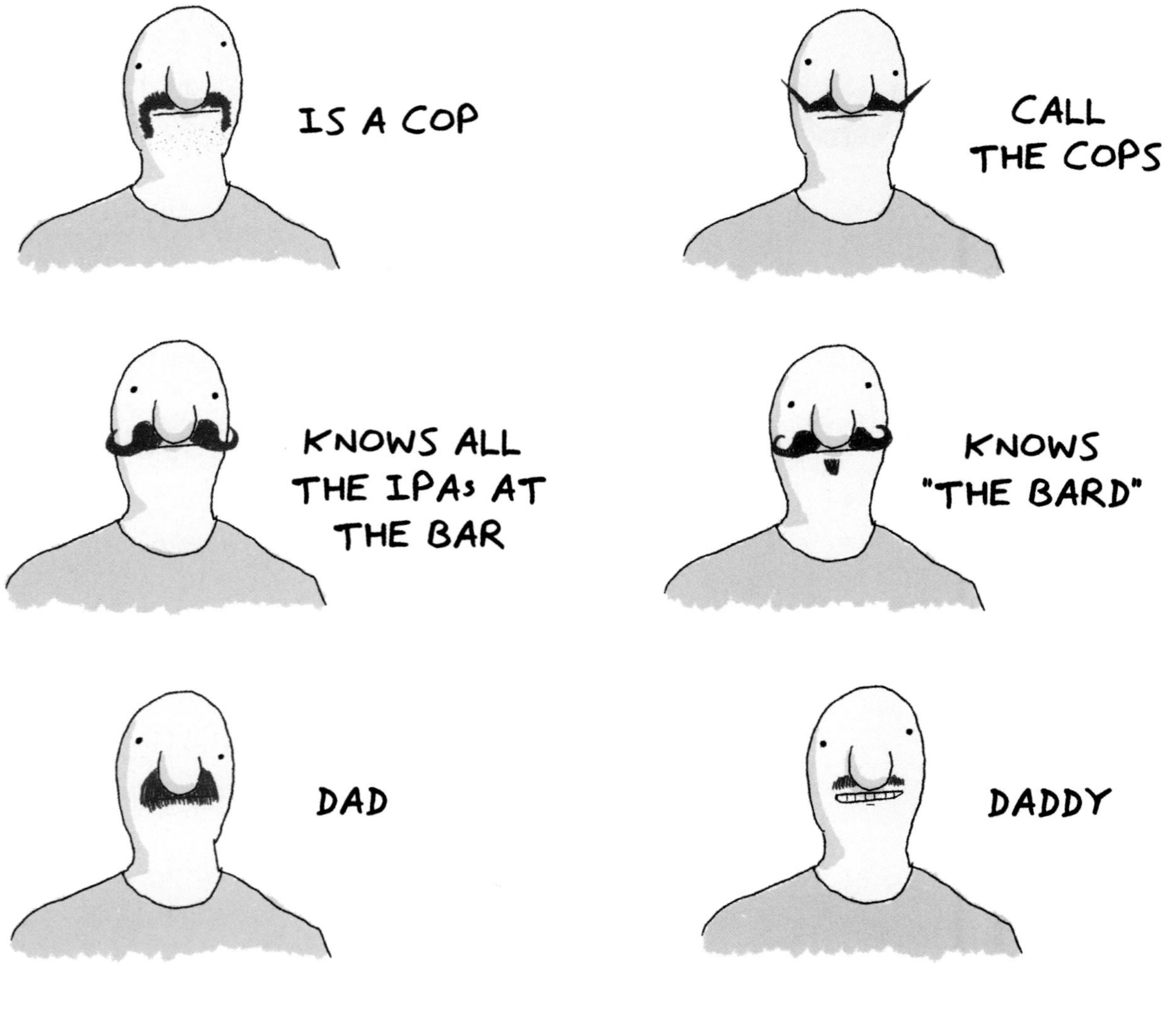
IS A COP
CALL THE COPS
KNOWS ALL THE IPAs AT THE BAR
KNOWS "THE BARD"
DAD
DADDY

WHAT YOUR COFFEE DRINK OF CHOICE SAYS ABOUT YOU

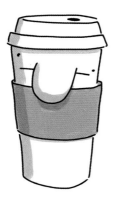

COFFEE WITH CREAM AND SUGAR

- YOU'RE A GROWN-ASS ADULT WHO STILL EATS CHICKEN NUGGETS

ESPRESSO

- THOUGH FREELANCE, YOU ENJOY PRETENDING TO BE IN A HURRY

ENERGY COFFEE

- HAS BEEN IN A FIST FIGHT AT A 311 CONCERT

COLD BREW

- YOU'RE DEAD INSIDE

- AND THIS WILL MAKE YOU FEEL NOTHING

STARBUCKS CARAMEL MACCHIATO

- HARD AS YOU MAY TRY, YOU'LL NEVER BECOME AN INSTAGRAM INFLUENCER

CORTADO

- THIS IS CORRECT

- BUT YOU'RE A REAL PAIN IN THE ASS OUTSIDE OF NYC AND LOS ANGELES

WHAT IS THAT ROCKER THINKING???

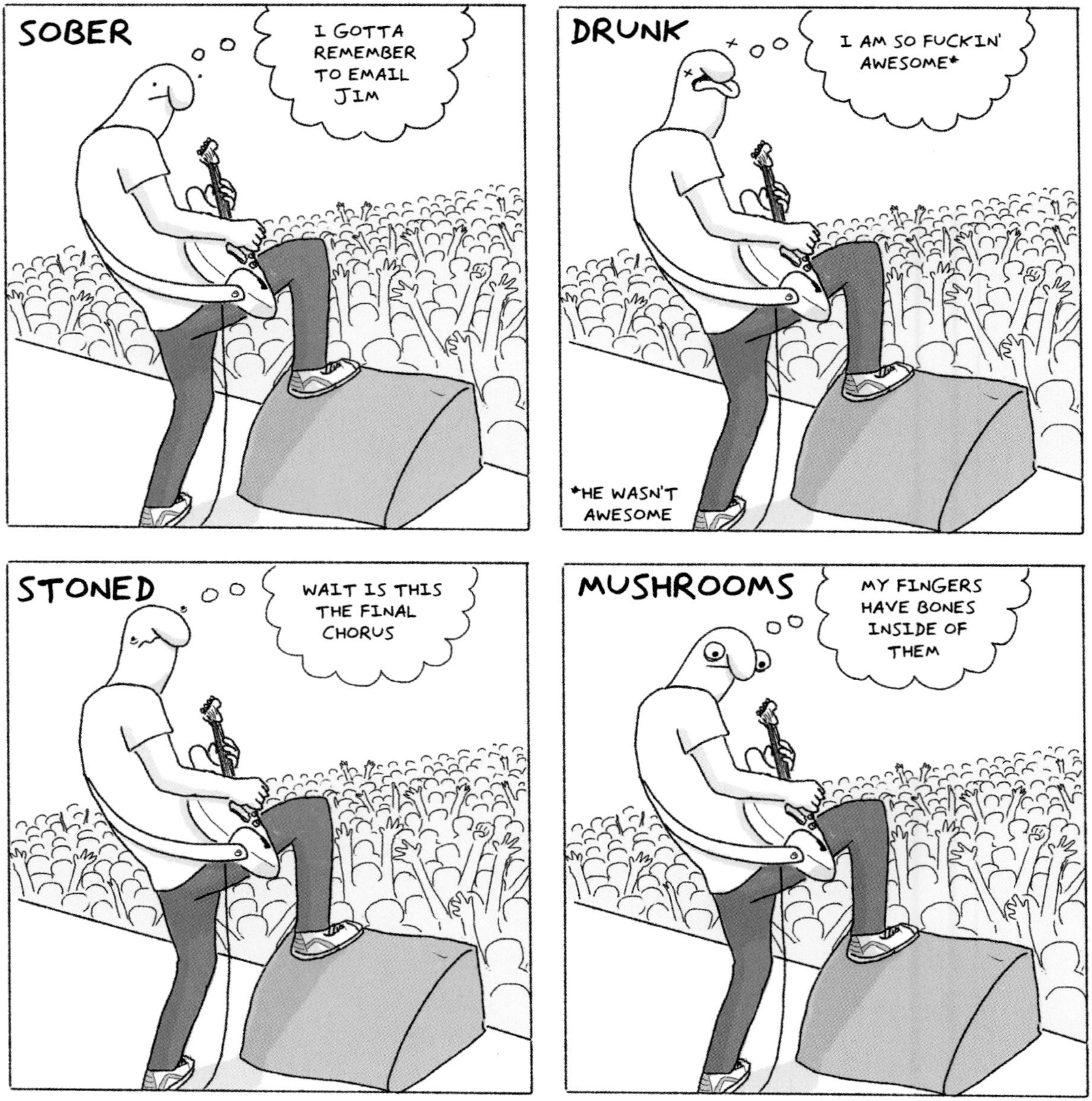
SOBER
I GOTTA REMEMBER TO EMAIL JIM
DRUNK
I AM SO FUCKIN' AWESOME*
*HE WASN'T AWESOME
STONED
WAIT IS THIS THE FINAL CHORUS
MUSHROOMS
MY FINGERS HAVE BONES INSIDE OF THEM

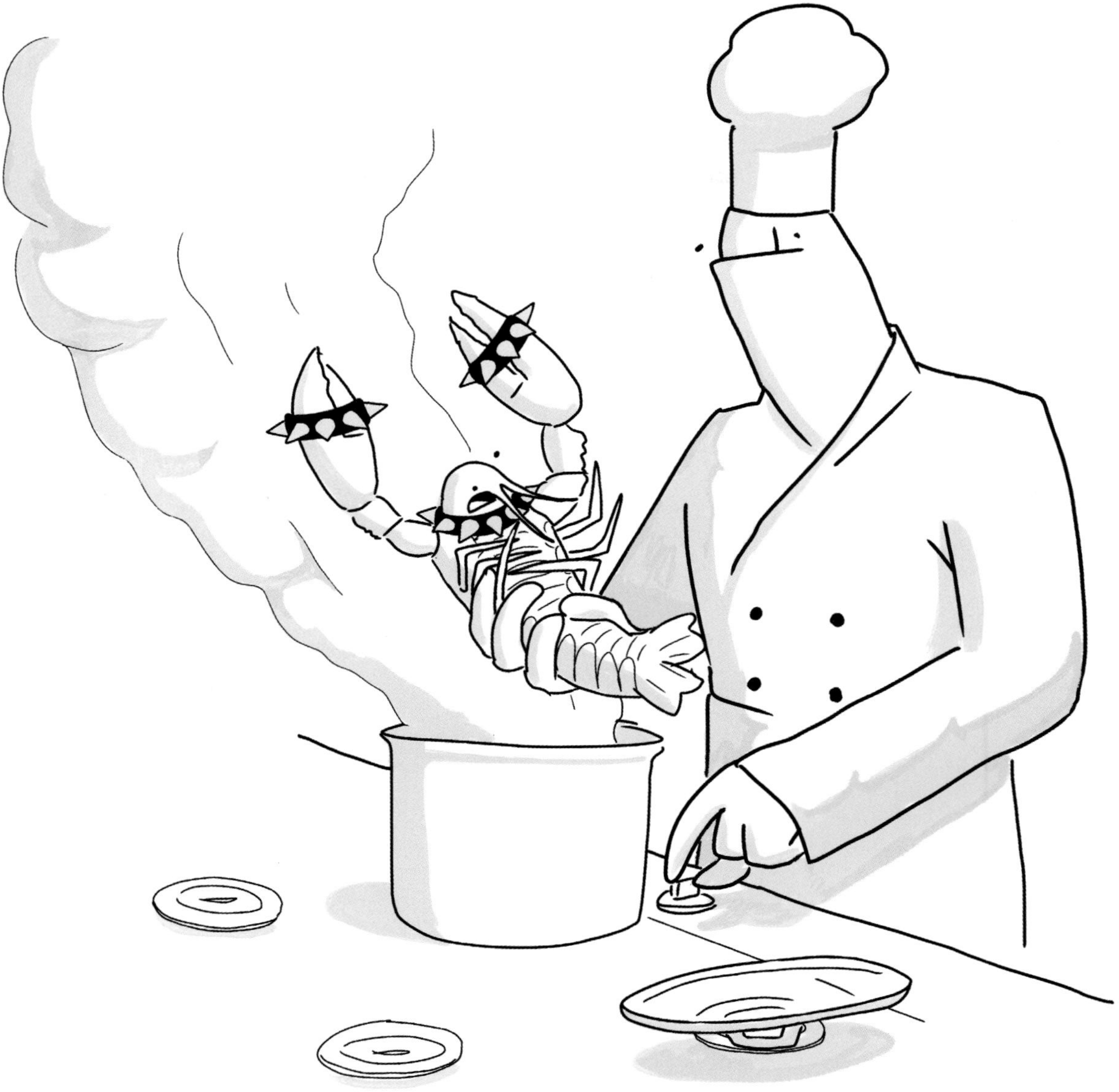

WHOA WHOA WHOA. I HAVEN'T EVEN TOLD YOU MY SAFE WORD YET!

Juul pieces of you

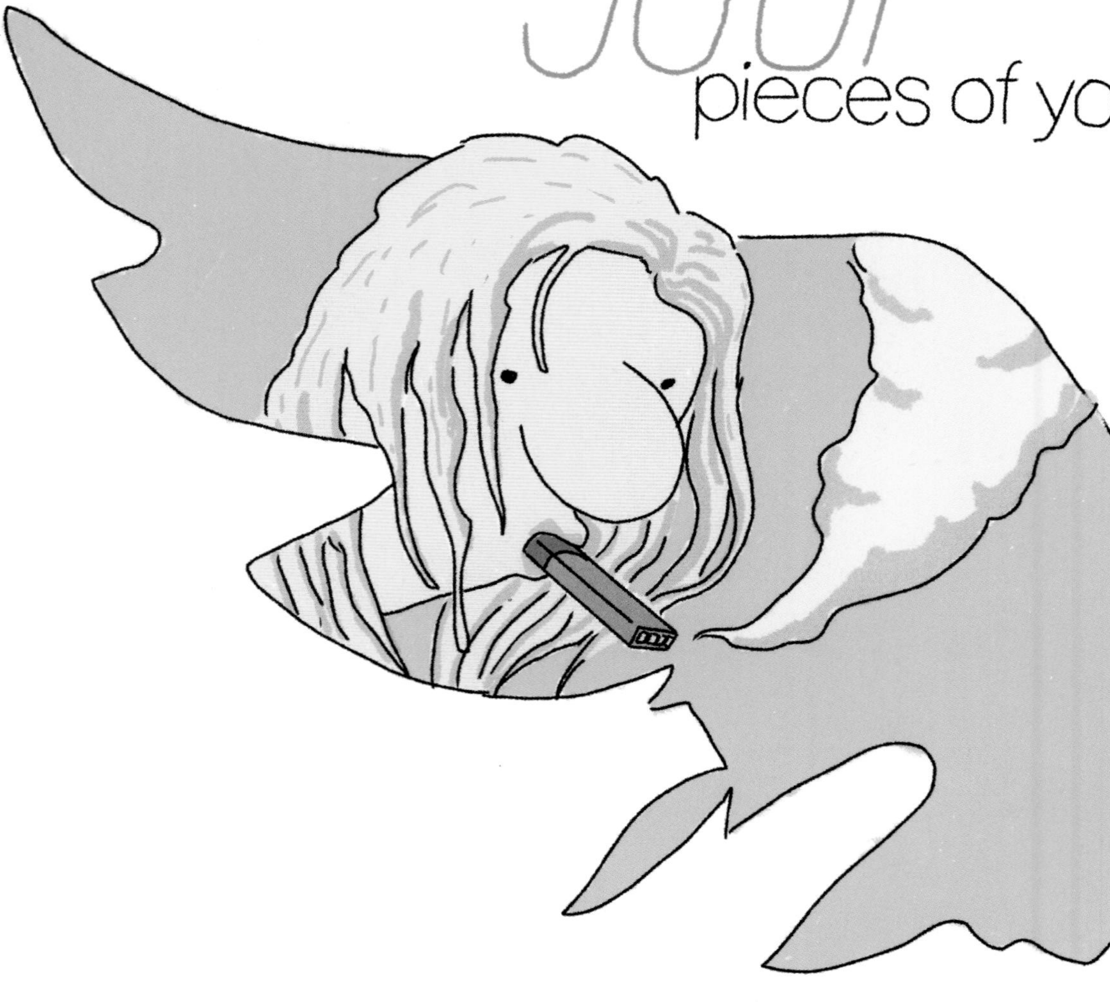

who will vape your soul?

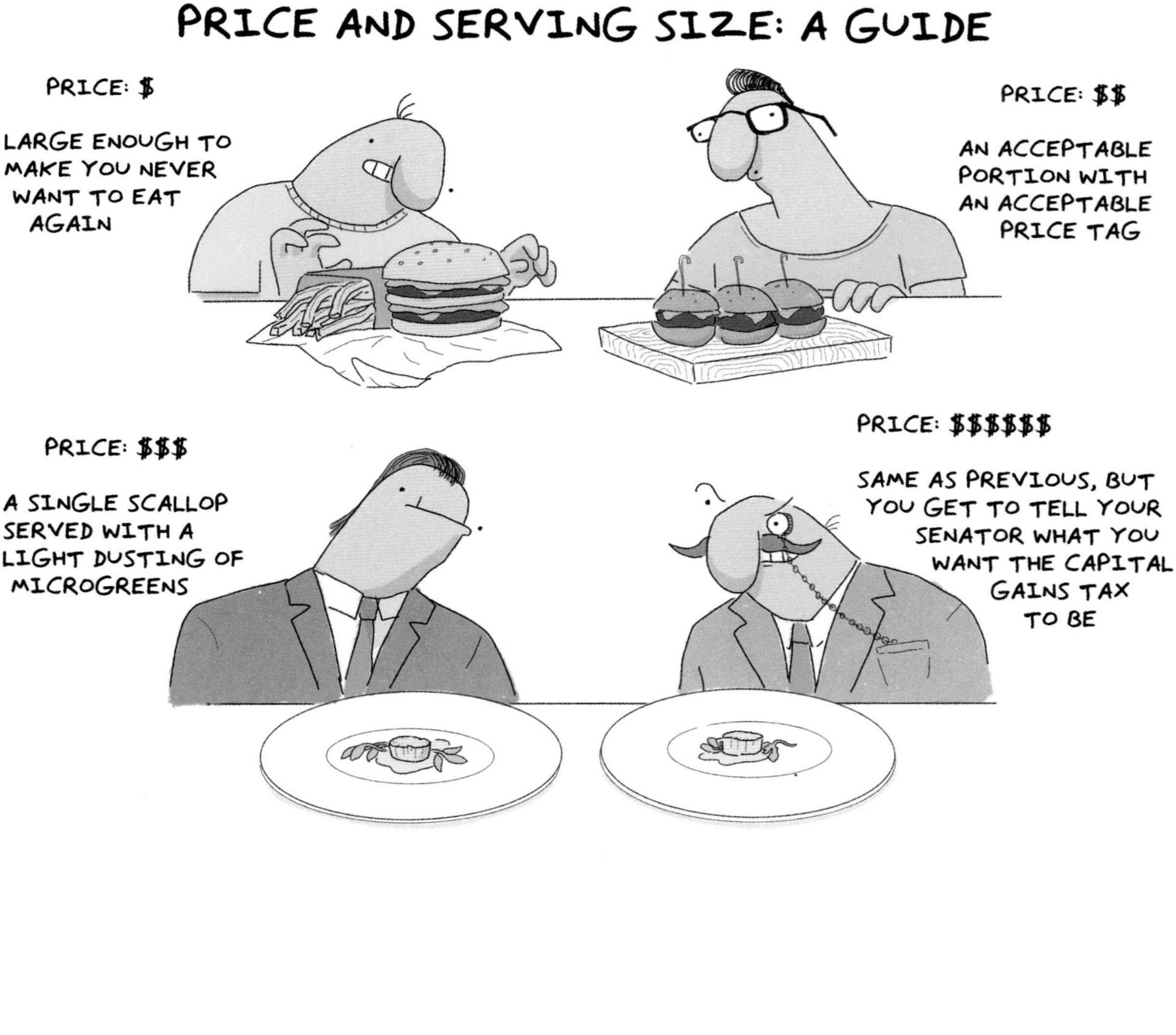
PRICE AND SERVING SIZE: A GUIDE
PRICE: $
LARGE ENOUGH TO MAKE YOU NEVER WANT TO EAT AGAIN
PRICE: $$
AN ACCEPTABLE PORTION WITH AN ACCEPTABLE PRICE TAG
PRICE: $$$
A SINGLE SCALLOP SERVED WITH A LIGHT DUSTING OF MICROGREENS
PRICE: $$$$$$
SAME AS PREVIOUS, BUT YOU GET TO TELL YOUR SENATOR WHAT YOU WANT THE CAPITAL GAINS TAX TO BE

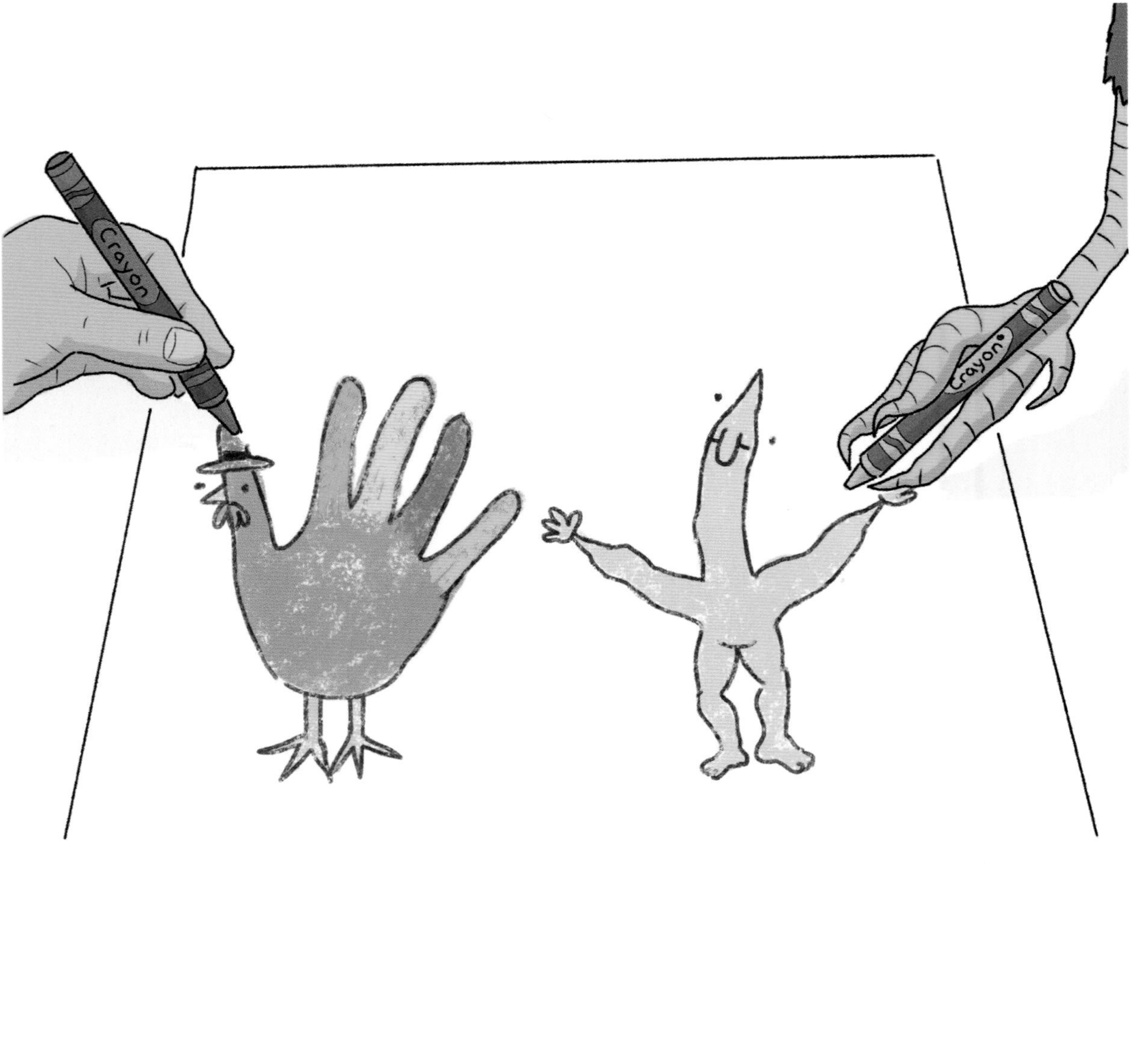
Crayon
Crayon

A GUIDE TO CURING YOUR FRIEND'S DEPRESSION

THERE, THERE. DON'T FEEL BAD!
I MEAN, THERE ARE PLENTY OF GOOD REASONS TO FEEL BAD.
BUT YOUR REASONS ARE BAD.

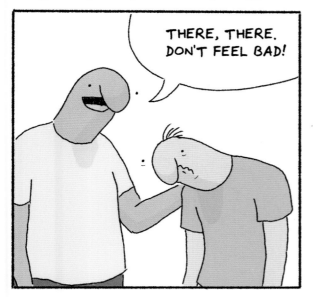

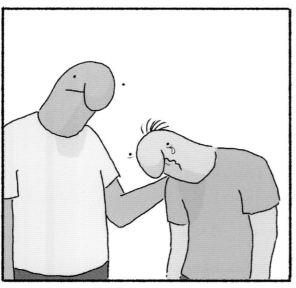

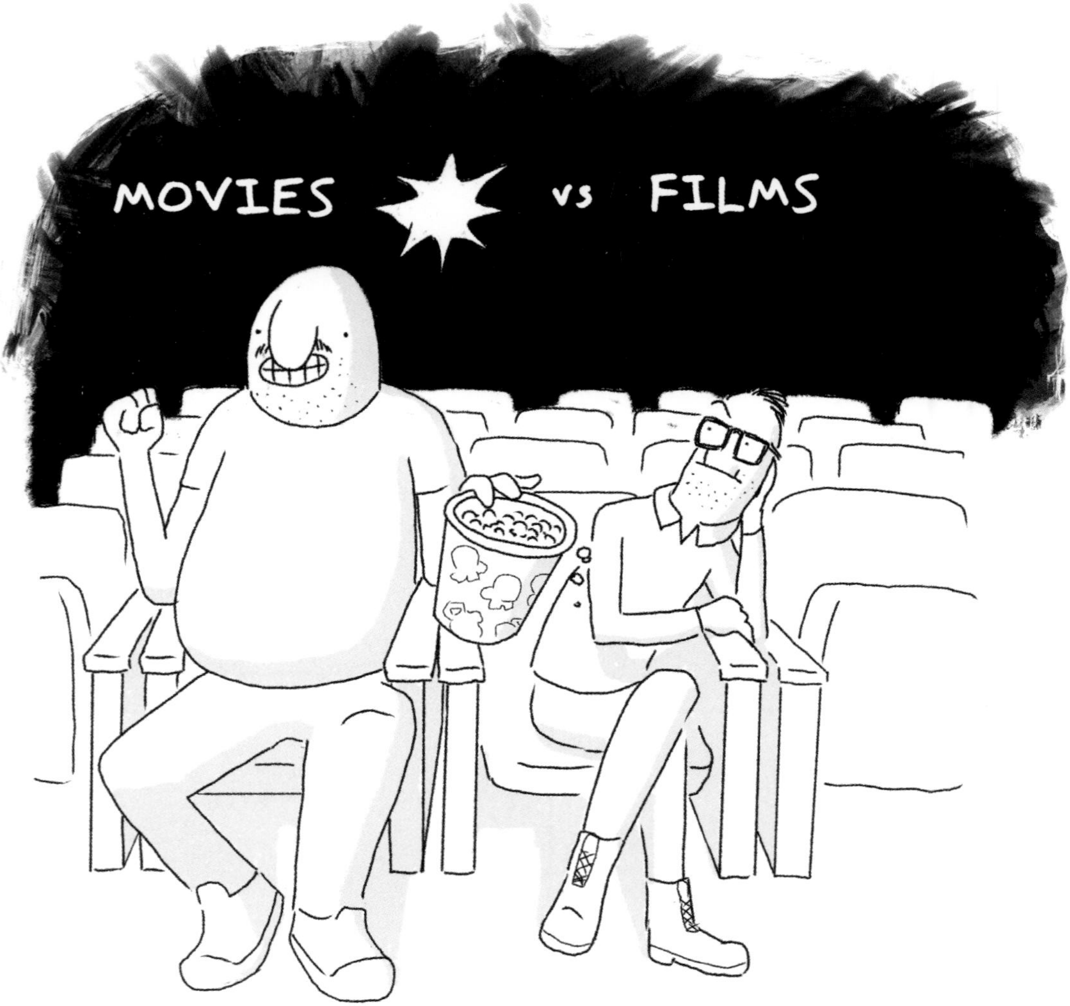
MOVIES vs FILMS

- "THE ROCK" IS IN ALL OF THEM
- BIG TRUCK EXPLODE
- EXPLODE GOOD

- DANIEL DAY-LEWIS IS IN ALL OF THEM
- NOTHING EXPLODES
- SOUNDTRACK HAS NO SMASH MOUTH :(

HA! THIS YOUNGER MILLENNIAL IS SO ABSORBED IN SOCIAL MEDIA THAT HE CANNOT APPRECIATE HIS YOUTH, UNLIKE I, AGING MILLENNIAL, WHO CANNOT APPRECIATE HIS THIRTIES.

WINE DESCRIPTIONS: A GUIDE

"TANNIC"

TASTES LIKE A MOUTHFUL
OF GODDANG GRAPE STEMS

"EARTHY"

TASTES LIKE A GODDANG
PILE OF LEAVES

"SMOKY"

THIS TASTES LIKE A
DAMN HAM, MA'AM

"BUTTERY"

NO WINE TASTES LIKE BUTTER.
YOU'RE JUST DRUNK AND
WEARING A TURTLENECK

FALL, IN SUMMARY

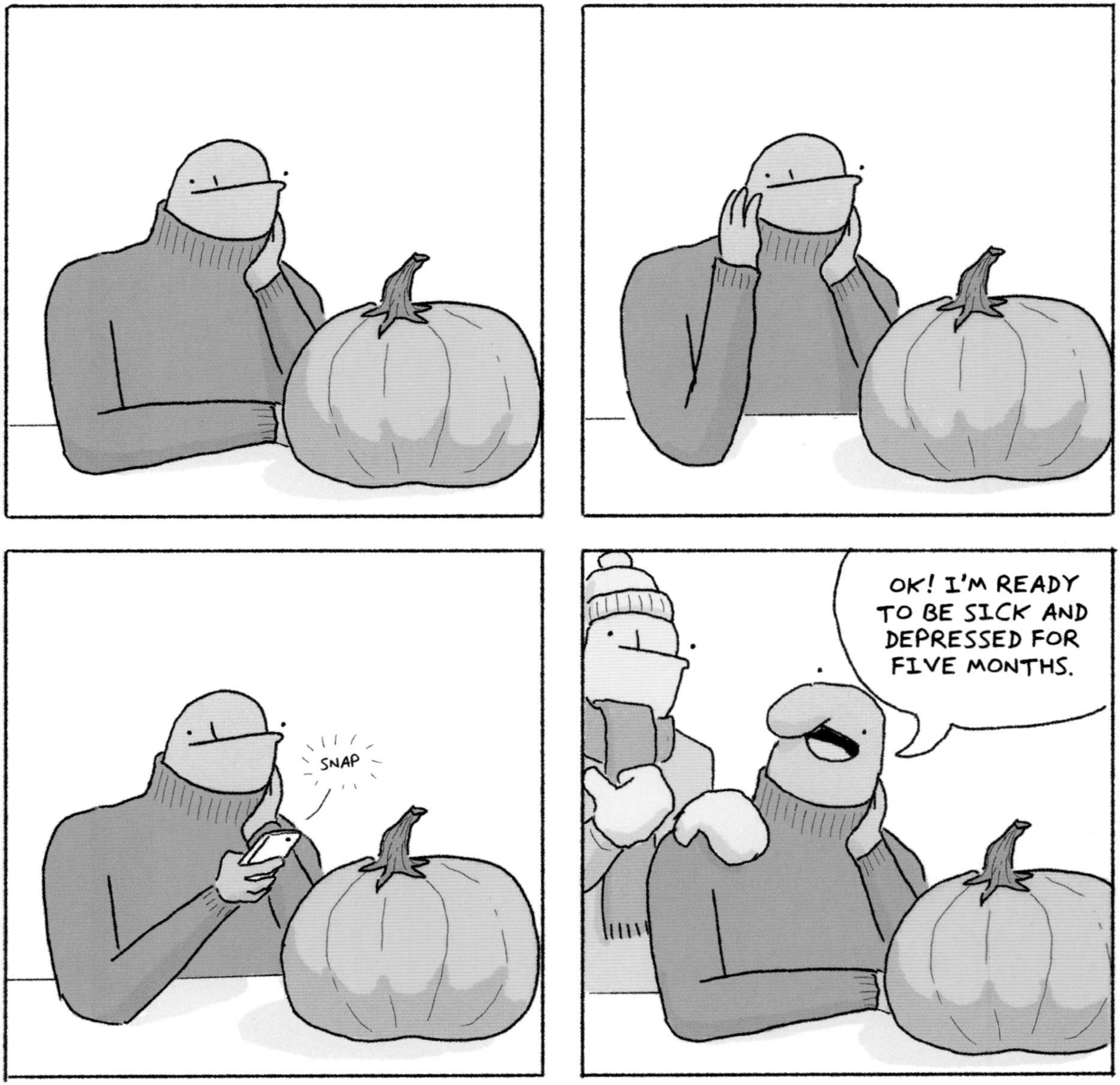
SNAP
OK! I'M READY TO BE SICK AND DEPRESSED FOR FIVE MONTHS.

WHAT YOUR HOUSEPLANT SAYS ABOUT YOU

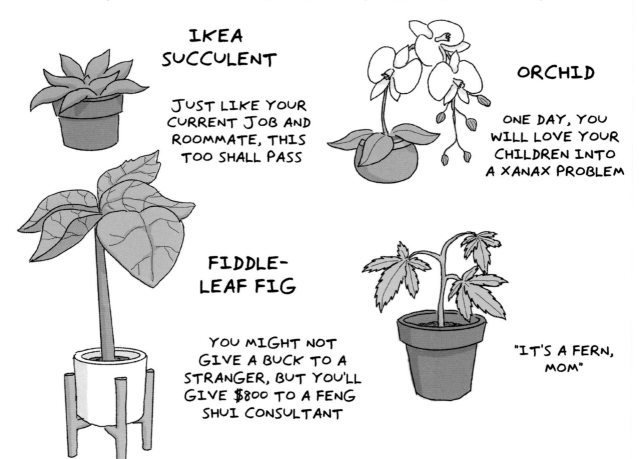

IKEA SUCCULENT

JUST LIKE YOUR CURRENT JOB AND ROOMMATE, THIS TOO SHALL PASS

ORCHID

ONE DAY, YOU WILL LOVE YOUR CHILDREN INTO A XANAX PROBLEM

FIDDLE-LEAF FIG

YOU MIGHT NOT GIVE A BUCK TO A STRANGER, BUT YOU'LL GIVE $800 TO A FENG SHUI CONSULTANT

"IT'S A FERN, MOM"

I should note that I don't know anything about houseplants, and relied heavily on my friend Jessie's expertise here. If you're thinking of starting a 500-days-of-comics project, make sure you have an in-house horticulturalist.

THE HAMSTER WHEEL

The first 30 days of the daily drawing challenge felt like a year all by themselves.

I tried to build a backlog of ideas to make the workload feel less overwhelming, but it was never *quite* enough that I could ever coast, and the jokes always needed tightening. Even in the first month, it felt like I was a hamster on a wheel that kept spinning regardless of whether I kept running along with it. I tried to keep a notebook of ideas around, and usually, I was at least a couple of weeks ahead on *concepts.* But sometimes the hamster wheel moved faster than my brain, and I ended up whipping up a comic that pleased me alone while inducing terror and confusion among my followers, like the masterpiece[1] featured on this page.

WHAT'S THE MATTER, HANK?
DON'T LIKE DANCING?

---

1. For reasons I do not understand, and probably don't want to understand, this one was one of my early personal favorites, in spite of the hundreds of comments protesting its existence, and remains so.

Though it was stressful to keep up with the daily challenge and find a rhythm, the beginning of the project also felt like a frantic, hyper-compressed technical art education crammed into a single manic month. I was forced to learn Photoshop out of urgent necessity, which I had been putting off for years. I learned the mechanics of transforming my own handwriting into a computer font. I made more strides in my drawing ability in one month than I had in the previous 10 years. And a few weeks into the project, I got retweeted and regrammed by Ringo! A real live Beatle! I could finally draw human hands![2] And the rest of the human body! Sort of!

The biggest technical change happened six months in, when I transitioned from scanning my hand-drawn comics to using an iPad. At first, it felt totally unnatural and boxy, just like learning to self-produce and record my own music on a computer had seemed at first. That feeling lasted about a week but was eventually overridden by the obvious advantage of being able to manipulate layers and individual elements of a drawing. Though I started out clumsily drawing everything with my finger, it exponentially multiplied the sorts of ideas I was able to tackle on a daily crunch. I could easily color and shade! And then change the colors or intensity of shading, without affecting my line drawings! To be sure, there was a meditative, tactile quality I missed from my previous Luddite methods. But overall, embracing our robot overlords was a huge step forward.[3]

Not having a budget to pay someone to be a full-time figure model, I also learned that my new digital environment meant that I could easily use myself as a model for otherwise difficult-to-imagine human poses. Often, if I needed to study a certain pose, I would set up a camera timer and use myself as a model.

---

2. It is a dark and terrible secret in the art world that no one can draw hands without looking at their own hands and then just continuing to stare and think about how weird hands are.
3. Now when I use pen and paper, I often become visibly enraged that I can't move characters around the page after drawing them and catch myself instinctively reaching for the nonexistent undo button.

You might have already thought ahead a couple of steps, and if so, you're probably sweating. You've done the mental math. Well, you're about to get confirmation of your deepest fears: I am the man who lives in the potato chip can. The Chip Man™ is me.

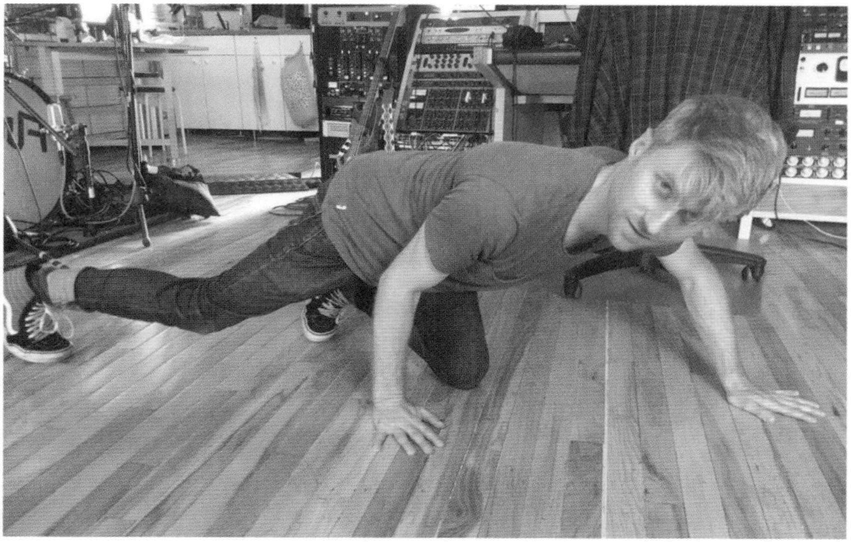

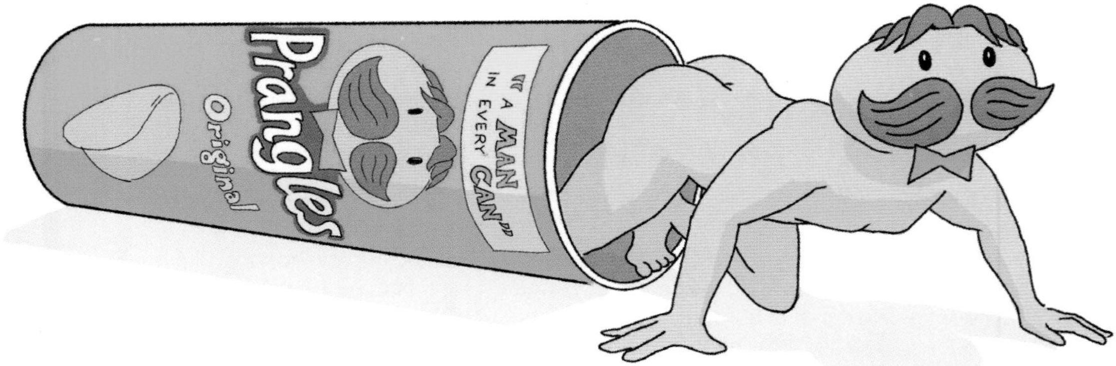
Prangles
Original
A MAN
IN EVERY CAN

Let's move on, once again. It's all we can do.

A TIP FROM THE ARTIST

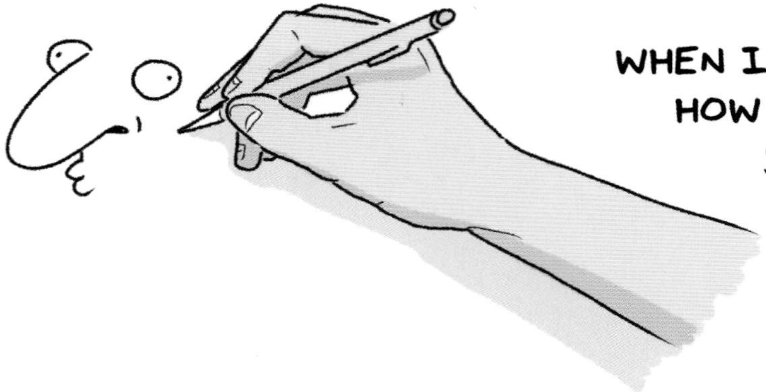

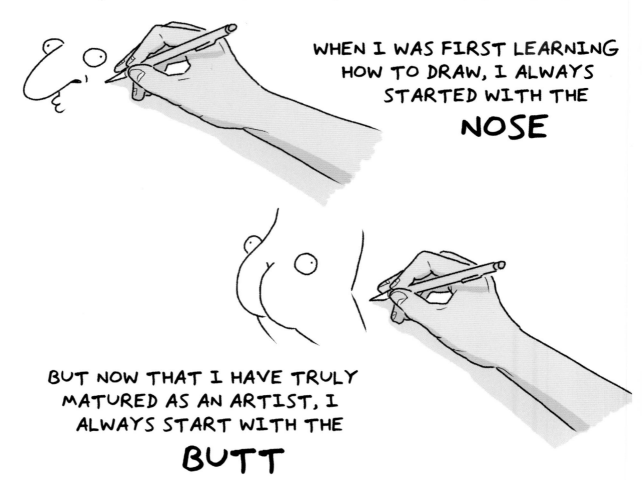

WHEN I WAS FIRST LEARNING HOW TO DRAW, I ALWAYS STARTED WITH THE

NOSE

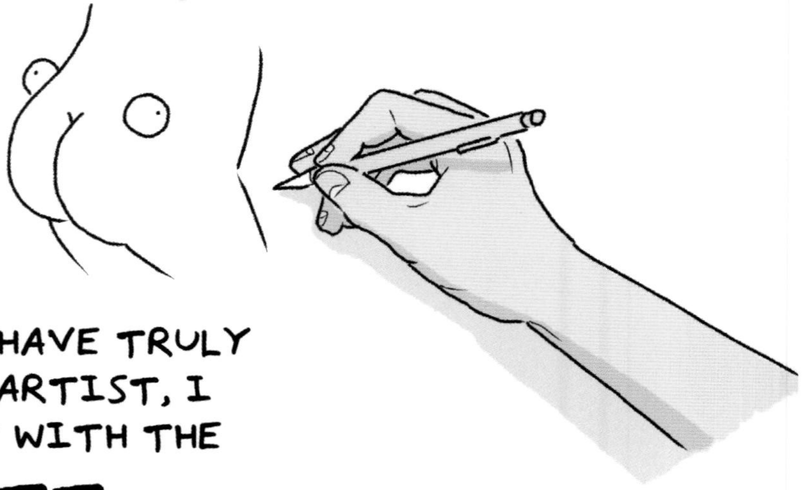

BUT NOW THAT I HAVE TRULY MATURED AS AN ARTIST, I ALWAYS START WITH THE

BUTT

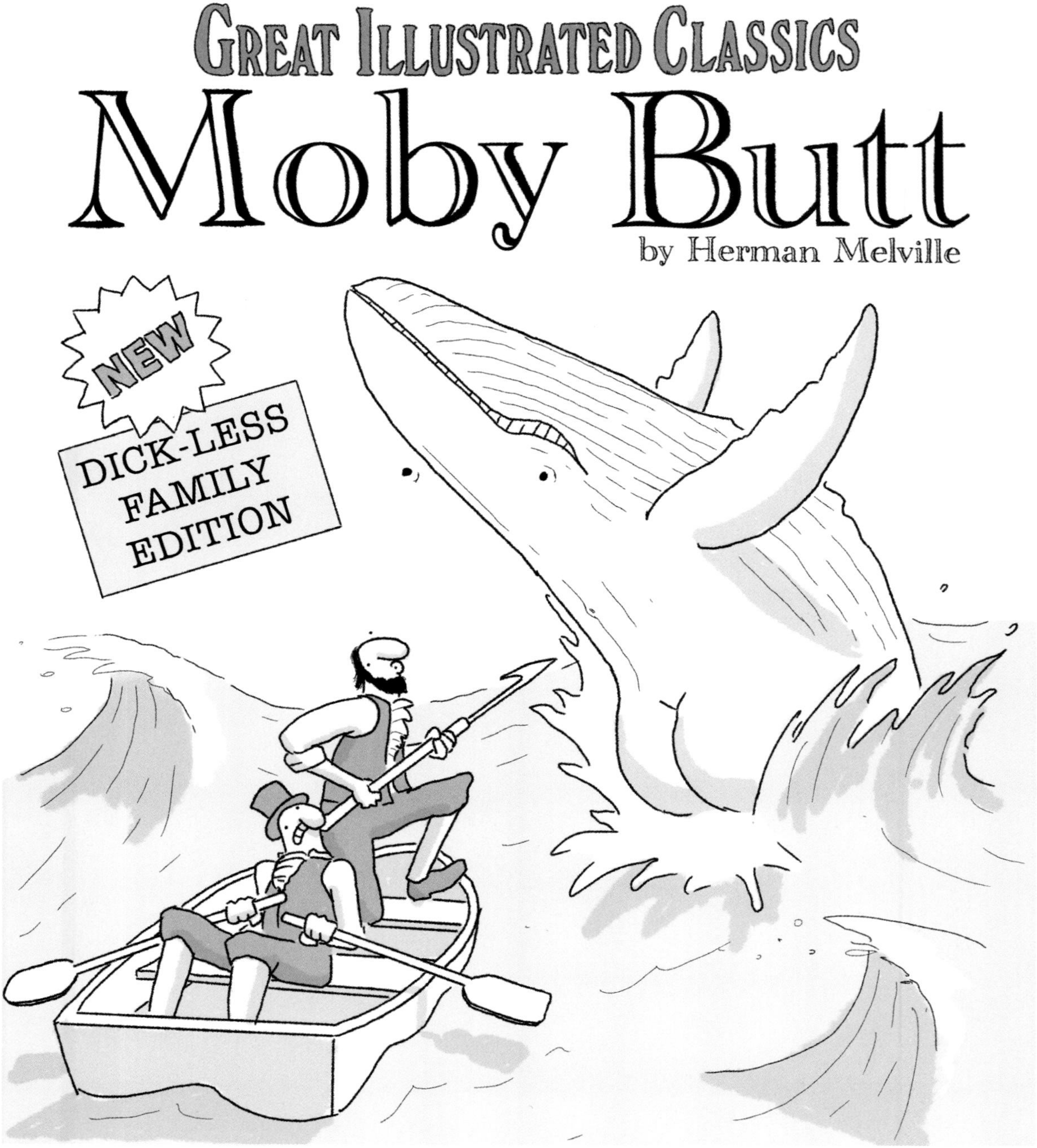
GREAT ILLUSTRATED CLASSICS
Moby Butt
by Herman Melville
NEW
DICK-LESS
FAMILY
EDITION

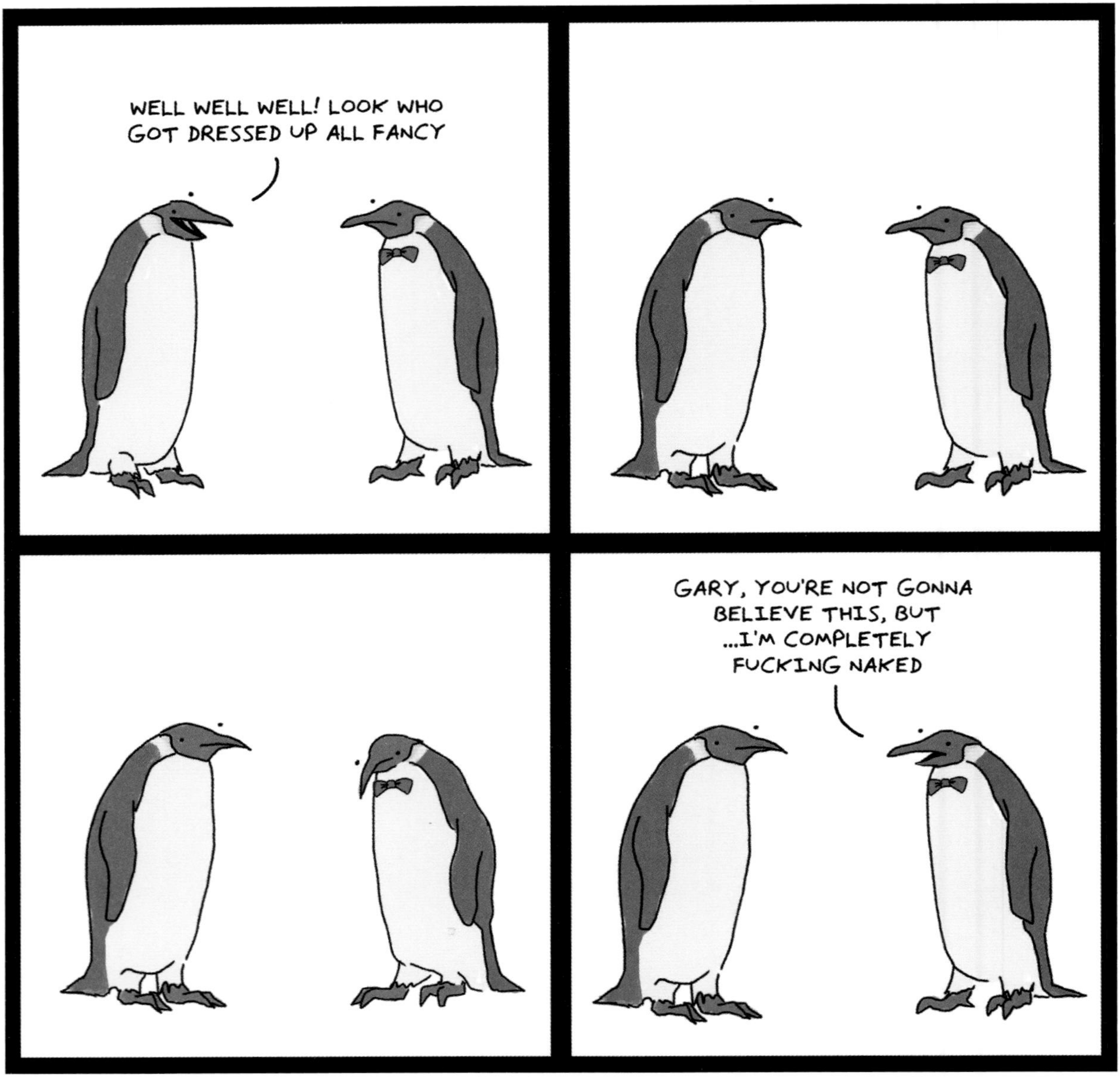
WELL WELL WELL! LOOK WHO GOT DRESSED UP ALL FANCY
GARY, YOU'RE NOT GONNA BELIEVE THIS, BUT ...I'M COMPLETELY FUCKING NAKED

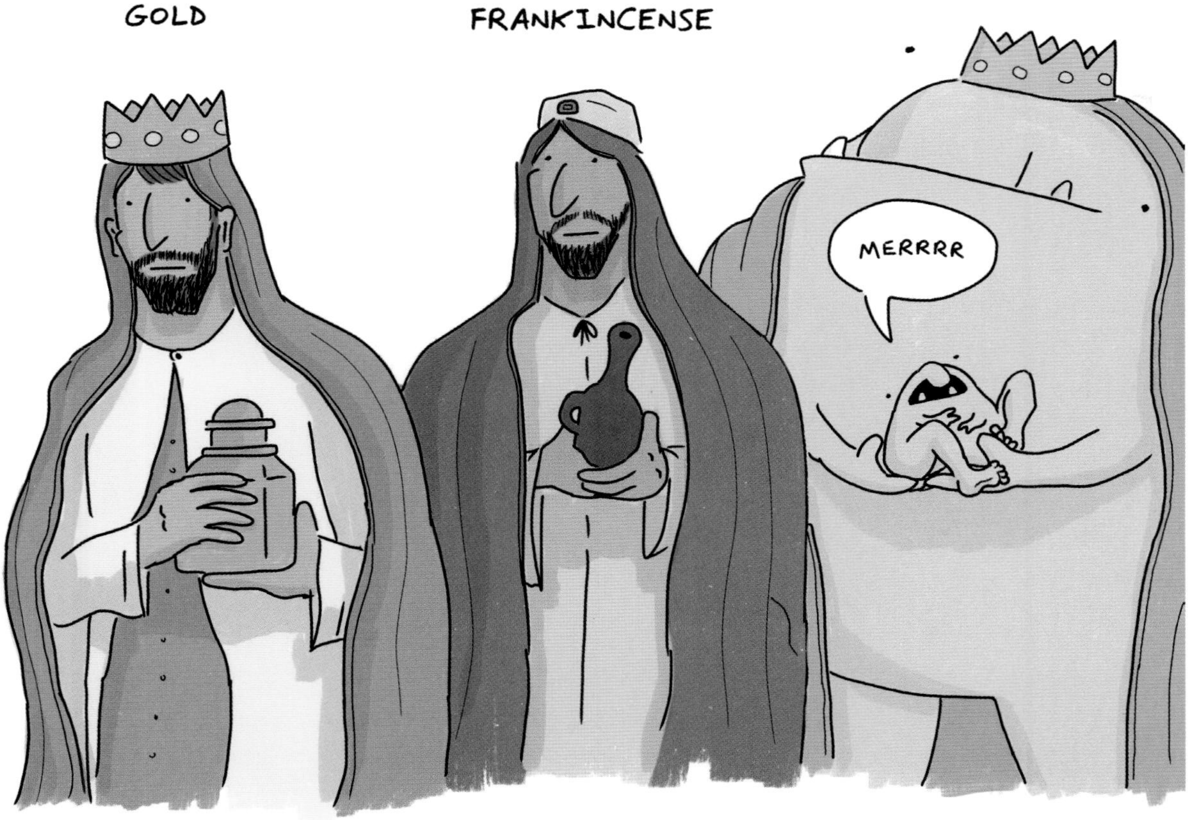
GOLD
FRANKINCENSE
MERRRR

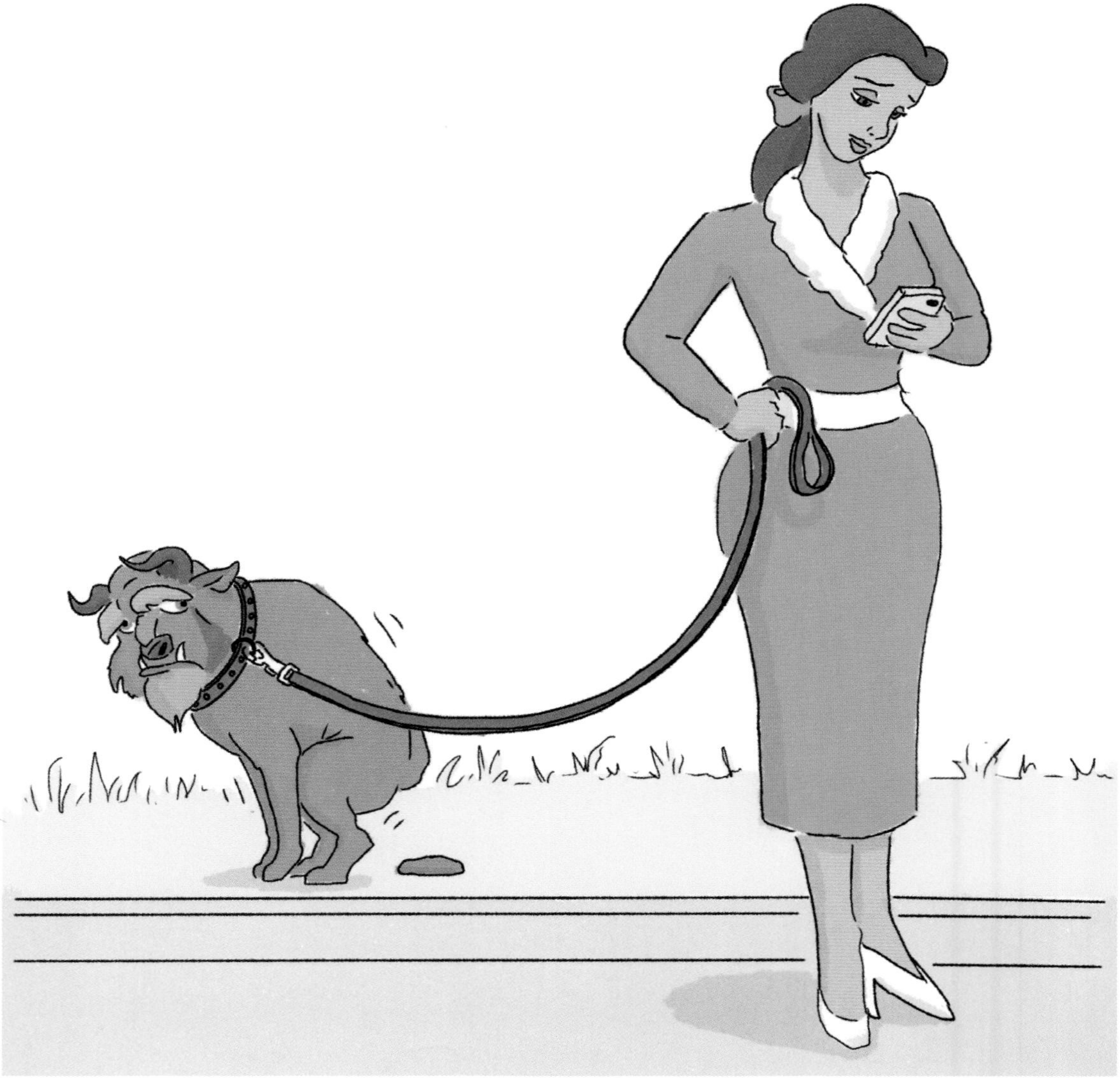

A lot of people seemed to think this was some kind of commentary on modern masculinity being constrained by feminism, and a lot of other people seemed to think it was a ham-handed feminist statement, but I have to let both of them down by admitting that I just thought it would be funny to see the Beast pooping and that my friend Dan actually came up with the idea in the first place.

FOOTBALL vs FOOTBALL

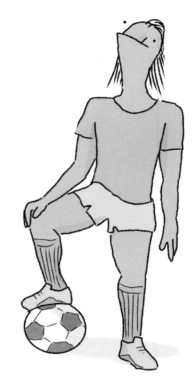

- EACH POINT WORTH SIX POINTS, FOR SOME REASON

- BIG BOYS GOING HOG WILD AND PRETENDING NOT TO GET CONCUSSIONS

- IT'S NICE TO BE ABLE TO MAKE SMALL TALK WITH UNCLE LARRY

- NO ONE HAS EVER SCORED A POINT

- SMALL, BEAUTIFUL BOYS PRETENDING THEY ARE MORTALLY WOUNDED

- IT'S NICE TO BE ABLE TO MAKE SMALL TALK OUTSIDE OF AMERICA

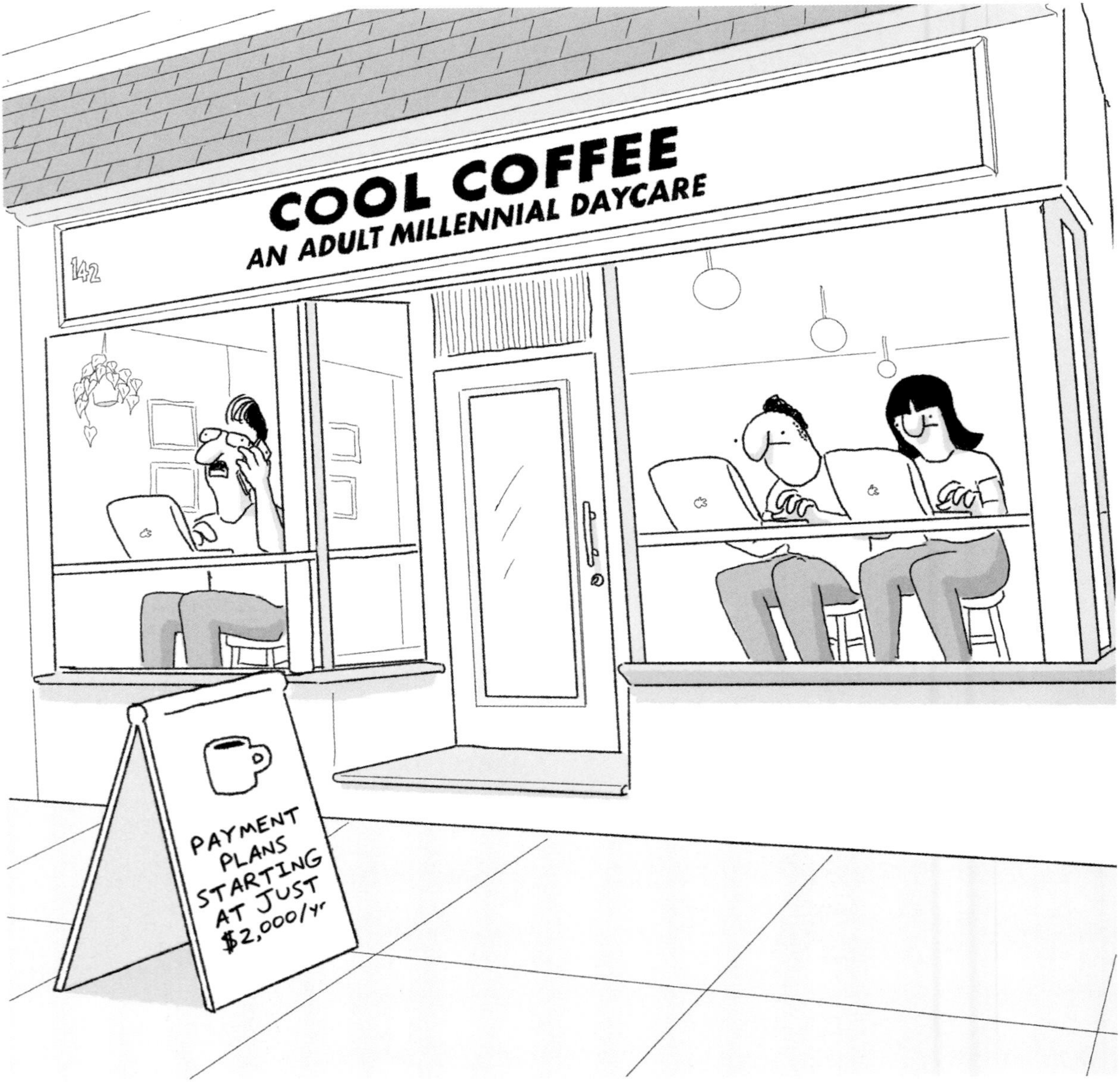

COOL COFFEE
AN ADULT MILLENNIAL DAYCARE
142
PAYMENT PLANS STARTING AT JUST $2,000/yr

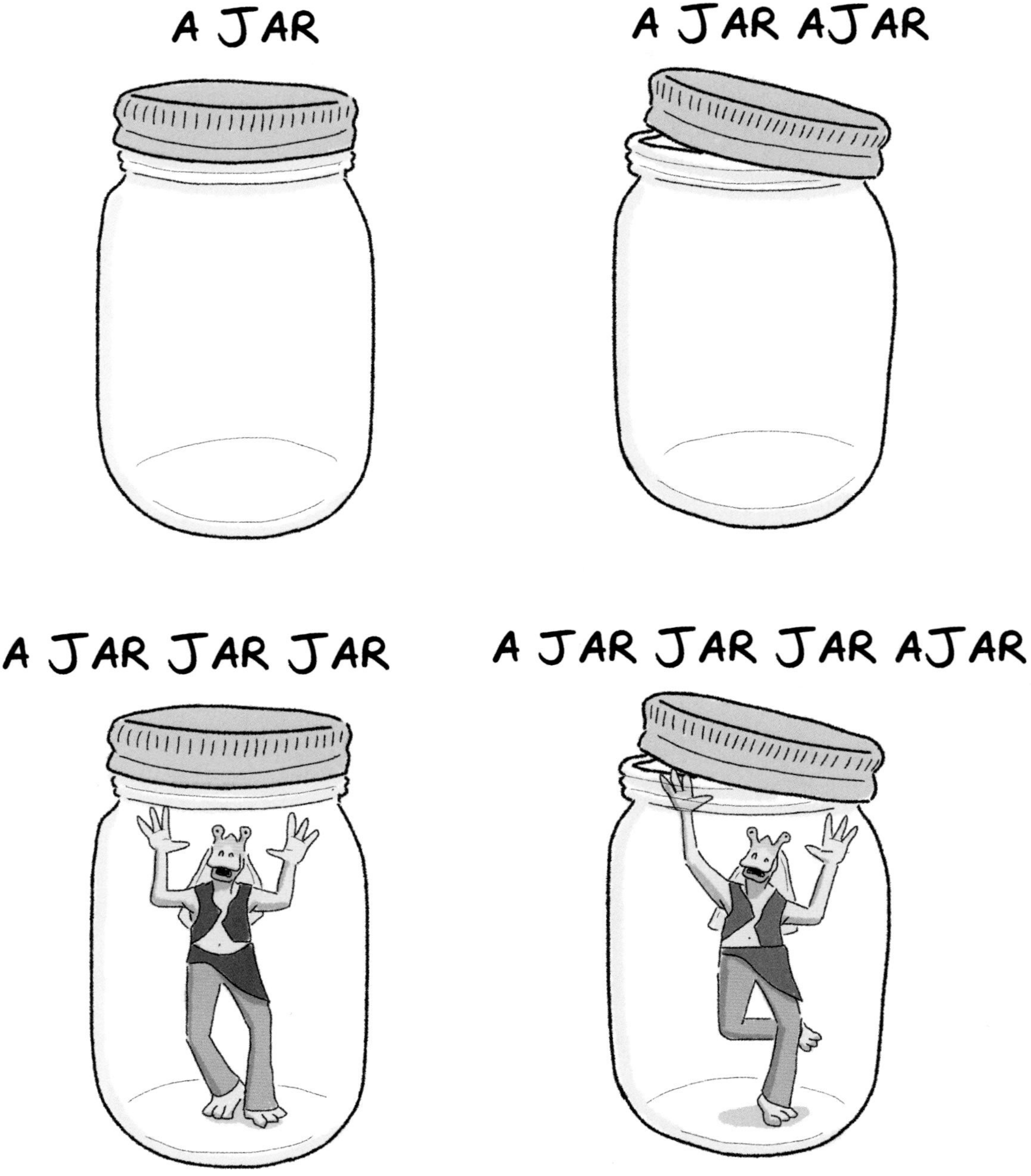
A JAR
A JAR AJAR
A JAR JAR JAR
A JAR JAR JAR AJAR

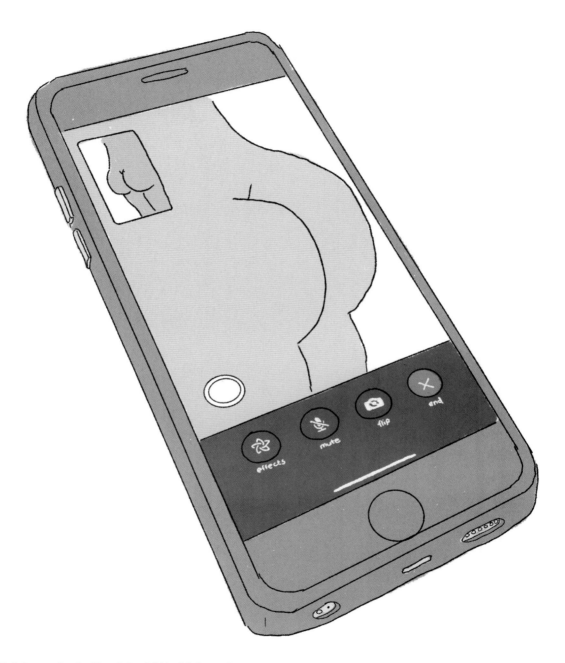

Buttdial. Or maybe AssTime? Get it? Yeah? Great. Let's move on.

WHAT YOUR SANDALS SAY ABOUT YOU: A GUIDE

HAS PURCHASED UNDERWEAR
IN A HURRY FROM A CVS

ROCK-HARD ABS AND
BABY-SOFT HANDS

DIDN'T LIKE THE DEAD
'TIL JOHN MAYER JOINED

STOPPED LIKING THE DEAD
WHEN JOHN MAYER JOINED

HAS BEEN IN A DOUBLE
KAYAK WITH A GOLDEN LAB

EXPLAIN YOURSELF
OR I CALL THE POLICE

KNOW YOUR BREEDS

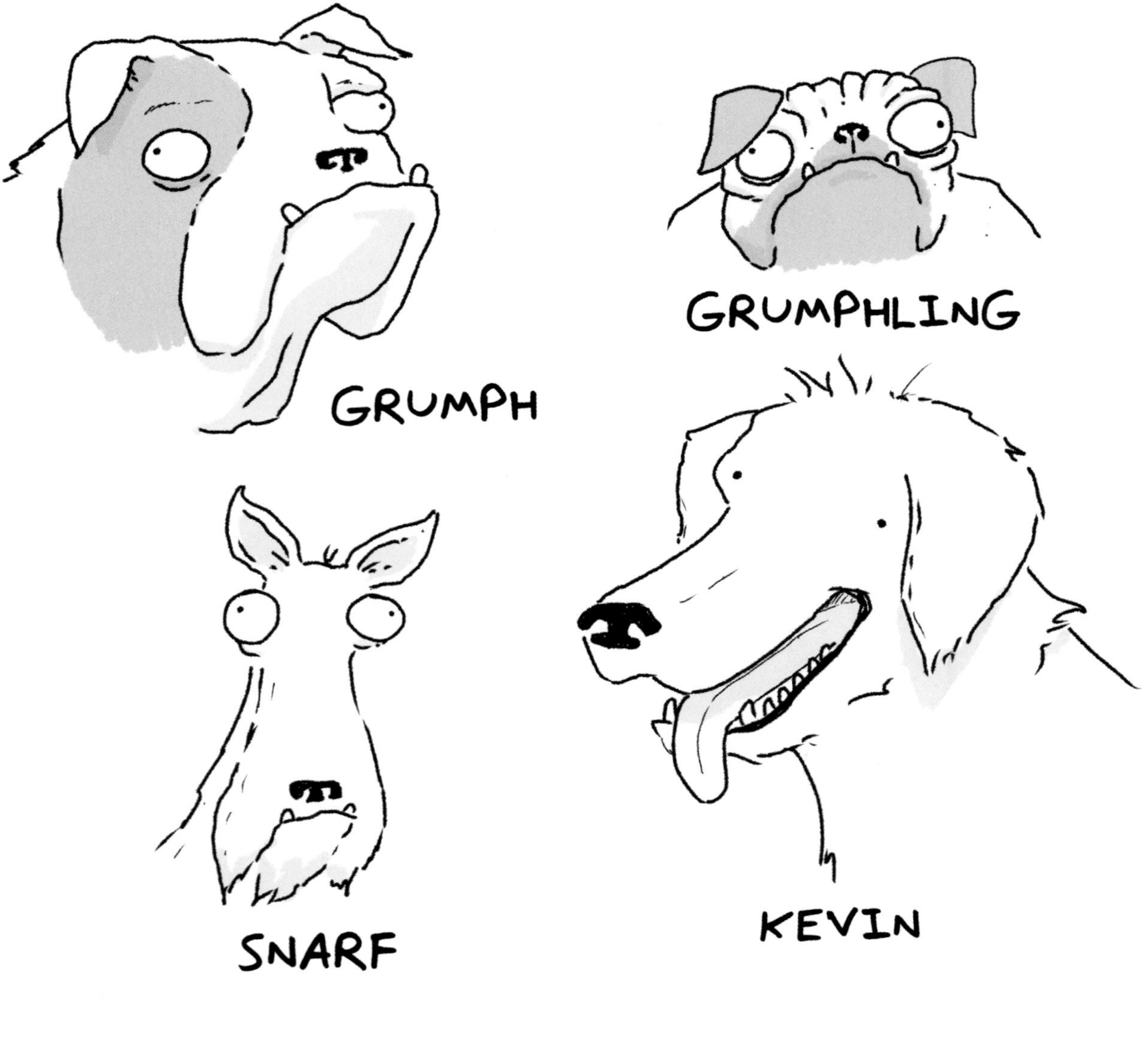
GRUMPH
GRUMPHLING
SNARF
KEVIN

WHICH HOGWARTS HOUSE ARE YOU?

WEEBLEDINK

- EXTREMELY ONLINE, EXTREMELY SAD
- "YOU AWAKE? HAHA"

GRUMPLEWORM

- INSTAGRAMS YOGA POSES AND DAILY AFFIRMATIONS
- BUT AS A CRY FOR HELP

SNAGGLEHORN

- LOVES MURDER PODCASTS
- BUT ONLY TO DROWN OUT THE CEASELESS, SHRIEKING VOICES WITHIN

CHUMBAWUMBA

- DRINKS A WHISKEY DRINK
- DRINKS A VODKA DRINK
- DRINKS A LAGER DRINK
- DRINKS A CIDER DRINK

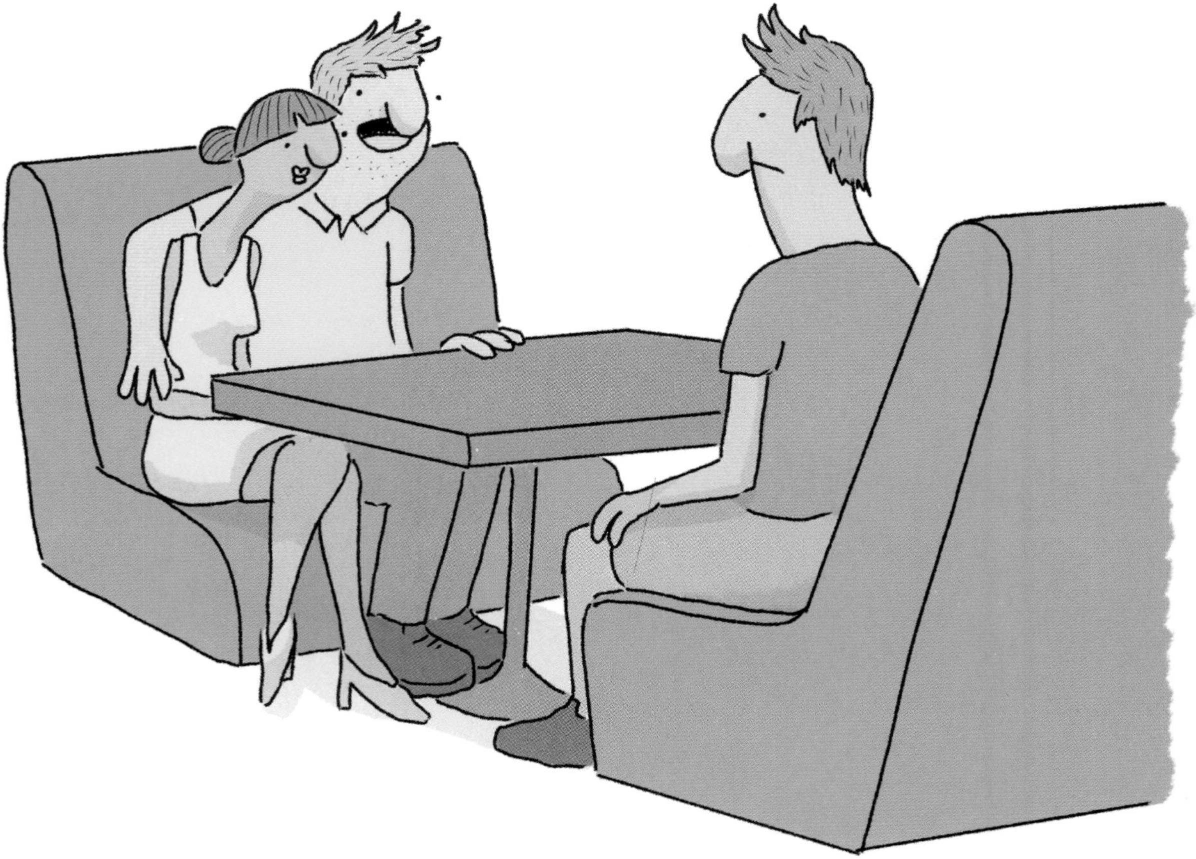

FUNNY YOU SHOULD ASK! I WAS TAKING A DUMP AND INDISCRIMINATELY SWIPING RIGHT!

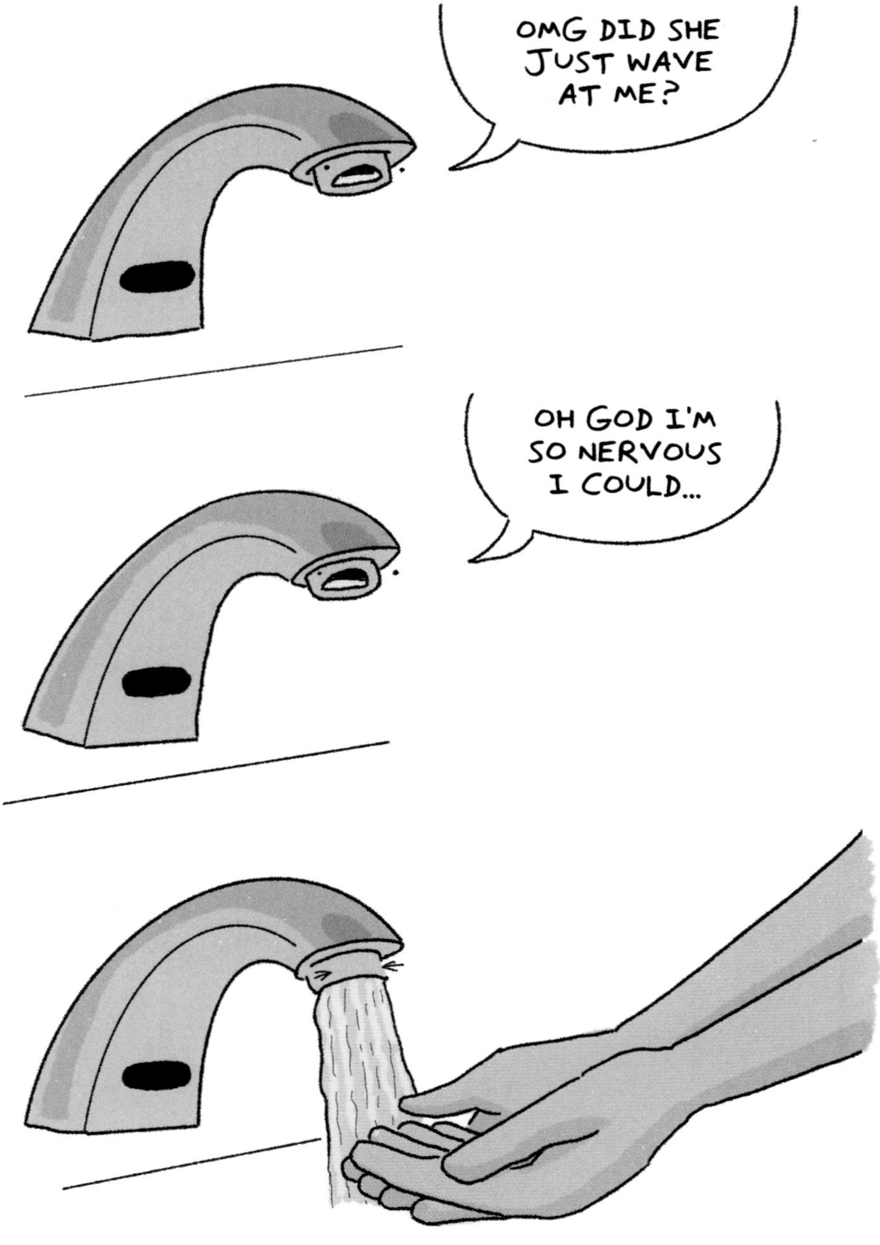
OMG DID SHE JUST WAVE AT ME?
OH GOD I'M SO NERVOUS I COULD...

YOGDA

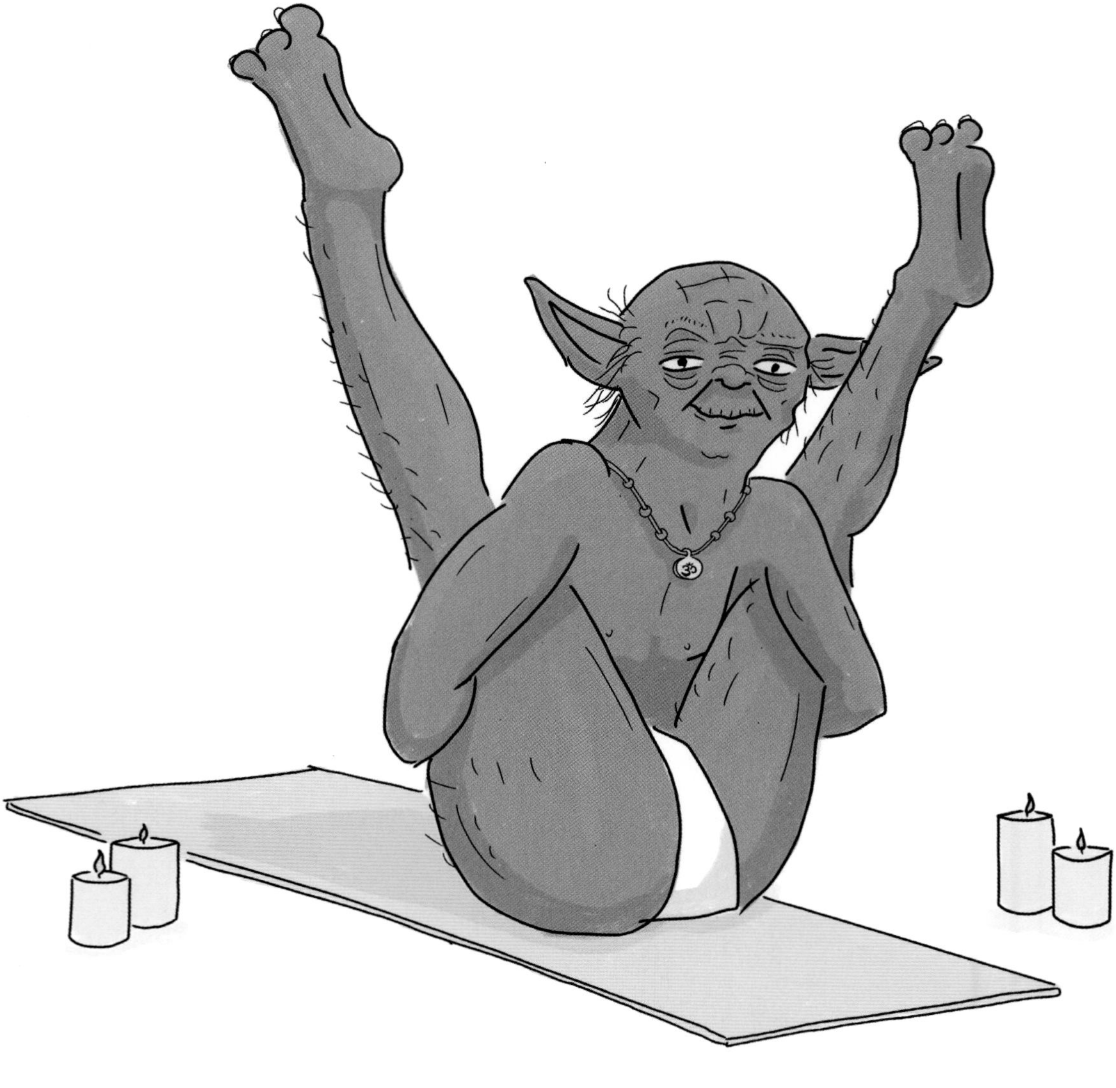

A GUIDE TO PAPER-FREE HAND DRYERS

SPRAY YOUR GERMS
ON THE WALL

SPRAY YOUR GERMS
DOWN TO THE CENTER
OF THE EARTH

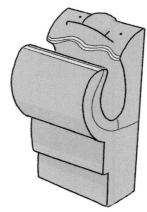

SPRAY OTHER PEOPLE'S
GERMS ON YOUR GERMS

WIPE YOUR GERMS ON
A HIGHLY ABSORBENT
GOLDEN RETRIEVER

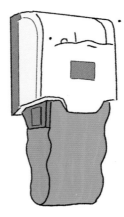

UNDER NO CIRCUMSTANCES
SHOULD YOU TOUCH THIS
CURSED OBJECT

If you haven't seen the last one in person, you've truly lived a charmed life. I was told by commenters that these ones are actually more eco-friendly and sanitary than electric hand dryers, but the one at the Horseshoe Tavern in Toronto that sags all the way to the bathroom floor begs to differ.

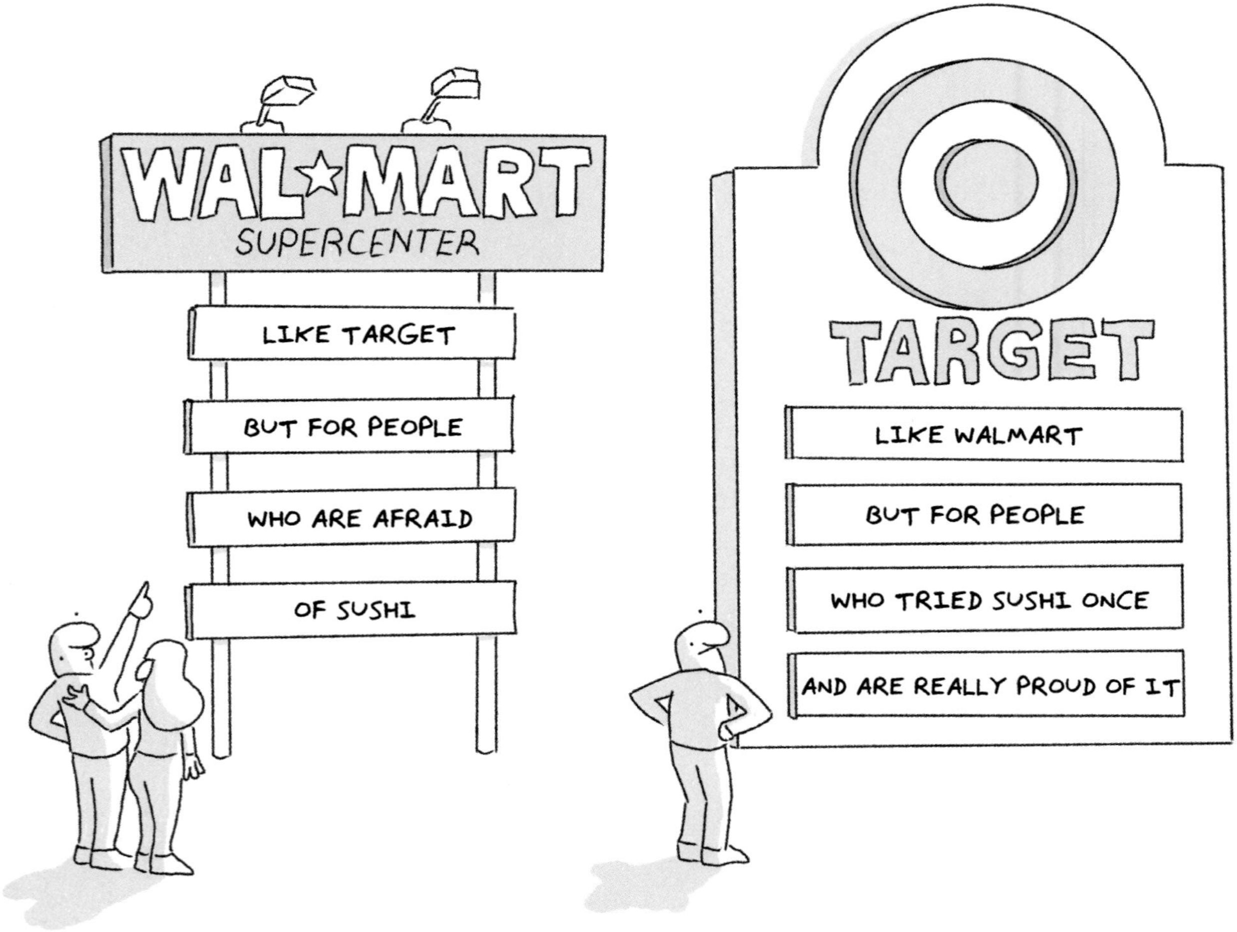
WAL★MART
SUPERCENTER
LIKE TARGET
BUT FOR PEOPLE
WHO ARE AFRAID
OF SUSHI
TARGET
LIKE WALMART
BUT FOR PEOPLE
WHO TRIED SUSHI ONCE
AND ARE REALLY PROUD OF IT

MEN'S FALL FASHION: A GUIDE

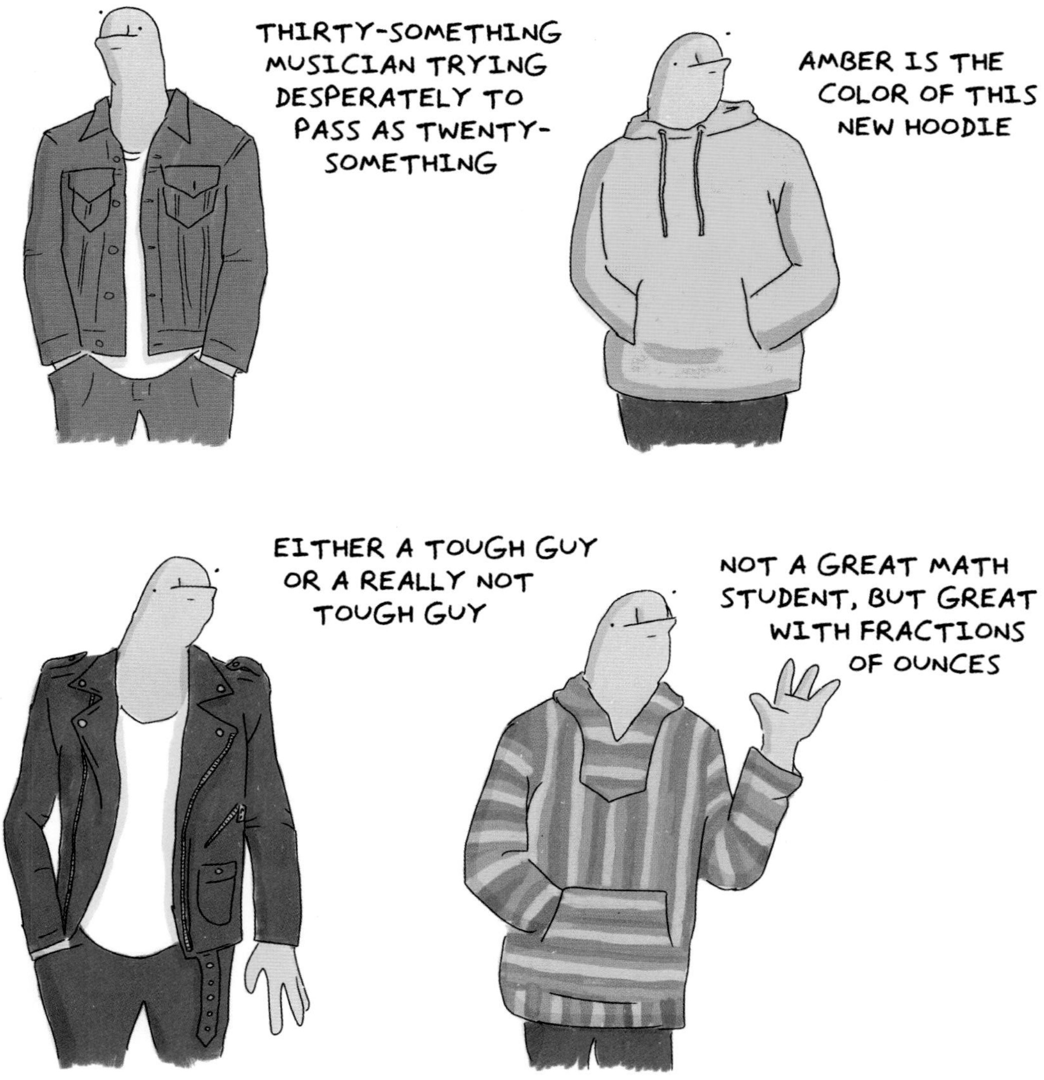
THIRTY-SOMETHING MUSICIAN TRYING DESPERATELY TO PASS AS TWENTY-SOMETHING
AMBER IS THE COLOR OF THIS NEW HOODIE
EITHER A TOUGH GUY OR A REALLY NOT TOUGH GUY
NOT A GREAT MATH STUDENT, BUT GREAT WITH FRACTIONS OF OUNCES

I'll give you a wild guess which one I am.

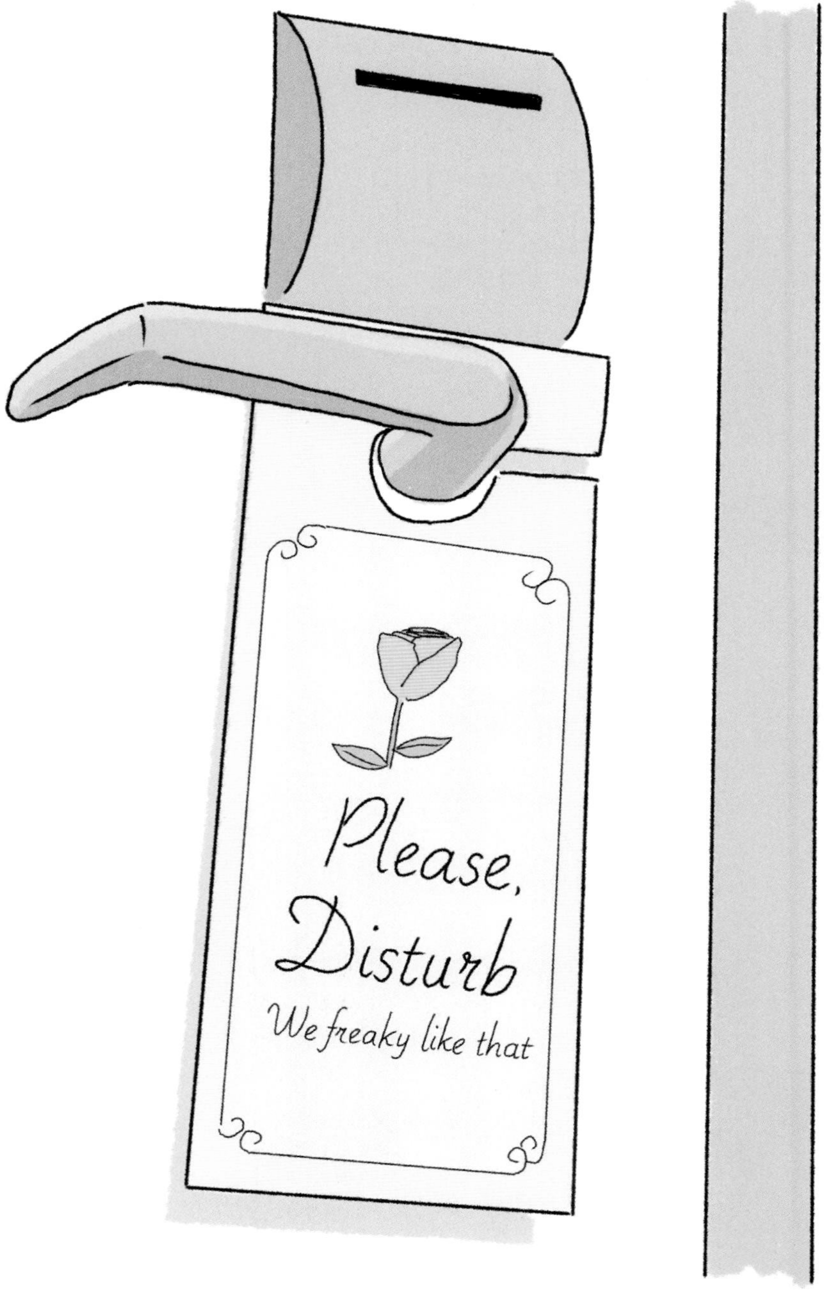
Please, Disturb
We freaky like that

HOW TO COPE IN...

LOS ANGELES

VS

NEW YORK

- PSYCHEDELICS AND SURFING

- "I LOVE THE FREEDOM OF HAVING A CAR"

- PRETENDING TO HAVE A GLUTEN ALLERGY

- COFFEE AND THERAPY

- "I LOVE THE CHANGE OF SEASONS"

- PRETENDING NOT TO HAVE A GLUTEN ALLERGY

A GUIDE TO GLASSES

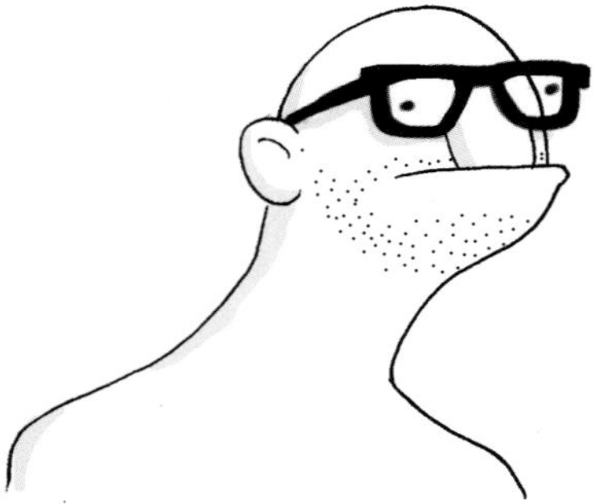

DEFINITELY HAS FINAL CUT PRO

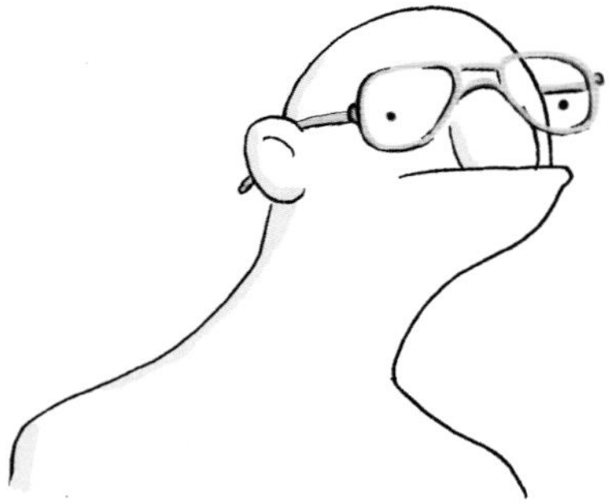

EITHER REALLY COOL OR REALLY UNCOOL

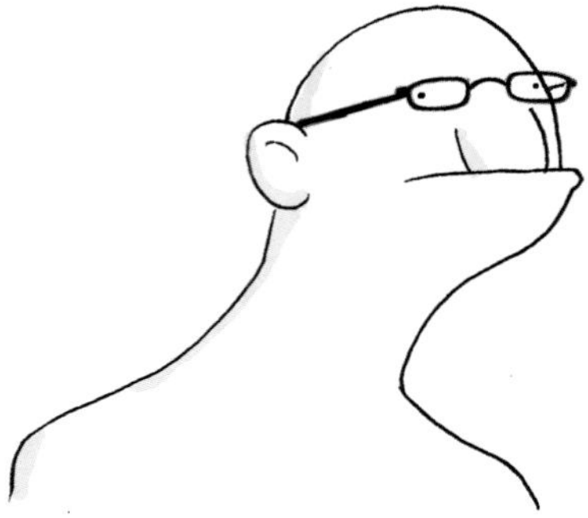

"JUST TRYING TO SEE HERE, MAN"

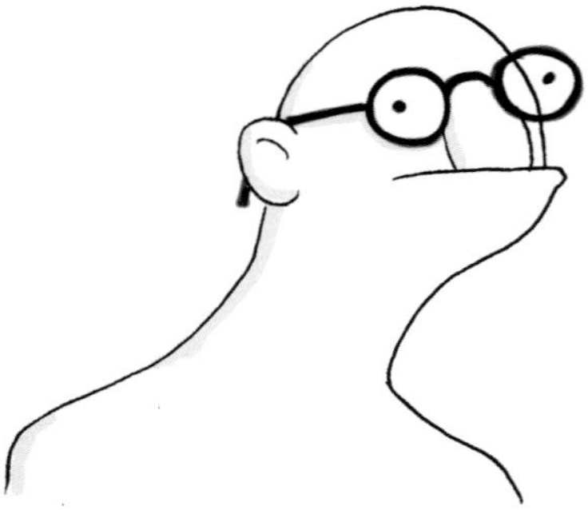

GOING FOR LENNON BUT WILL SETTLE FOR POTTER

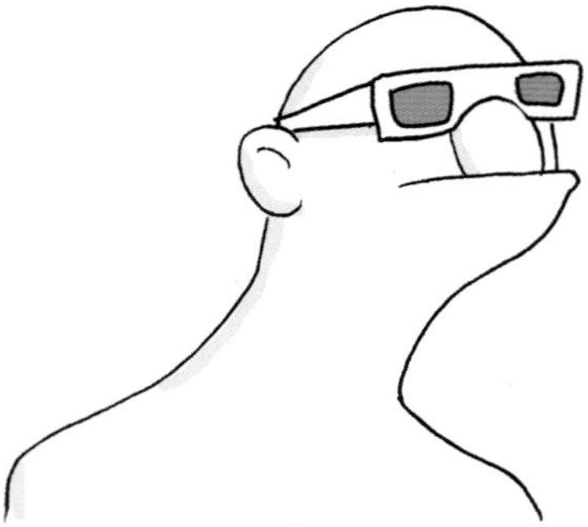

MOVIE'S FINISHED, THE DRUGS ARE NOT

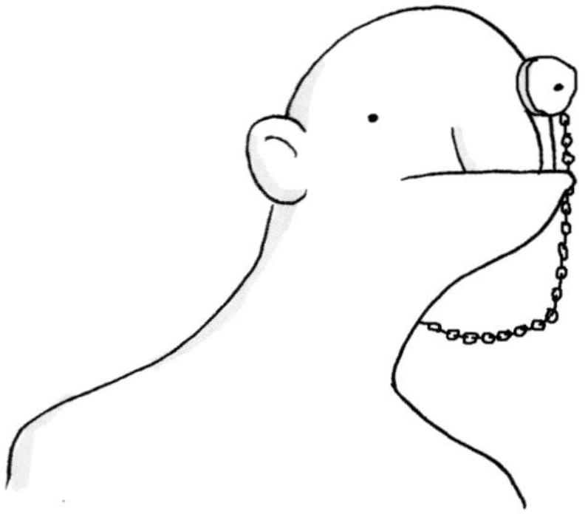

EGADS!

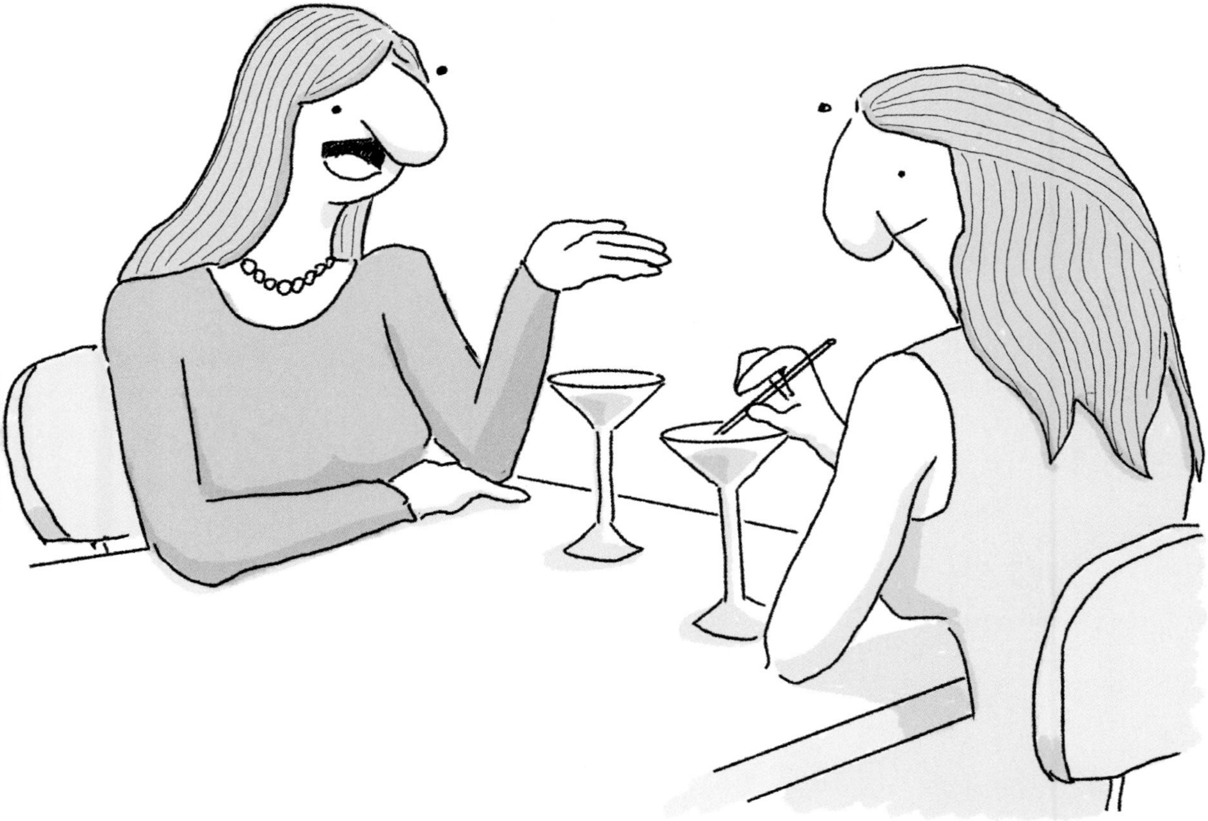

HONESTLY, EVER SINCE I WITHDREW FROM THE WORLD AND SUBMERGED MYSELF IN VIDEOS OF ROUND ANIMALS, I'VE BEEN FEELING SO MUCH BETTER!

WHISKEY: A TASTING GUIDE

TENNESSEE

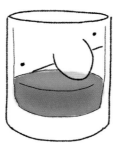

TASTES LIKE
HAM, Y'ALL

BOURBON

TASTES LIKE A
HONEY-BAKED
HAM, Y'ALL

RYE

DAMN, MA'AM!
THIS TASTES LIKE
A SPICED HAM

IRISH

FECK, THIS TASTES
LIKE A SMOOTH HAM

SCOTCH

OCH AYE, THIS TASTES
LIKE SMOKED HAM,
LADDIE

JAPANESE

WAIT THIS IS
JUST SCOTCH

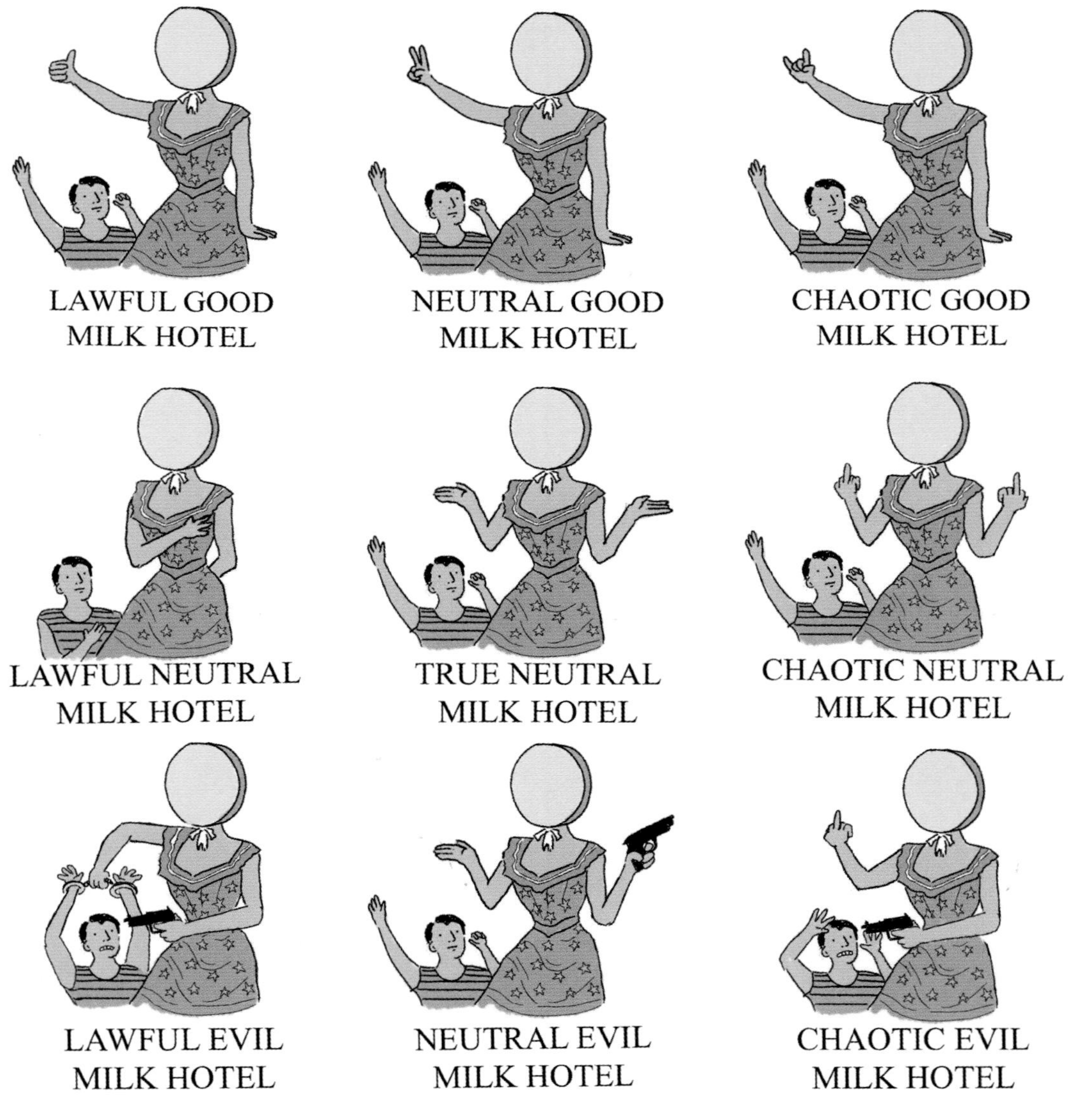
LAWFUL GOOD MILK HOTEL
NEUTRAL GOOD MILK HOTEL
CHAOTIC GOOD MILK HOTEL
LAWFUL NEUTRAL MILK HOTEL
TRUE NEUTRAL MILK HOTEL
CHAOTIC NEUTRAL MILK HOTEL
LAWFUL EVIL MILK HOTEL
NEUTRAL EVIL MILK HOTEL
CHAOTIC EVIL MILK HOTEL

Don't get this one? Well, first, you need to listen to Neutral Milk Hotel's sophomore album *In the Aeroplane Over the Sea*. Second, you need to closely study the *Dungeons and Dragons* alignment chart. If you complete these tasks, you will understand this comic. Congratulations on having wasted a lot of time, and I hope it was worth it.

TOO GOTH?

HOW TO THINK OF 500 COMICS IN 500 DAYS

I also got asked often: "How did you think of so many ideas for comics?"

On a practical level, I always kept a notebook on me with a running list of ideas, because I never knew when something was going to come to mind. But, I should note that my "ideas" generally consisted of barely legible, vague prompts like "A COMIC ABOUT NO PARKING SIGNS??" Or "A T-REX WITH A HUMAN NOSE AND A BIG BUTT???" My close friends also became a lifeline, particularly my best friend, Dan, who was generous enough to pitch great ideas of his own (many of which are featured in this book) and donate a not-insignificant percentage of his workday to answering my flurries of frantic text messages every morning. Early on in the project, I also bought myself some time by doing a comic about every sign of the zodiac, and my backup plan in case of total inspiration disaster was to buy myself 50 days by doing a comic about every state in the United States. Thankfully, I was never forced to do this, but I should in this moment extend my sincerest apologies to Indiana for depriving them of their very first published comic.

But as the project wore on, I found that the process for harvesting ideas for comics had a lot in common with my (much longer) experience with songwriting inspiration. If you do creative art of some kind, you know that inspiration is a slippery thing, appearing when you least expect it, and often disappearing when you need it most. For me, the most effective method is this: Don't think.

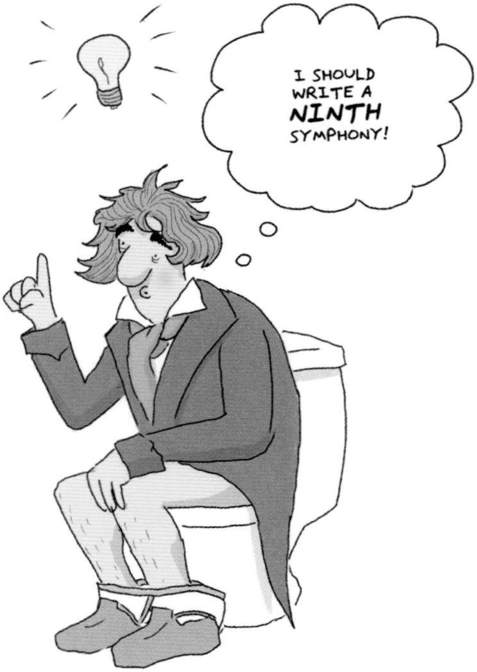
I SHOULD WRITE A NINTH SYMPHONY!

It seems counterintuitive, but I found that the most direct way to conjure ideas was to deliberately do nothing at all. Nearly all of my best ideas came while on long walks or while running. While meditating. Or rather, while *trying* to meditate.[1] Or similarly, while sitting on the toilet. Ideas did *not* come when I allowed my digital addictions to take over. And if they did, they were mutated reflections of the cultural landscape that I didn't necessarily feel full creative ownership over. Usually, those ones were just half-baked regurgitations of popular memes that, in hindsight, look more like cries for attention than capital-A "Art."[2]

I am a big believer that anyone can channel creativity, but it requires a willingness to drop everything and allow space for new ideas to percolate. In my experience, new ideas only form when you've allowed room for new ones

---

1. As I understand it, all meditation is just a process of "trying" to meditate, generally unsuccessfully, and anyone who describes this incredibly difficult task as something they easily "do" is probably just trying to curate a specific personality brand as a coping mechanism for their perceived shortcomings. Namaste.
2. I am still unsure where the naked Stacked-Potato-Chip-Man™ belongs in the "lowercase-a" art versus "uppercase-A" Art binary.

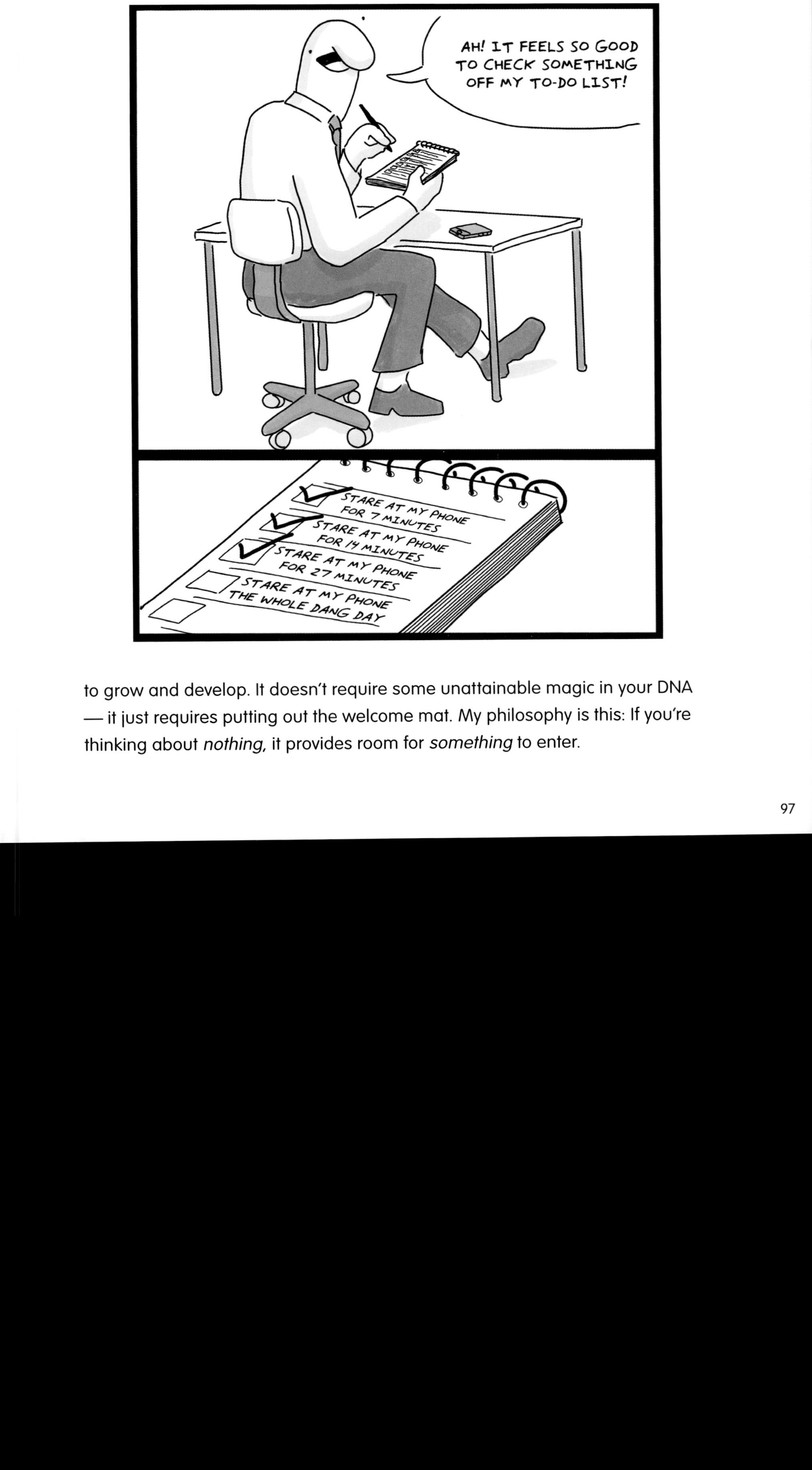
AH! IT FEELS SO GOOD TO CHECK SOMETHING OFF MY TO-DO LIST!
STARE AT MY PHONE FOR 7 MINUTES
STARE AT MY PHONE FOR 14 MINUTES
STARE AT MY PHONE FOR 27 MINUTES
STARE AT MY PHONE THE WHOLE DANG DAY

to grow and develop. It doesn't require some unattainable magic in your DNA — it just requires putting out the welcome mat. My philosophy is this: If you're thinking about *nothing,* it provides room for *something* to enter.

Paradoxically, as I was getting better at harnessing my creative energy for comics, that vast and empty headspace that nurtures new ideas started to feel threatened as the online following for my work began demanding more and more of my attention. As I got more and more followers, every comic I published had hundreds of comments to sift through. Emails to respond to. Social media metrics to study and maximize. Debates in the zeitgeist that begged a response. Notifications I "needed" to check. How could I have the time to do *nothing* when there was so much *something* to do?

My best idea during the project came right around the year mark. At that point, I was feeling a lot more confident in my drawing style, but I still felt like something was missing. I had assumed at some point that I would stumble upon a regular cast of characters I wanted to stick with and explore, but every time I tried to consciously think about it, I kept coming up dry.

That is, until Valentine's Day. Likely while doing nothing,[3] I thought of this quick gag involving conversation hearts:

---

3. I think, at least. It's hard to remember exactly when and where you were doing nothing.

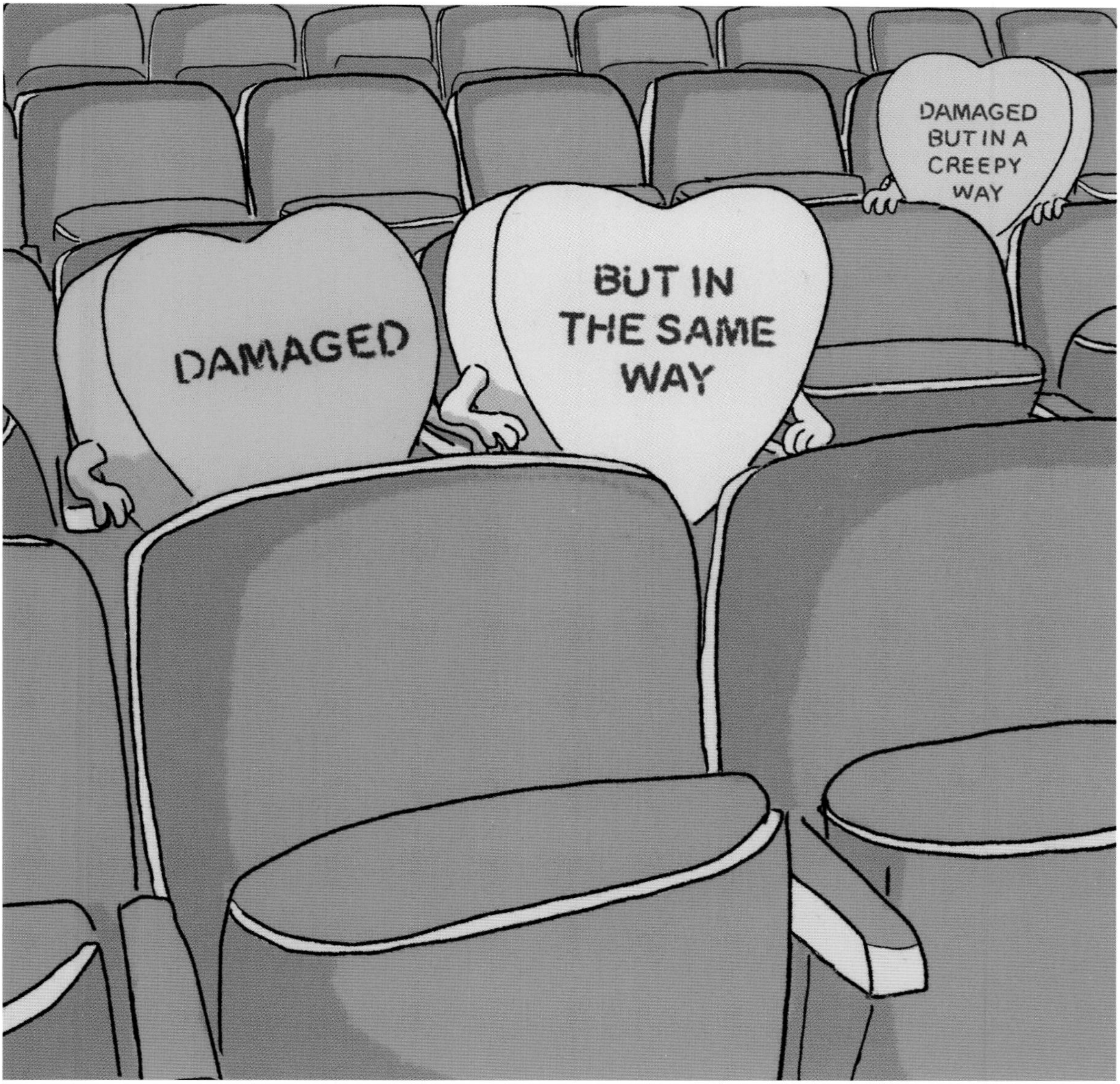
DAMAGED
BUT IN THE SAME WAY
DAMAGED BUT IN A CREEPY WAY

After seeing a big reaction to the comic online, it occurred to me that the text on the front of conversation hearts could be, well, just about anything. I hastily scraped together another one:

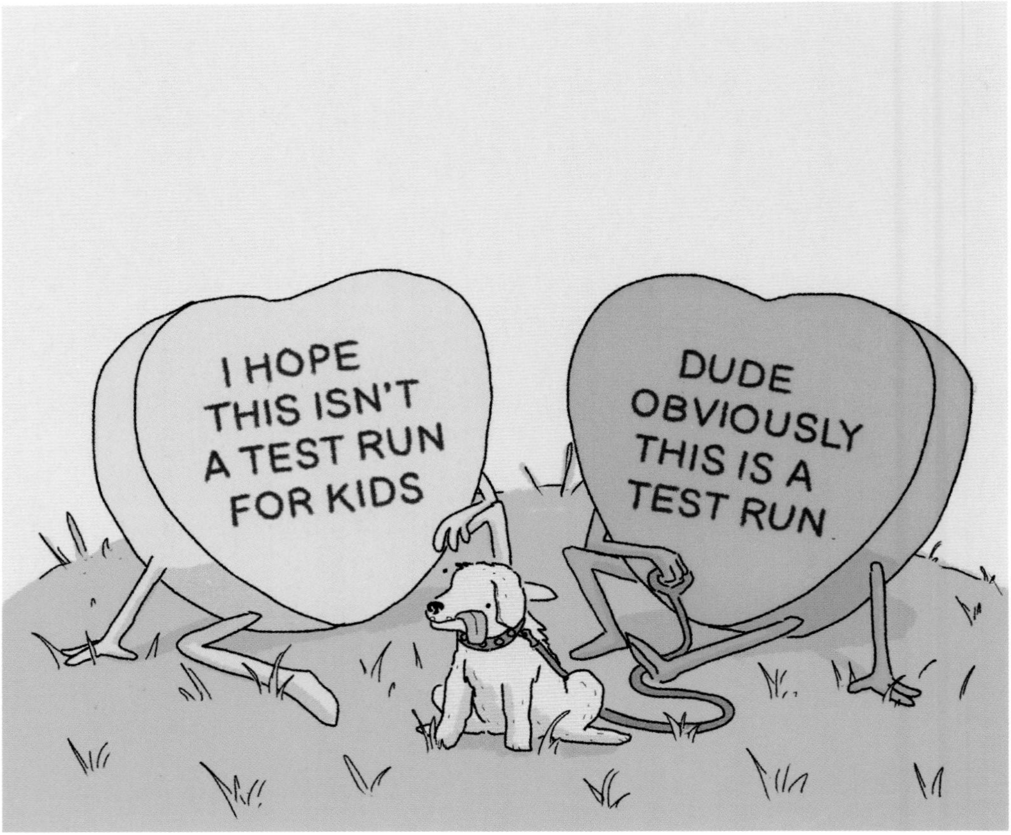
I HOPE THIS ISN'T A TEST RUN FOR KIDS
DUDE OBVIOUSLY THIS IS A TEST RUN

All of a sudden, the possibilities felt infinite. In fact, I may or may not be simultaneously working on a book composed entirely of candy hearts. But I wouldn't go around spreading rumors. . . .

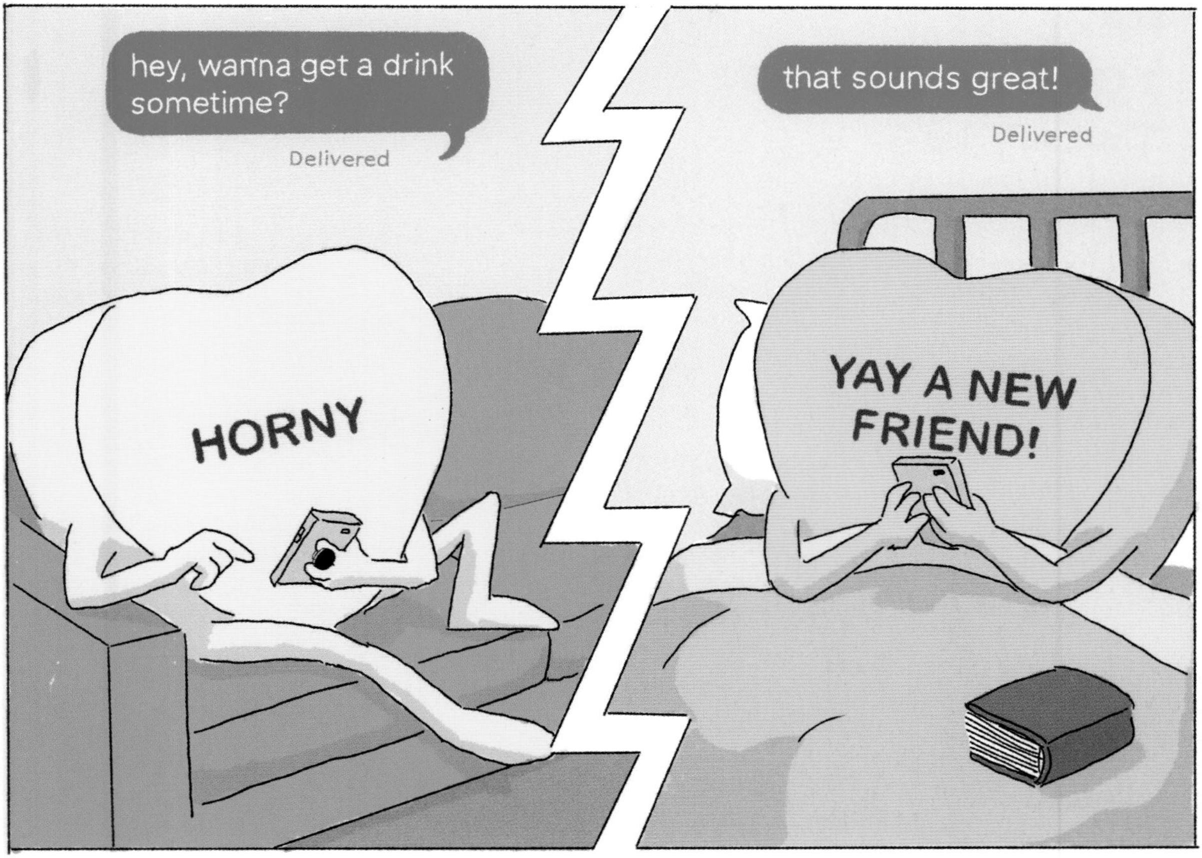
hey, wanna get a drink sometime?
Delivered
HORNY
that sounds great!
Delivered
YAY A NEW FRIEND!

THINGS YOU'LL DEFINITELY HAVE BY YOUR LATE TWENTIES

A GIGANTIC RUBBER BAND BALL

A PLASTIC BAG FILLED WITH YOUR OLD PLASTIC BAGS

A GROWING SENSE OF THE LARGER ARC OF YOUR LIFE, WHICH DOESN'T RESEMBLE WHAT YOU IMAGINED

SIMULTANEOUS FEAR OF DYING ALONE AND FEAR OF COMMITMENT

A VARIETY OF TOOTH EXTRACTION TOOLS

DO NOT OPEN!!

THESE TEETH ARE EXTREMELY FRAGILE

A COLLECTION OF TEETH YOU DUG UP OVER THE COURSE OF THE LAST TEN YEARS FROM A NEARBY CIVIL WAR GRAVEYARD

AGAIN, YES. I'M A HORSE. NOW HOP ON.

CONTACTS vs GLASSES

CONTACTS	GLASSES
• PLACE A PIECE OF PLASTIC IN YOUR EYE AND TRY NOT TO BLINK CONSTANTLY	• ATTACH TWO PORTABLE TELESCOPES TO YOUR ENORMOUS DORK FACE
• GREAT IF YOU LIKE PRODDING YOUR EYEBALL WITH YOUR DIRTY FINGERS	• GREAT FOR EXPERIENCING THE WORLD LIKE A FISH INSIDE A MURKY AQUARIUM
• AT THE END OF THE DAY, YOUR EYES FEEL LIKE THE DANG SAHARA	• AT THE END OF THE DAY, YOUR WHOLE FRIGGIN' FACE HURTS
• GOING FOR A SWIM IS A GRAVE AND WORRISOME FINANCIAL LIABILITY	• GOING FOR A RUN LOOKS LIKE THE BLAIR WITCH PROJECT

HOLIDAY TIP! FUN FAMILY CONVERSATION STARTERS

- WHITE BABY BOOMERS' DESCENT INTO FASCISM HAS TURNED ME INTO A HARDCORE SOCIALIST

- FOX NEWS IS A BRAIN BINKY FOR OLD PEOPLE WHO LACK INTELLECTUAL CURIOSITY

- MARIJUANA SHOULD BE FULLY LEGAL AND PSYCHEDELICS ARE NEXT IN LINE

- THE U.S. MILITARY HASN'T BEEN INVOLVED IN A JUSTIFIABLE CONFLICT SINCE 1945

- GENDER IS LARGELY A SOCIAL CONSTRUCT

I was amused to see this one reached over a million people on Facebook, which means I think I actually ruined Christmas.

TOADSTOOL

SQUIRREL OTTOMAN

NEWT BEANBAG

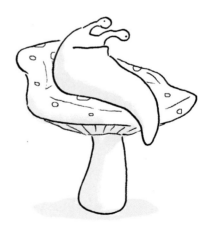

SLUG CHAISE LOUNGE

SEAHORSE vs SEA COW

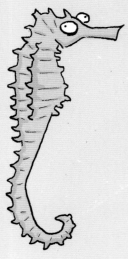

- NOT A HORSE

- NOT EVEN CLOSE

- WHATEVER IT IS, IT IS CREATING UNREALISTIC EXPECTATIONS FOR HUMAN MALES DURING THEIR PARTNER'S PREGNANCY

- AH. YES. THIS IS A COW

- A MERMAID COW

- DON'T DRINK THE MILK THOUGH

- AND IF YOU DO, ASK NICELY

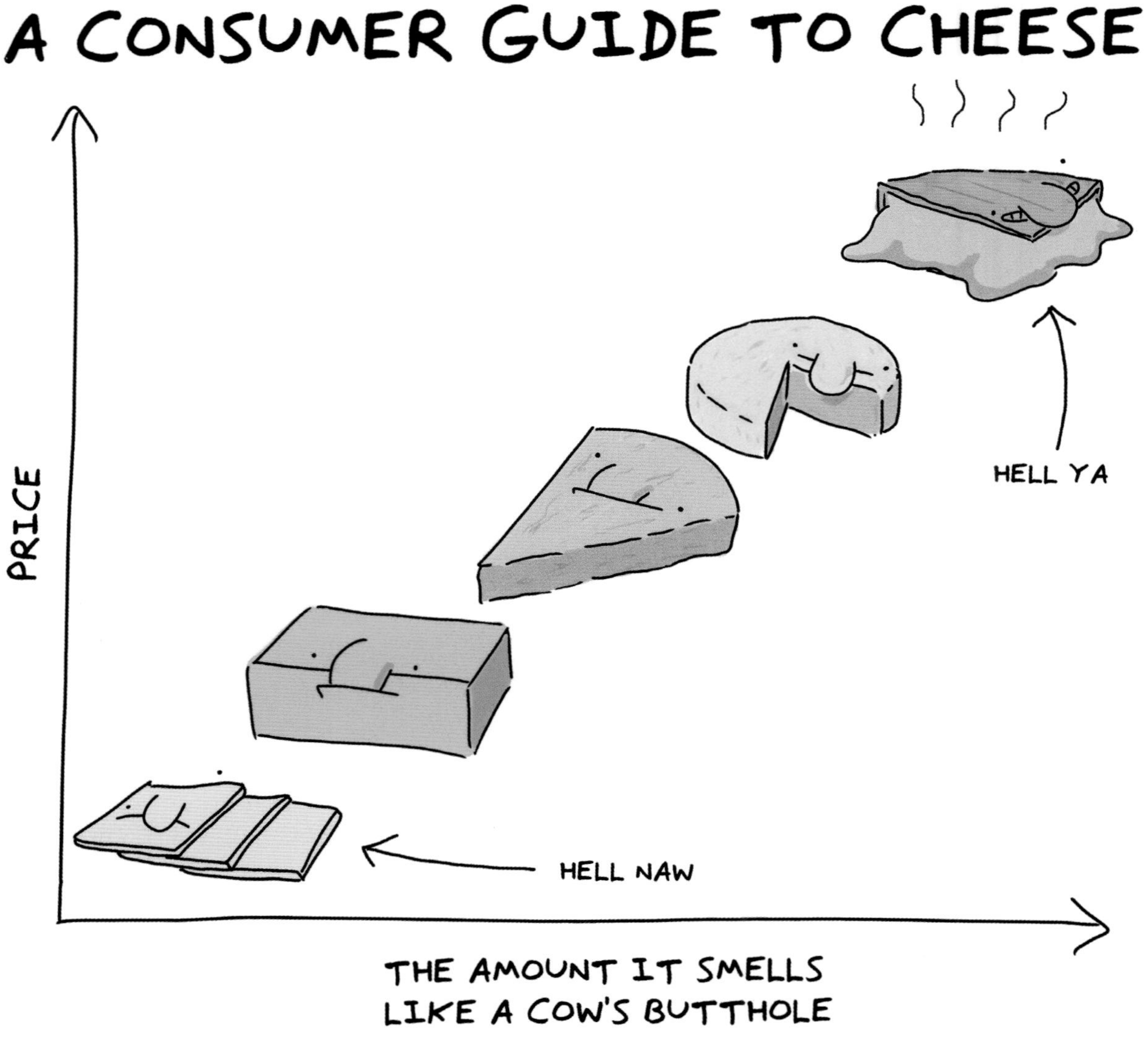
A CONSUMER GUIDE TO CHEESE
PRICE
HELL YA
HELL NAW
THE AMOUNT IT SMELLS LIKE A COW'S BUTTHOLE

Many commenters seemed to think I was just being funny with this chart, but this is actually how I feel about cheese.

SCRAMBLED EGGS

vs

CEREAL

- START YOUR DAY WITH PROTEIN AND AMINO ACIDS

- DOCTORS RECOMMEND, UNTIL THEY DECIDE NOT TO AGAIN

- PRETTY GOOD FOR A PILE OF LUKEWARM, UNFERTILIZED CHICKEN EMBRYOS

- START YOUR DAY WITH 70% SUGAR AND 30% SAWDUST

- TALKING ANIMALS STRONGLY RECOMMEND

- PRETTY GOOD FOR SOGGY HORSE FOOD

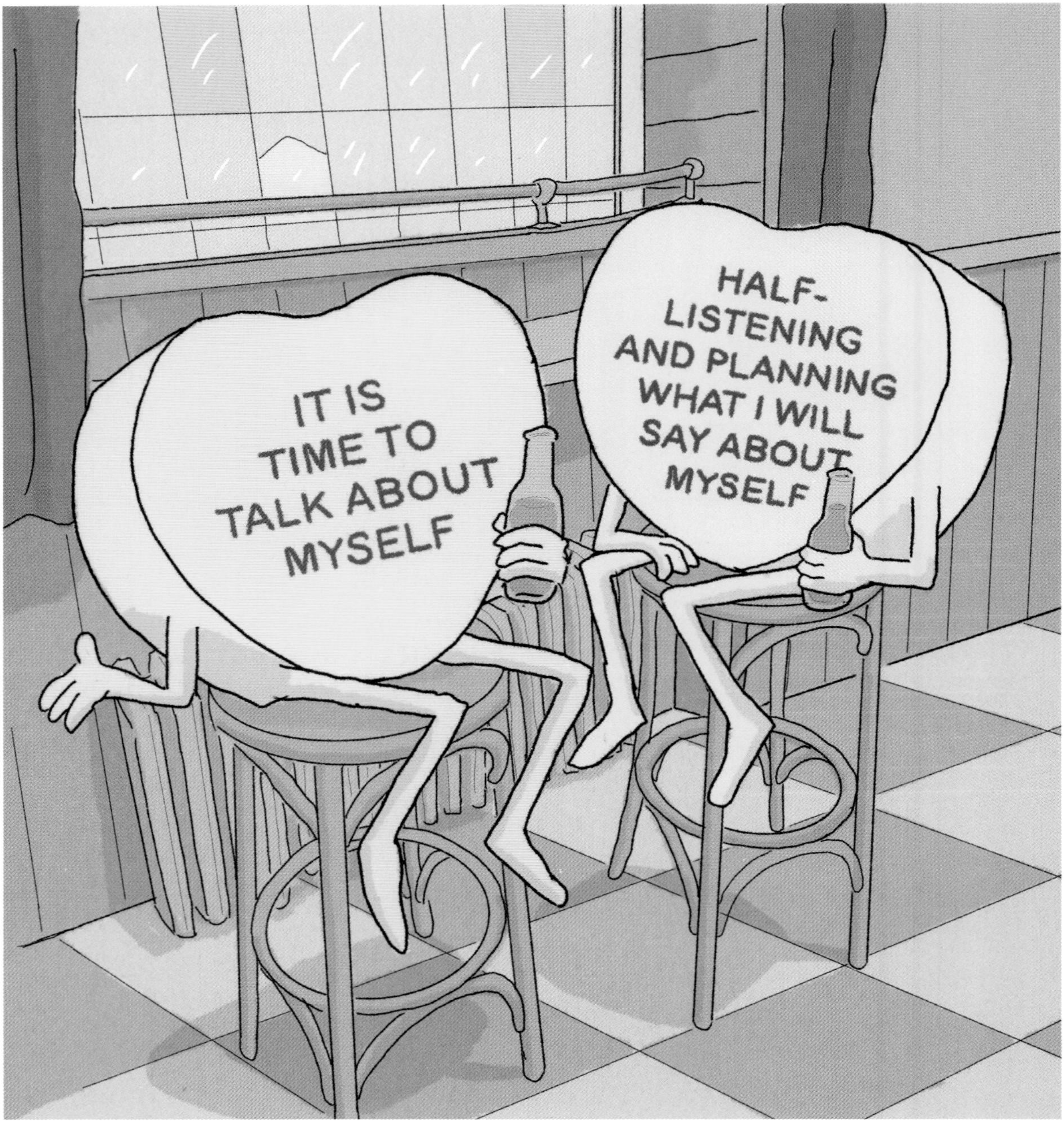
IT IS
TIME TO
TALK ABOUT
MYSELF
HALF-
LISTENING
AND PLANNING
WHAT I WILL
SAY ABOUT
MYSELF

BABIES vs DOGS

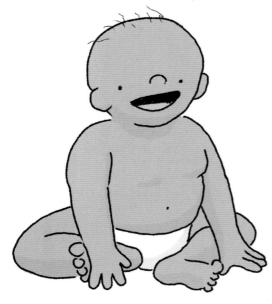

- IF YOU NAME IT "HAM," EVERYONE WILL SAY YOU ARE A BAD PERSON

- FAREWELL SLEEP AND TRAVEL

- HARD WORK, BUT IN 18 YEARS YOU CAN KICK BACK AND RELAX

- YOU CAN NAME IT "HAM"

- FAREWELL SLEEP AND TRAVEL

- HARD WORK, AND IN 10-15 YEARS YOU WILL BE INCONSOLABLE

FINISHED YOUR FALL FETISH CHECKLIST?

STAND IN A LINE TO INSTAGRAM
A PILE OF WARTY GOURDS

FUJI
APPLES
$40/lb

DRIVE TWO HOURS TO
BUY EXPENSIVE APPLES

DOCUMENT THE
COLORFUL ANGUISH OF
THE DYING FOREST

LEAVE A PERFECTLY
GOOD, GIANT VEGETABLE
OUT TO ROT

DRINK A CUP OF WARM,
SQUASH-FLAVORED
BEAN WATER

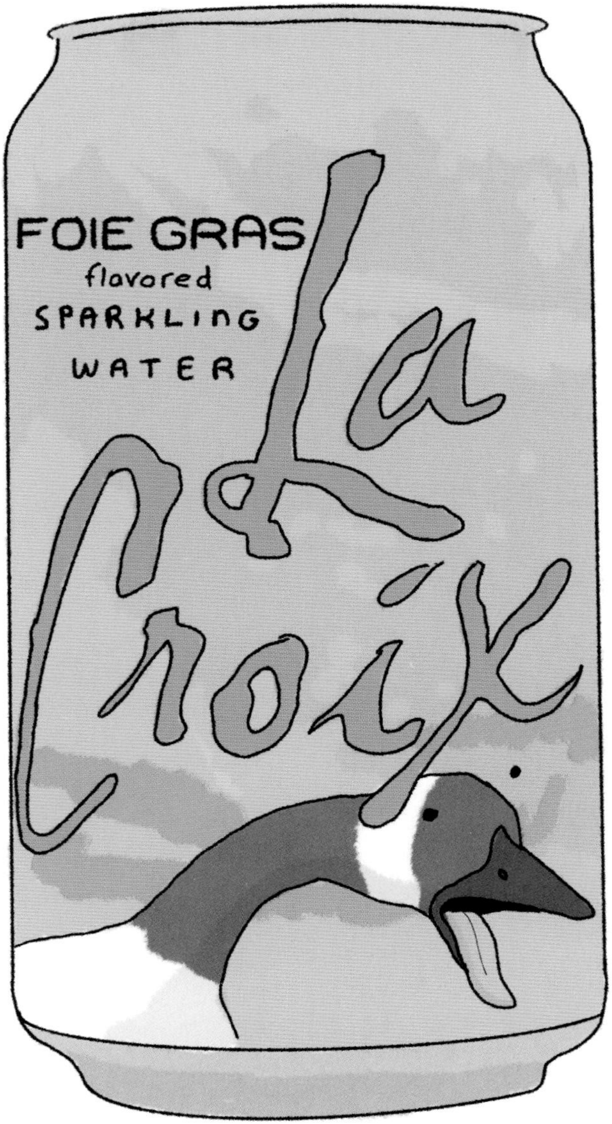
FOIE GRAS
flavored
SPARKLING
WATER
La
Croix

This one was a rare visual collaboration with Ben, the keyboardist of my band. Mostly I just like the expression on the goose.

"PLEASE RISE."

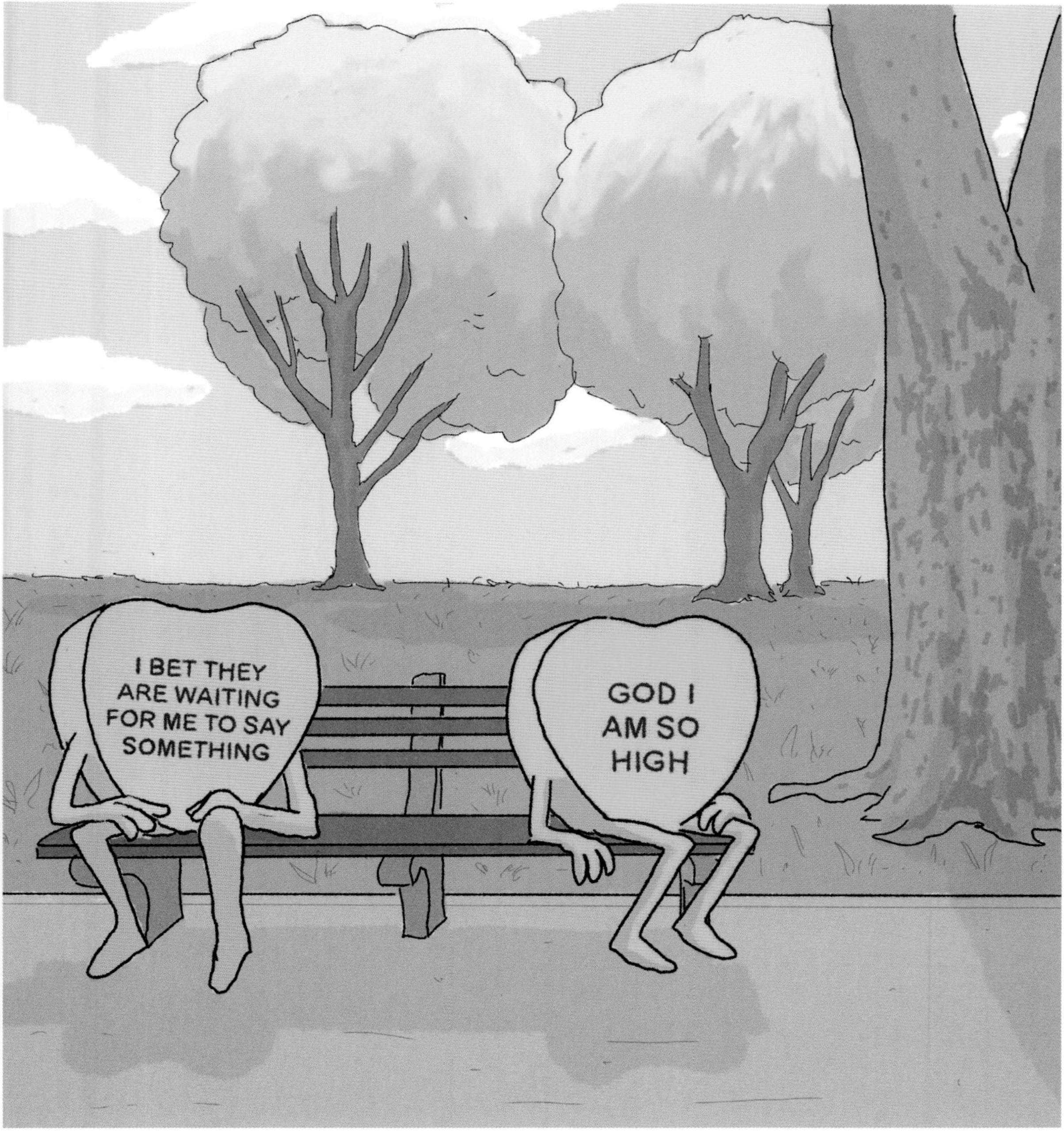
I BET THEY ARE WAITING FOR ME TO SAY SOMETHING
GOD I AM SO HIGH

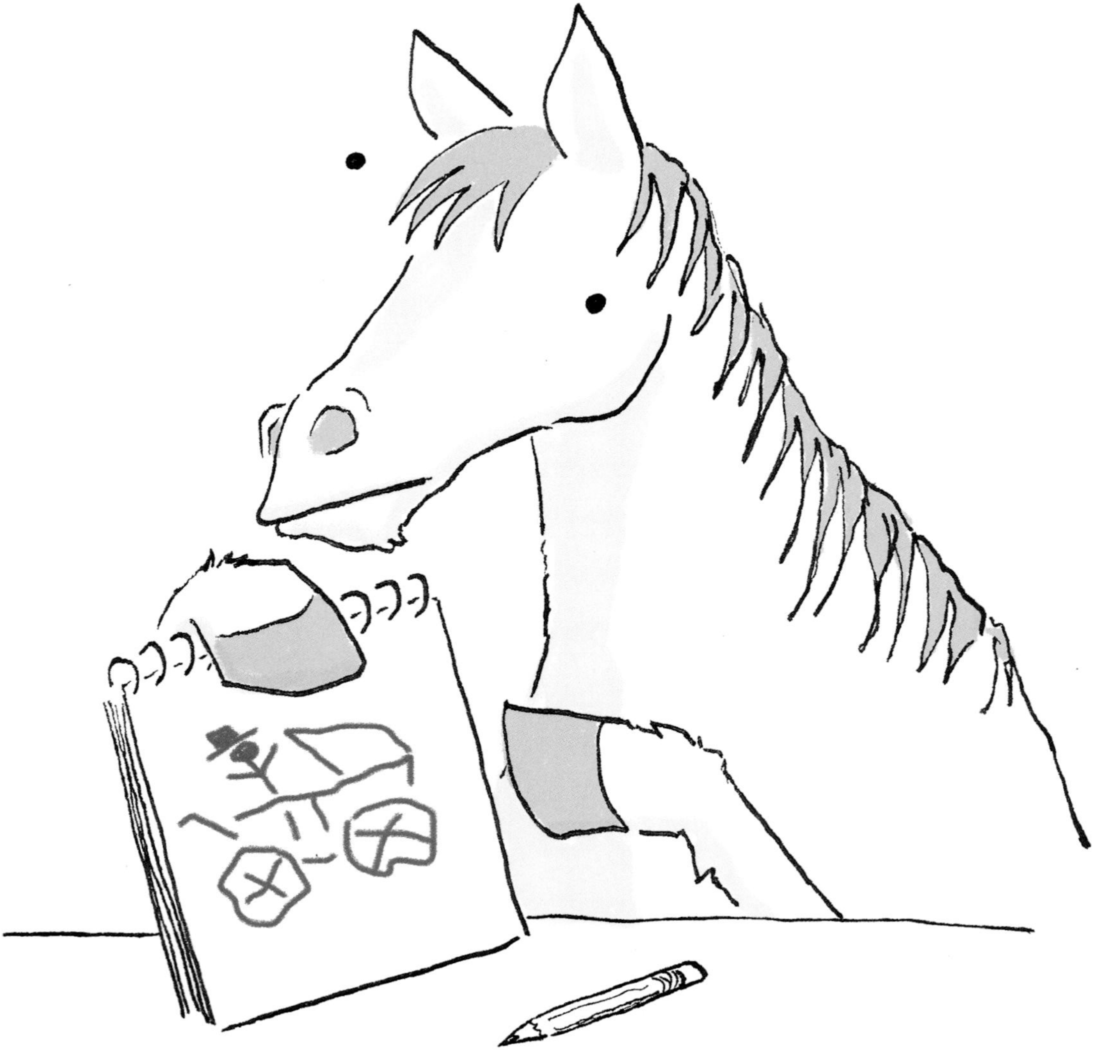

(A horse-drawn carriage)

NOSES: A COMPREHENSIVE GUIDE

OPEN
CARRY

CONCEALED
CARRY

I felt this needed clarification.

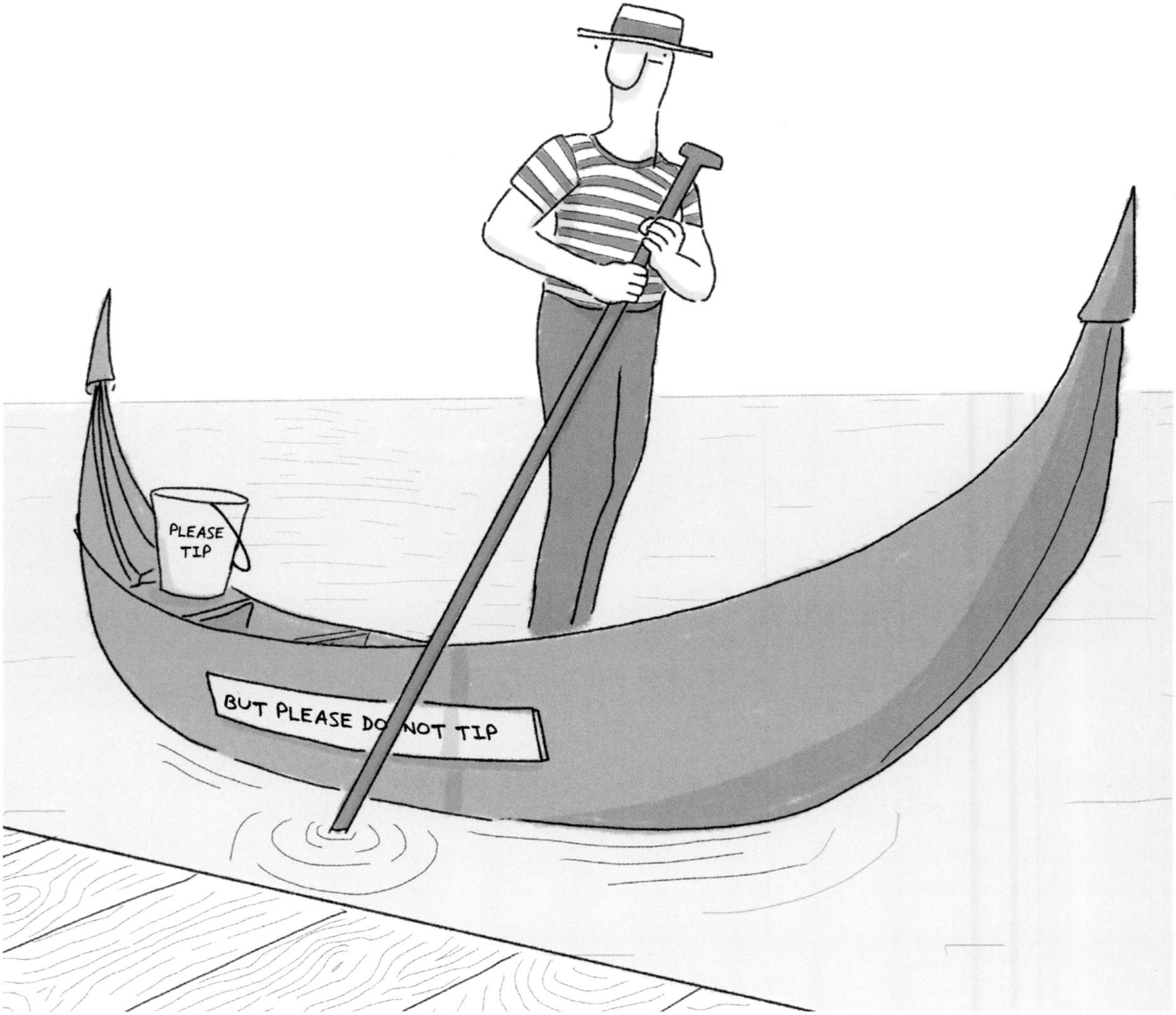
PLEASE TIP
BUT PLEASE DO NOT TIP

UNDIES vs SWIMSUIT

• CLOSE YOUR EYES, IT IS TOO SEXY	• OK YOU CAN OPEN YOUR EYES NOW
• FABRIC NOT QUITE AS THICK AS A SWIMSUIT, THIS IS NAUGHTY	• FABRIC MARGINALLY THICKER, ACCEPTABLE FOR INSTAGRAM AND GRANDMA
• RATED "R"	• YOU CAN WEAR IT TO CHURCH

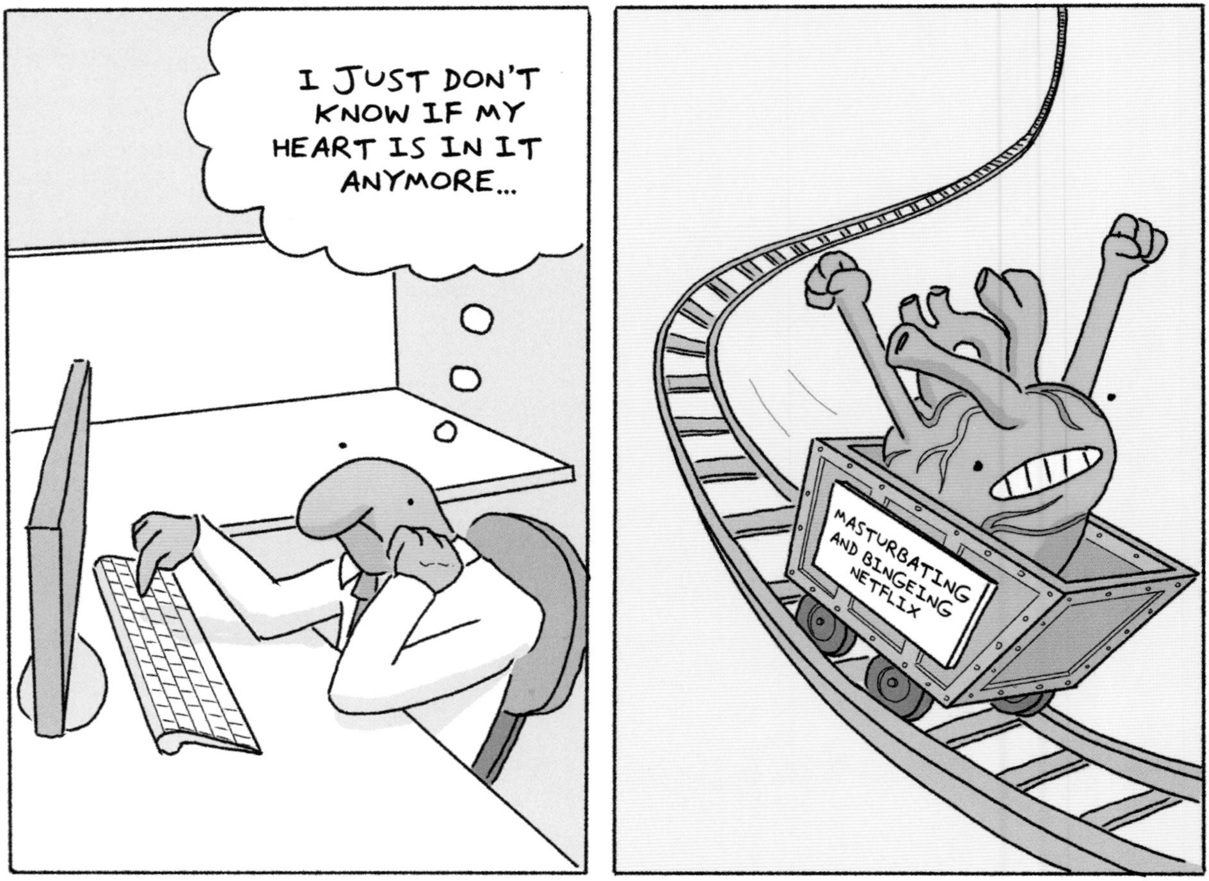
I JUST DON'T KNOW IF MY HEART IS IN IT ANYMORE...
MASTURBATING AND BINGEING NETFLIX

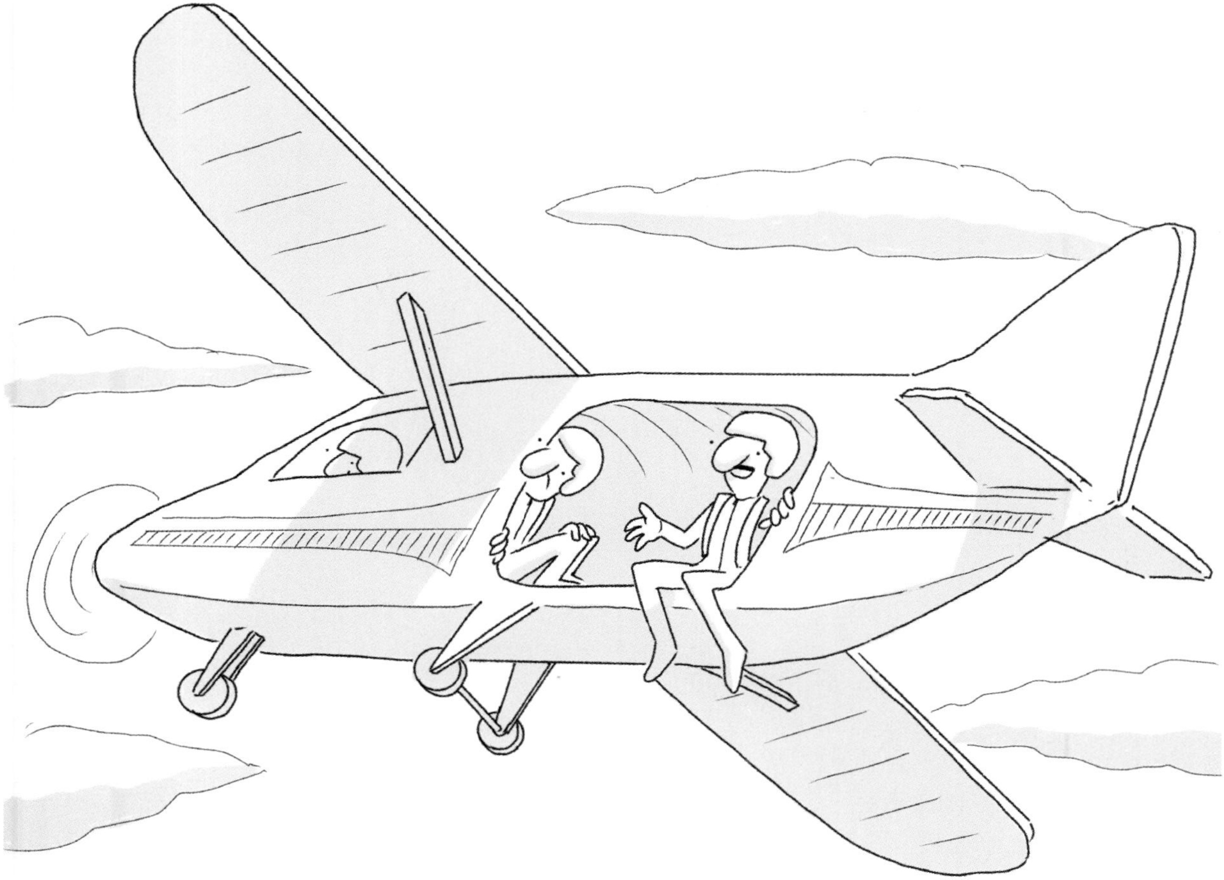

LIFE'S TOO SHORT TO NOT DO SOMETHING THAT HAS A HIGH LIKELIHOOD OF SHORTENING YOUR LIFE!

This one fits into a category of comics I often draw, which I would classify as "some extremely 1990s *New Yorker* shit."

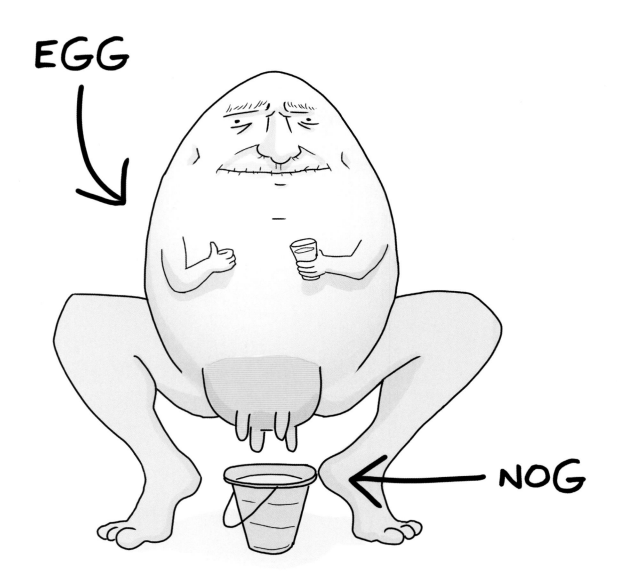

EGG

NOG

Did I really need to draw the milk mustache? No, I didn't. But I think it shows how deeply I care about my craft.

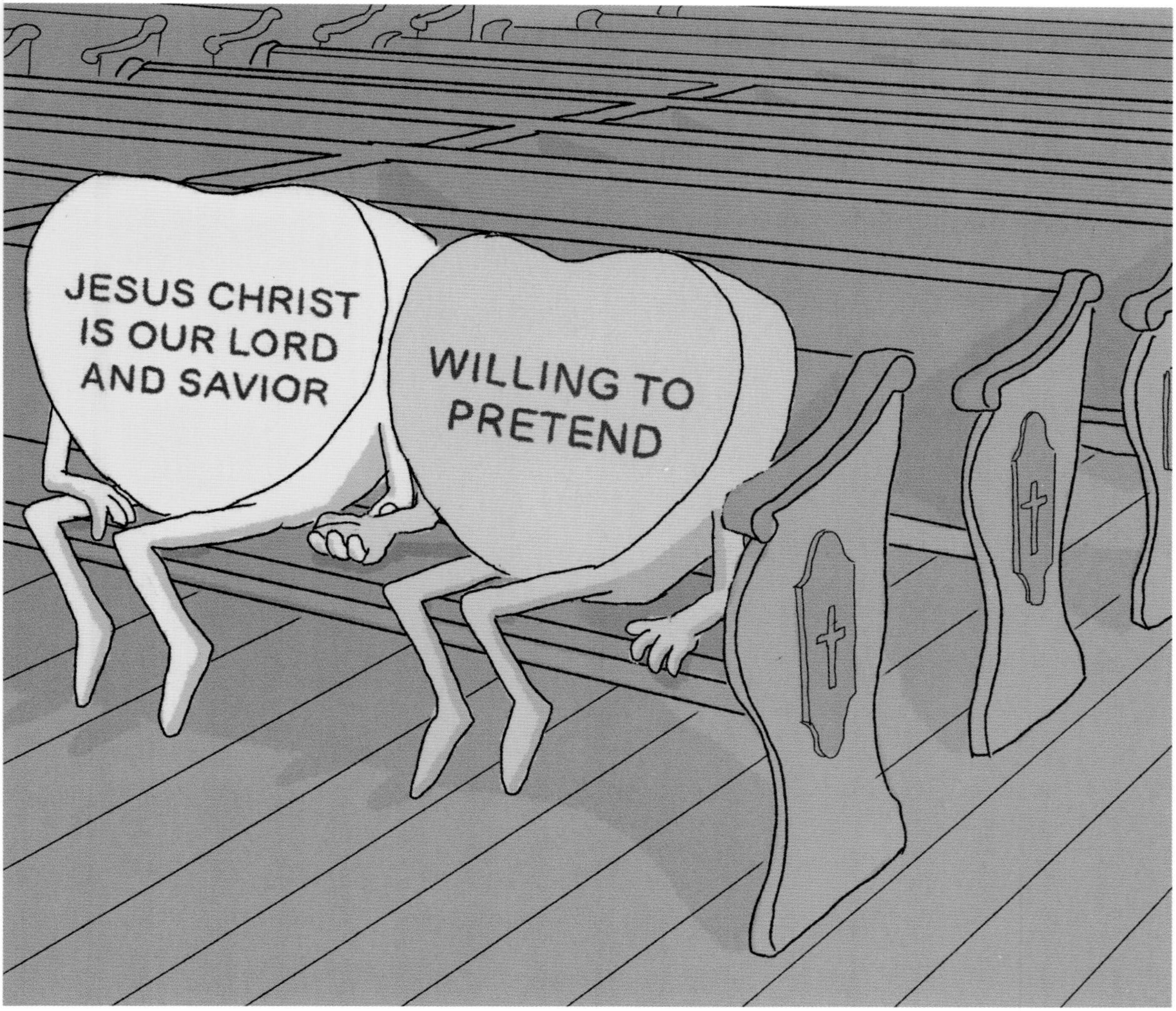
JESUS CHRIST IS OUR LORD AND SAVIOR
WILLING TO PRETEND

SUMMER AS A KID

- 700 FIREFLIES CAPTURED
- 135 HILLS ROLLED DOWN
- 97 GAMES OF MARCO POLO
- 73 TREES CLIMBED
- 41 WATER GUN FIGHTS
- 13 TADPOLES CAUGHT

VS

SUMMER AS AN ADULT

- WENT TO THE BEACH ONCE
- AND NOW IT'S OVER

GUESS
WHAT?

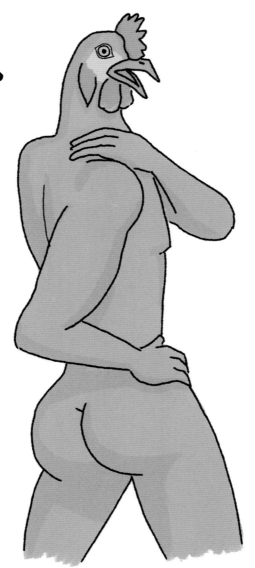

CHICKEN
BUTT.

There are some comics that don't get a lot of likes but do get a lot of people direct messaging them to one another.
This is one of those. And yes, I have access to those metrics. I see you out there spreading my cartoon smut in private.
I see you, you filthy animals.

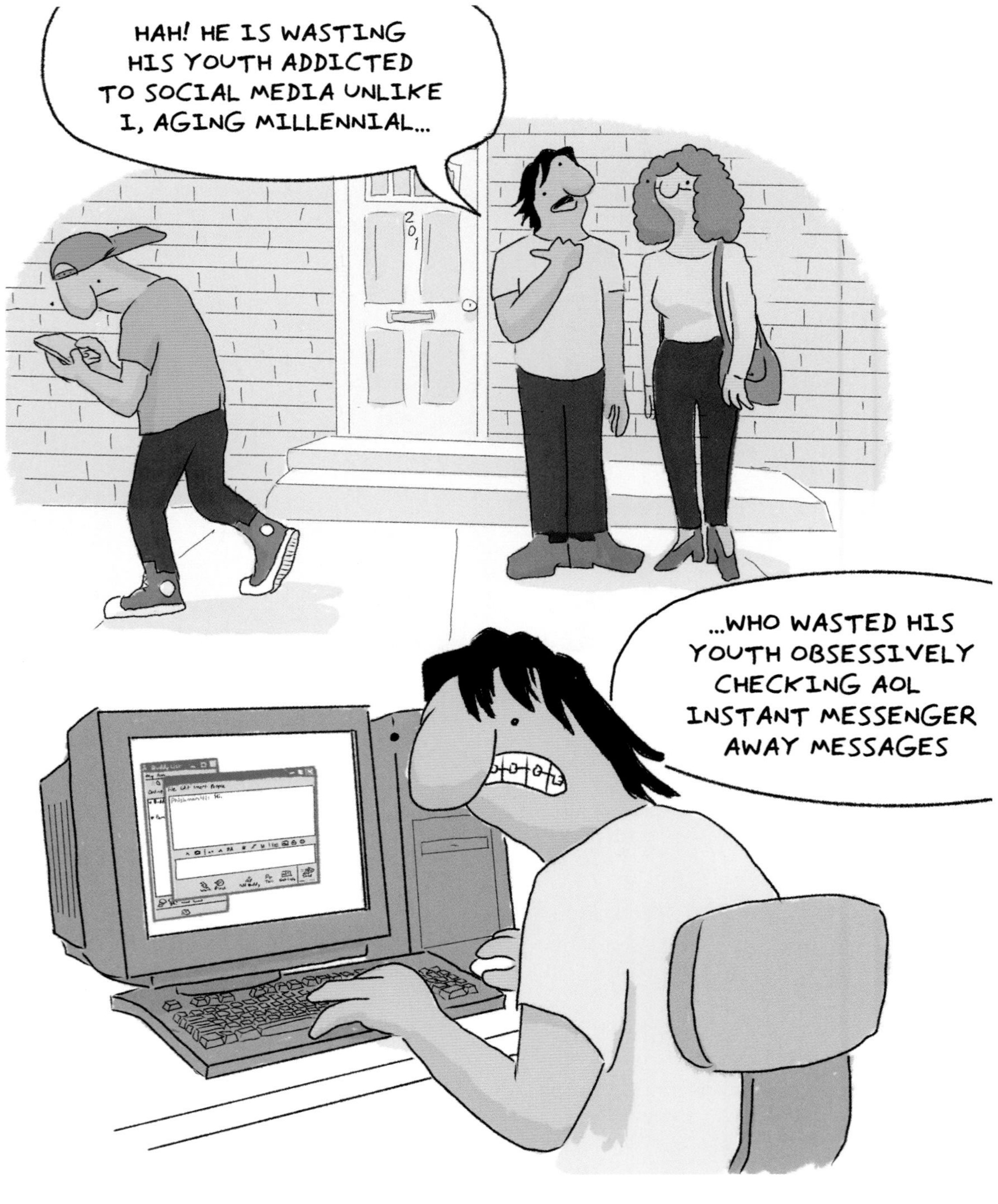
HAH! HE IS WASTING HIS YOUTH ADDICTED TO SOCIAL MEDIA UNLIKE I, AGING MILLENNIAL...
...WHO WASTED HIS YOUTH OBSESSIVELY CHECKING AOL INSTANT MESSENGER AWAY MESSAGES

HOW FACEBOOK STARTED WORLD WAR III AND I BARELY SOLD ANY MUGS: A MEMOIR

The project snowballed. More and more people were watching, and the stakes felt higher each day. I was getting better at drawing butts, among other things, in noticeable increments! I was riding a creative wave.

But, as I was continually tapping into the mentality of creating crowd-pleasing comics, I was also gaining deeper insight into being a social media manager, having volunteered for the daily responsibility of maintaining my comics on Facebook, Instagram, Twitter, Reddit, and Tumblr. And as a result, I began to gain a much deeper and darker understanding of how social media works — and its built-in biases. Our tech overlords might sneer at the idea of their algorithms being "biased" in any traditional sense, since they are *technically* just mathematical calculations based on user behavior. But it's not quite so simple, and the puppeteers of Silicon Valley aren't as smart as they think they are.[1]

---

1. Specifically, I don't think Mark Zuckerberg is particularly smart. I mean, have you *seen* that man's haircut?

To ride a ~~horse~~ ?? *is to fly without wings*

Let's say you drew a comic. And let's say, for example, that it's a rich, meaningful comic like the one on this page.

OK, fine. Maybe it's not a masterpiece to *you*. But before we move on, you must accept that you are wrong.[2]

When I post a cartoon, the algorithm shows it to people who it thinks *might* like it based on previous engagement with my account. The first batch of followers it gets shown to either hit like, or continue scrolling in disgust.

---

2. Have you accepted that you are wrong yet? No? Then I guess you'll just have to keep reading this footnote until you develop some good *taste*. How about now? How about **now**? C'mon, it's a horse with a big nose and a butt! That's high-quality stuff!

The algorithm then uses those early reactions to determine whether it will continue to show this cartoon to the rest of my followers.[3] So, contrary to what you might expect, just because you follow an account doesn't mean the algorithm will show you posts from that account with any regularity — your like was a vote for *potentially* viewing future content. More than anything, social media networks use the pages you follow as a carrot to dangle in front of your favorite artists and musicians. "Pay us," they say to creators, "and we'll *definitely* show your posts to your own followers! In fact, for only $300, we'll show this single comic to everyone who follows you!"

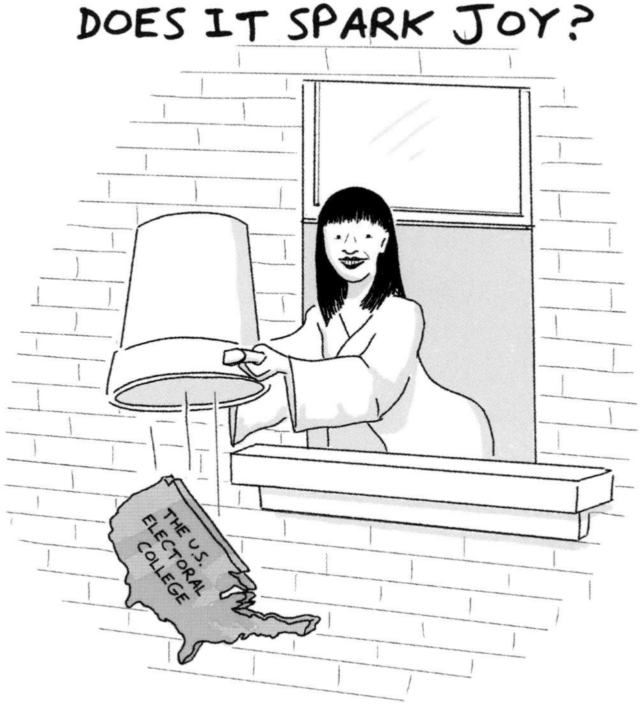
DOES IT SPARK JOY?
THE U.S. ELECTORAL COLLEGE

Now, in addition to being in the service of encouraging promoted posts, algorithms can also have an emotional bias, since they are based on something the tech world calls "engagement": Let's say I post a cartoon with a clear political target. For example, I thought the one featured on this page was solid, but maybe not my most imaginative.

For people who agreed with me, it triggered all

3. In this case, the comic was not "served" to many of my followers based on its initial performance. A loss that I am willing to accept in the name of artistic purity.

sorts of exciting synapses: "YES! I TOO AGREE!" And for those who disagreed, it provoked rage: "NO! I DO NOT AGREE!" The algorithm went hog wild[4] as a result, eventually reaching tens of millions of people.

Eventually, this comic even reached Official Spokesperson of Urban Millennials, Congresswoman Alexandria Ocasio-Cortez, who reposted it on Instagram and retweeted it, with credit, giving me the thrill of making a personal connection with one of my favorite progressive politicians. But on the flip side, I was suddenly "engaging" with her thousands of trolls, who made my Twitter entirely unusable for a couple of weeks, unless I was in the mood to debate someone with the username TrumpOrBust1776 while wading through physical threats and anti-Semitic slurs.[5]

Eventually, the zeitgeist around this comic hit the opinion page of the *Washington Post*, with an editorial titled "Does the electoral college spark joy?" appearing on March 20, 2019. I have no way of confirming that this combination of words came from my comic, but it sure smelled like it did. Moments like these made me feel as if my comics were moving the Overton window ever so slightly, infinitesimally nudging the needle of public opinion toward our country dumping an antiquated and undemocratic system. But I also wondered if I wasn't just contributing to a growing problem.

Comics like this revealed an interesting bias of the algorithm — their built-in formulas incentivize content that provokes an *extreme* reaction. Good or bad, as long as it's provoking a reaction, it goes straight to the top of the feed. The algorithms are there for a purpose: to capture our attention effectively to sell ads.

---

4. No one says this.
5. Related to this, a lesson I learned early was this: Block early, and block often. If someone smells like an internet troll on first glance, they probably are. I came here to draw butts, not to host a debate club.

And moderation doesn't sell. As it turns out, the engagement that keeps us coming back is tied in with some of our worst tribal instincts, which the algorithm will increasingly and exponentially encourage based on our online behavior. We can't help it![6] It's just the dopamine! And the cortisol!

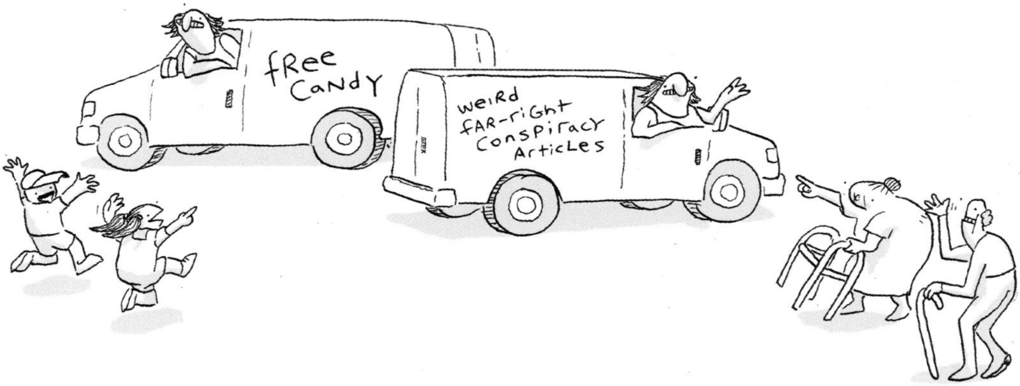
FREE CANDY
WEIRD FAR-RIGHT CONSPIRACY ARTICLES

It's the same structural weakness that enables Trump to dominate the internet, and how he broke above the noise of "reasonable" discourse that tried to take him down. Everything he does provokes an extreme reaction in one direction or the other. Which, inevitably, makes him the loudest voice in the room, even if everyone else is shouting him down. It's why political echo chambers are thriving. It's ushering in a new golden age of grifters and fictitious news sites. It's why it feels like you live in an alternate reality from your Uncle Steve when he starts talking about the Clinton Foundation at Thanksgiving as if it's a global terrorist organization. It's just his algorithm, baby! Well, among other things about Uncle Steve.

---

6. Facebook can't help it either! They just need to extract your maximal time and energy to harvest advertising revenue!

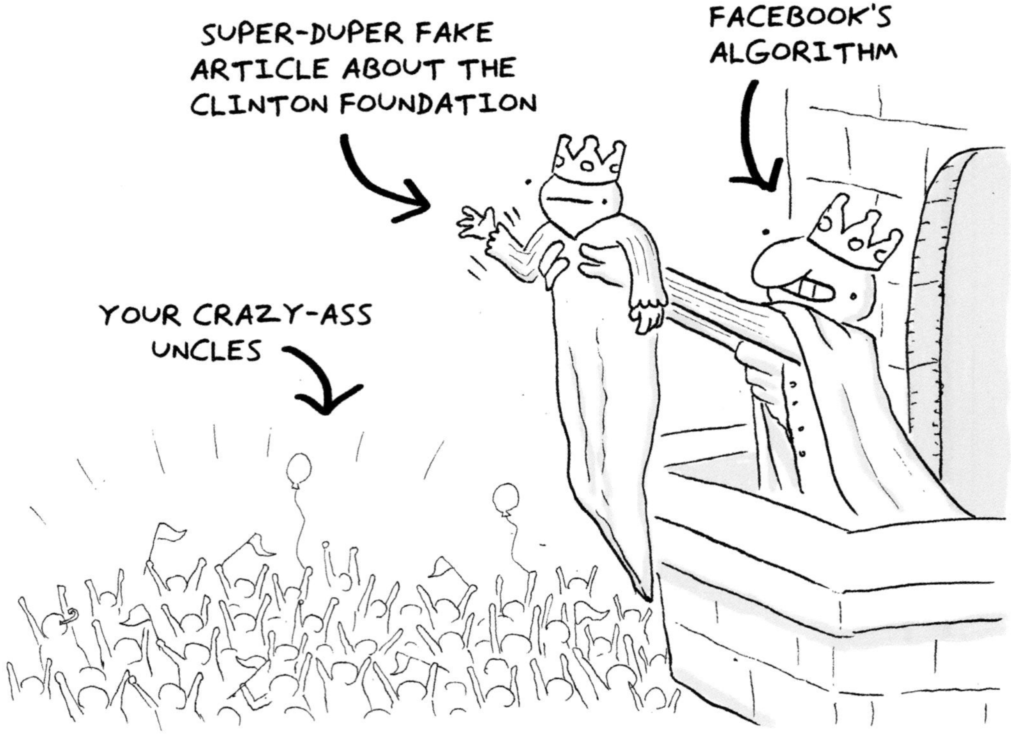
SUPER-DUPER FAKE ARTICLE ABOUT THE CLINTON FOUNDATION
FACEBOOK'S ALGORITHM
YOUR CRAZY-ASS UNCLES

The more I thought about it, the more disturbing the whole idea of social media platforms started to seem. Capitalism had finally wormed its way into the previously inaccessible, as tech pioneers had found a way to monetize basic human connection. And it had even found a way to psychologically manipulate creative showboats like me, who are aware of their own sick addiction but who will gladly work for free to get showered with abstract symbols of belonging.

My biggest revelation about social media's sleight of hand came early in the project, when a cartoon about coffee addiction went *extremely* viral on Facebook. If you ask me, the cartoon is . . . solid. It made me chuckle when I drew it, but it also felt like a fun throwaway gag.

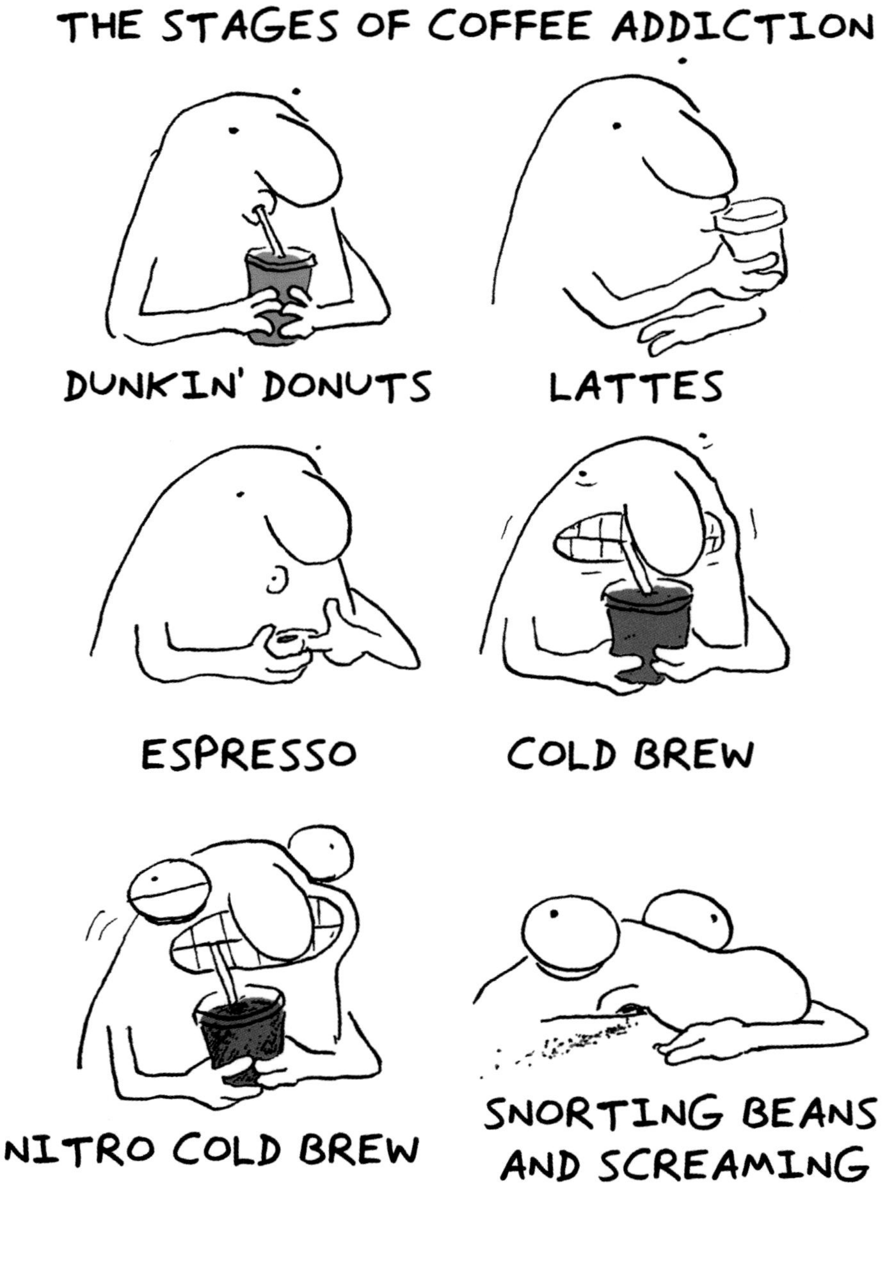
THE STAGES OF COFFEE ADDICTION
DUNKIN' DONUTS
LATTES
ESPRESSO
COLD BREW
NITRO COLD BREW
SNORTING BEANS AND SCREAMING

But on Facebook, it seemed to hit in just the right way. Watching it explode, I hastily added a link to purchase a coffee mug with the comic printed on it within the text body of the post.

When the internet tide receded, over 200 million people had seen the comic. And I had sold 17 mugs.

Suddenly, the inequity of the platforms came into starker view. Here were tech monopolies declaring that the "hosting" of arts meant that they deserved all the revenue from it (a Silicon Valley grift I already knew well as a musician). It didn't matter to them if it was someone's intellectual property uploaded against their will — it was all just fertile soil for targeted ads. And even worse, we as consumers and creators continue to grant them the ability to have a monopoly on a service that could and should be replicated and easily improved upon.

I also began to suspect that my art itself was beginning to be shaped by the algorithm. I couldn't help but take into account when a comic I posted received fewer likes than usual, and I noticed that I was consciously and subconsciously shifting my artwork based on those nudges.[7] Was I shaping the internet, or was it shaping me?

I began to feel deeply conflicted about being complicit in structures that seemed increasingly clear to me were having a largely negative impact on the world. But on the other hand: all the likes!

OK, enough griping about the social media landscape. Let's get back to comics, a significant portion of which are devoted to griping about the social media landscape.

---

7. Although I should admit that the biggest influence it had was that I started drawing fewer phallic noses, more butts, which I suppose is an honest and worthwhile improvement.

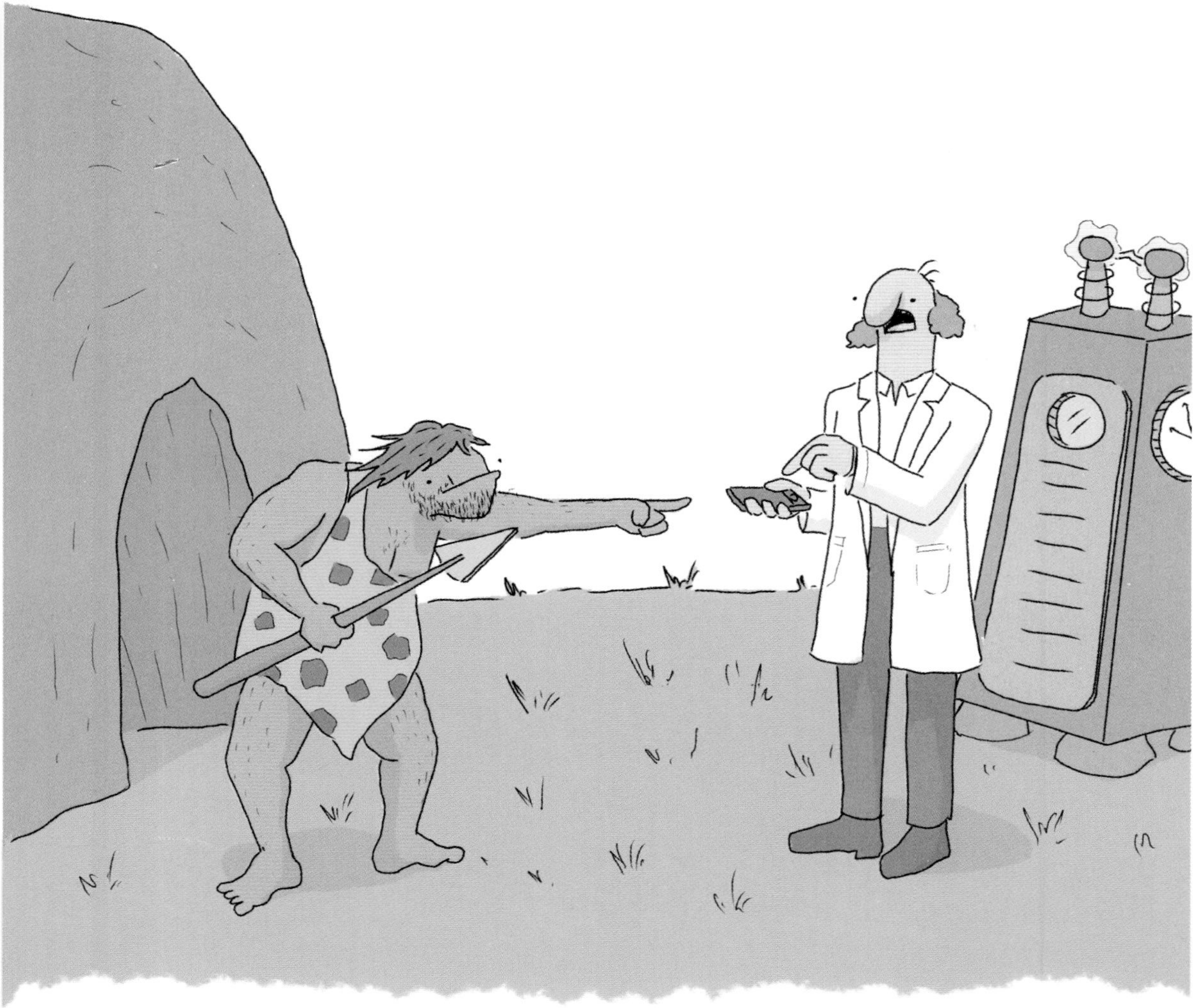

OH, THIS? IT CAN ACCESS EVERY PIECE OF KNOWLEDGE FROM THE HISTORY OF MANKIND AND I HATE IT.

YOU'LL BELIEVE ANYTHING
THE MAINSTREAM MEDIA SAYS!

NOW WATCH THIS YOUTUBE DOCUMENTARY
ABOUT THE DEEP STATE MADE BY AN ANONYMOUS
TEEN WITH BASIC IMOVIE SKILLS

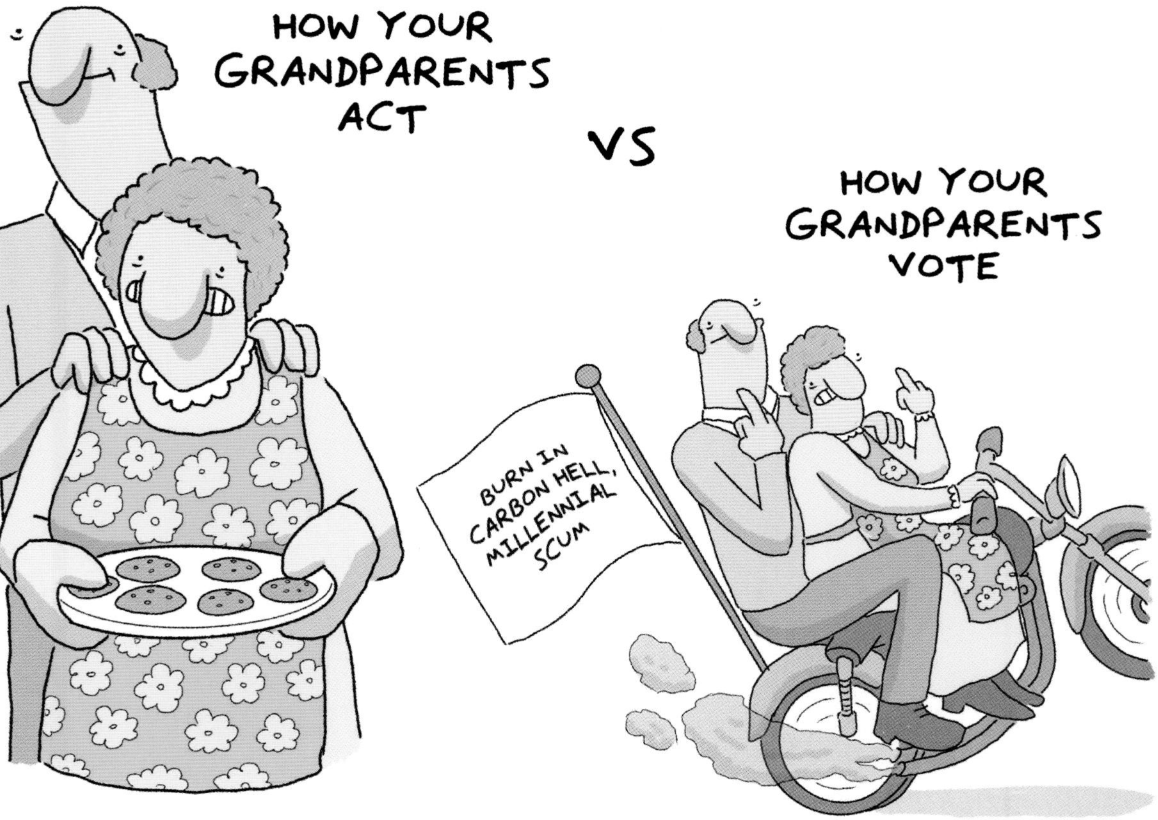
HOW YOUR GRANDPARENTS ACT
VS
HOW YOUR GRANDPARENTS VOTE
BURN IN CARBON HELL, MILLENNIAL SCUM

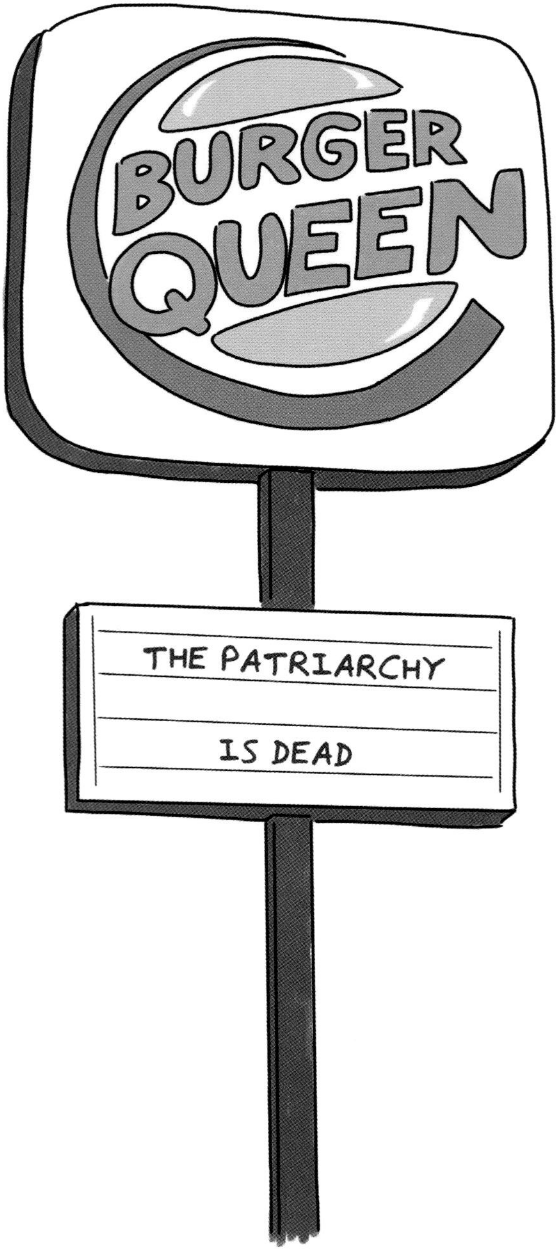
BURGER QUEEN
THE PATRIARCHY
IS DEAD

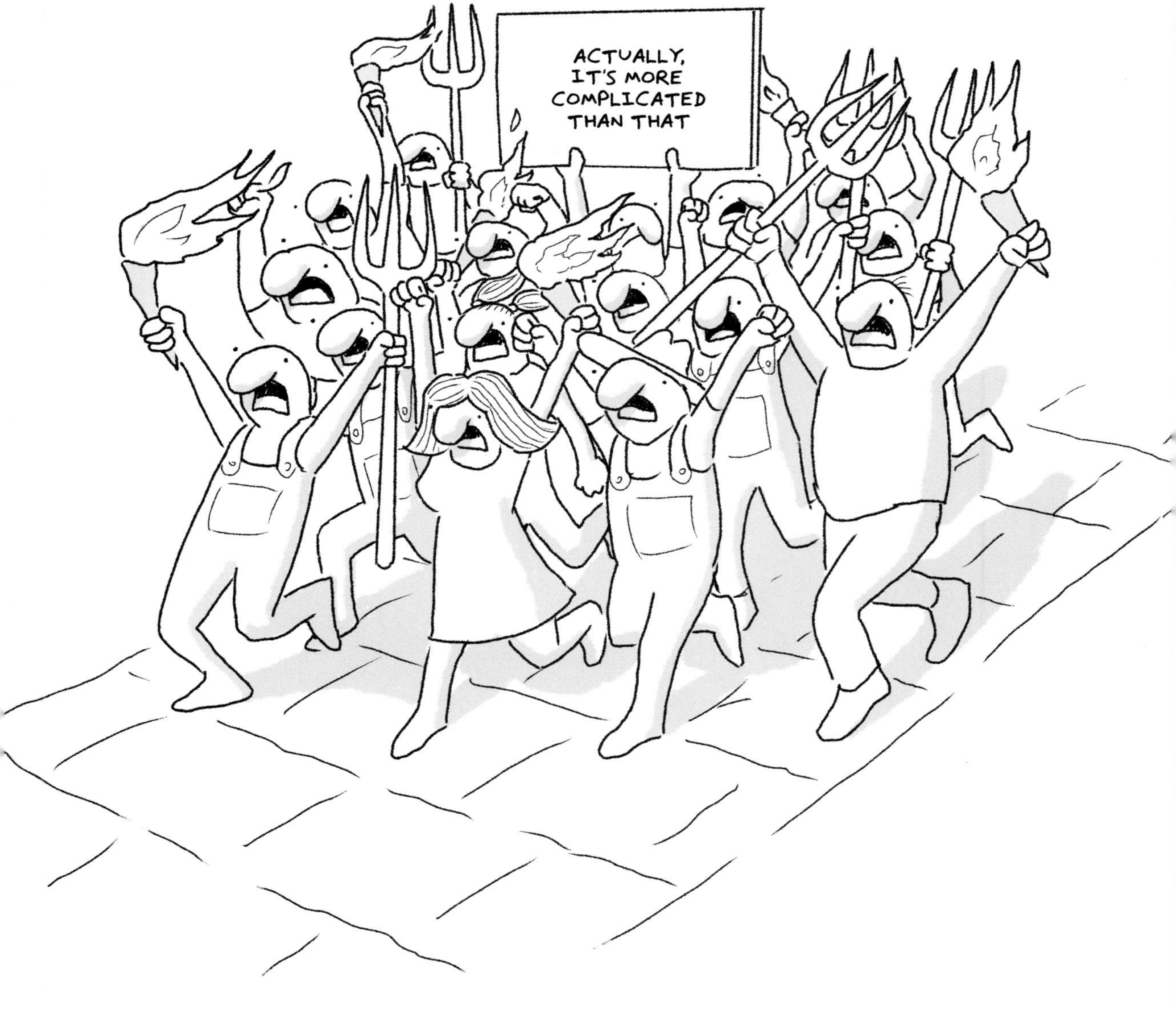
ACTUALLY, IT'S MORE COMPLICATED THAN THAT

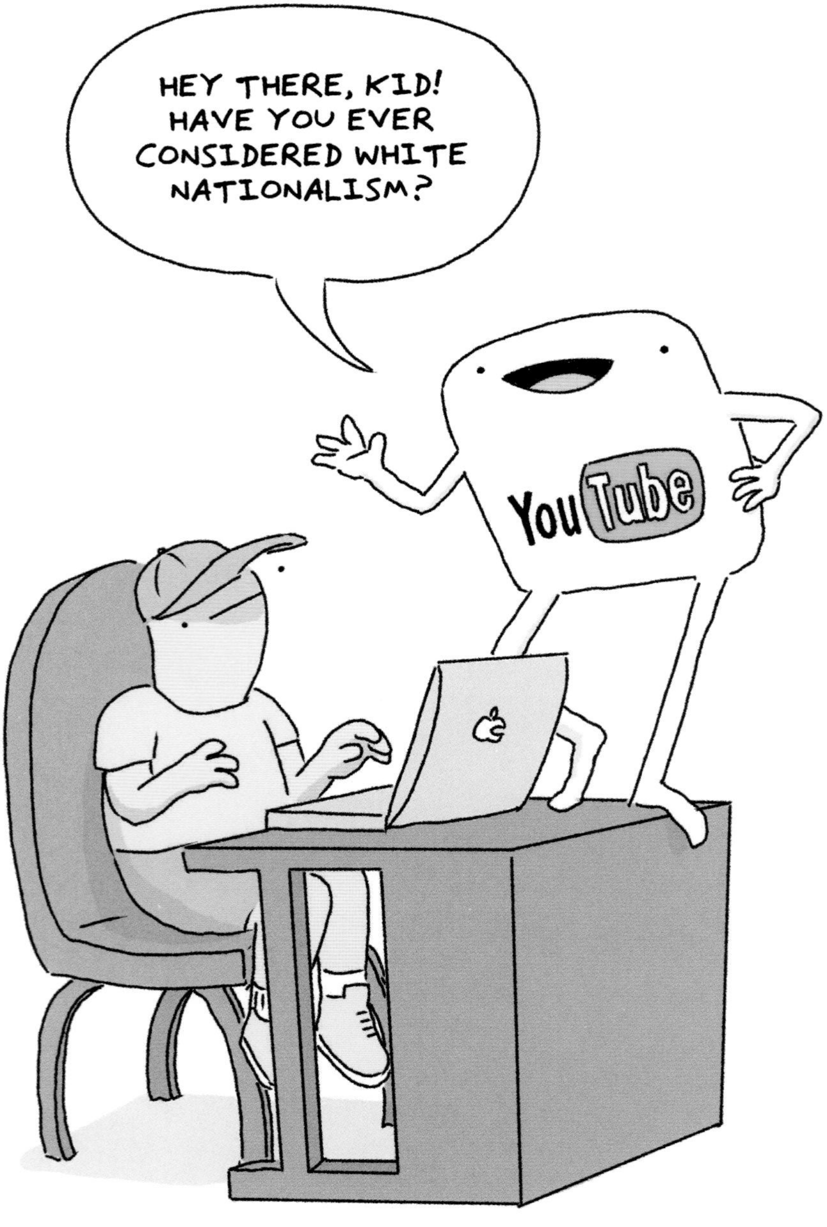
HEY THERE, KID! HAVE YOU EVER CONSIDERED WHITE NATIONALISM?
YouTube

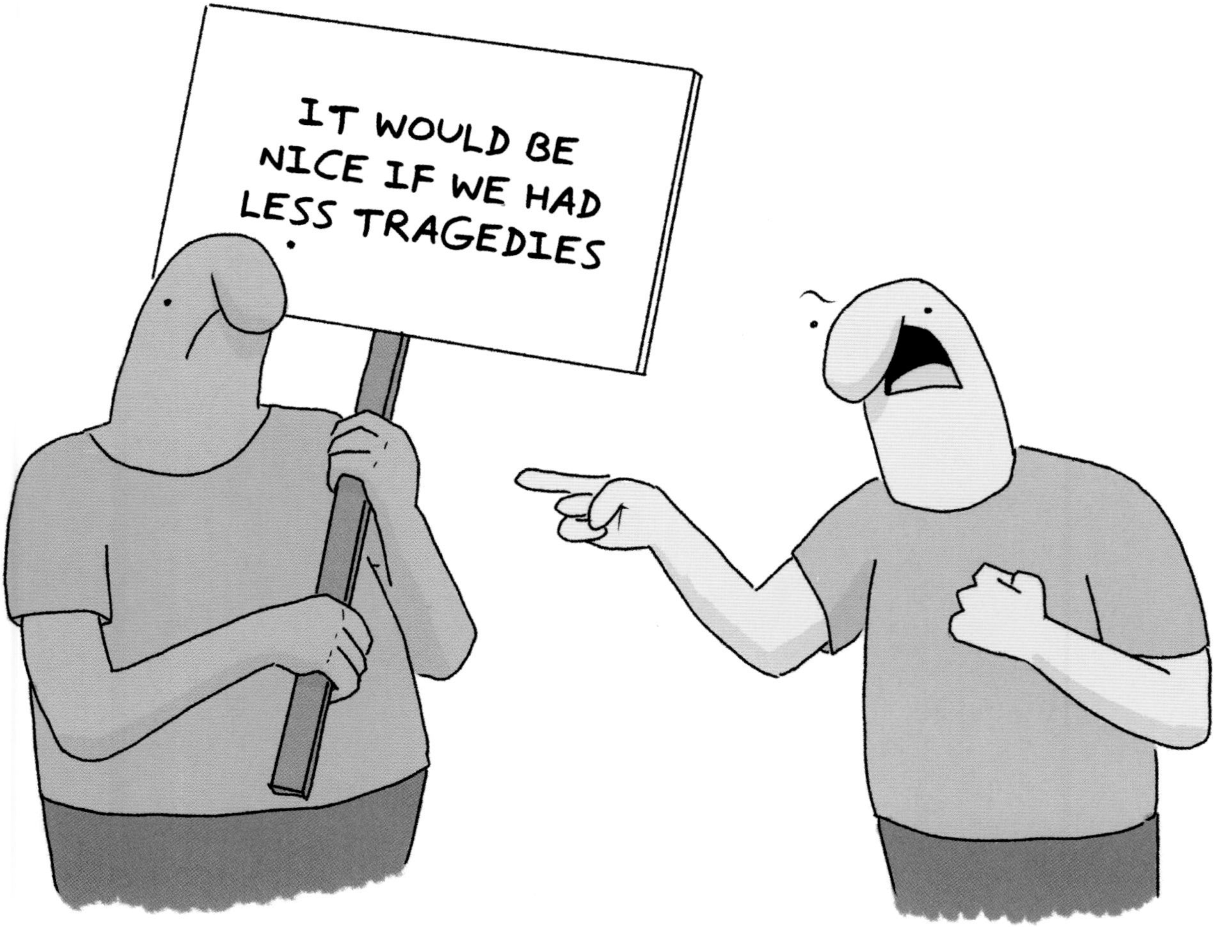
IT WOULD BE NICE IF WE HAD LESS TRAGEDIES.

HEY! STOP POLITICIZING THIS TRAGEDY!

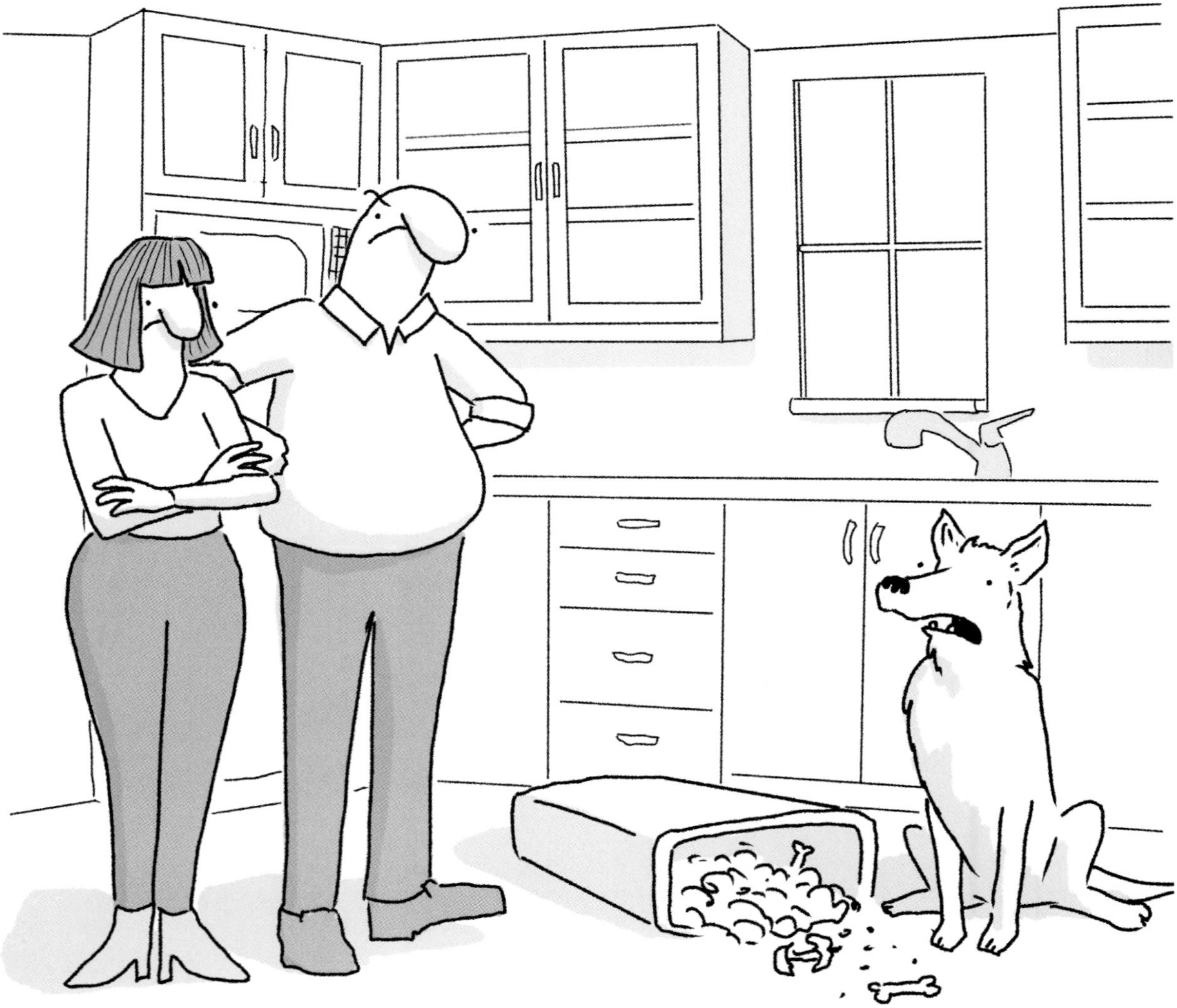

THIS IS A RIGGED WITCH HUNT, ORCHESTRATED BY THE CORRUPT DEMOCRATS AND THE DEEP STATE.

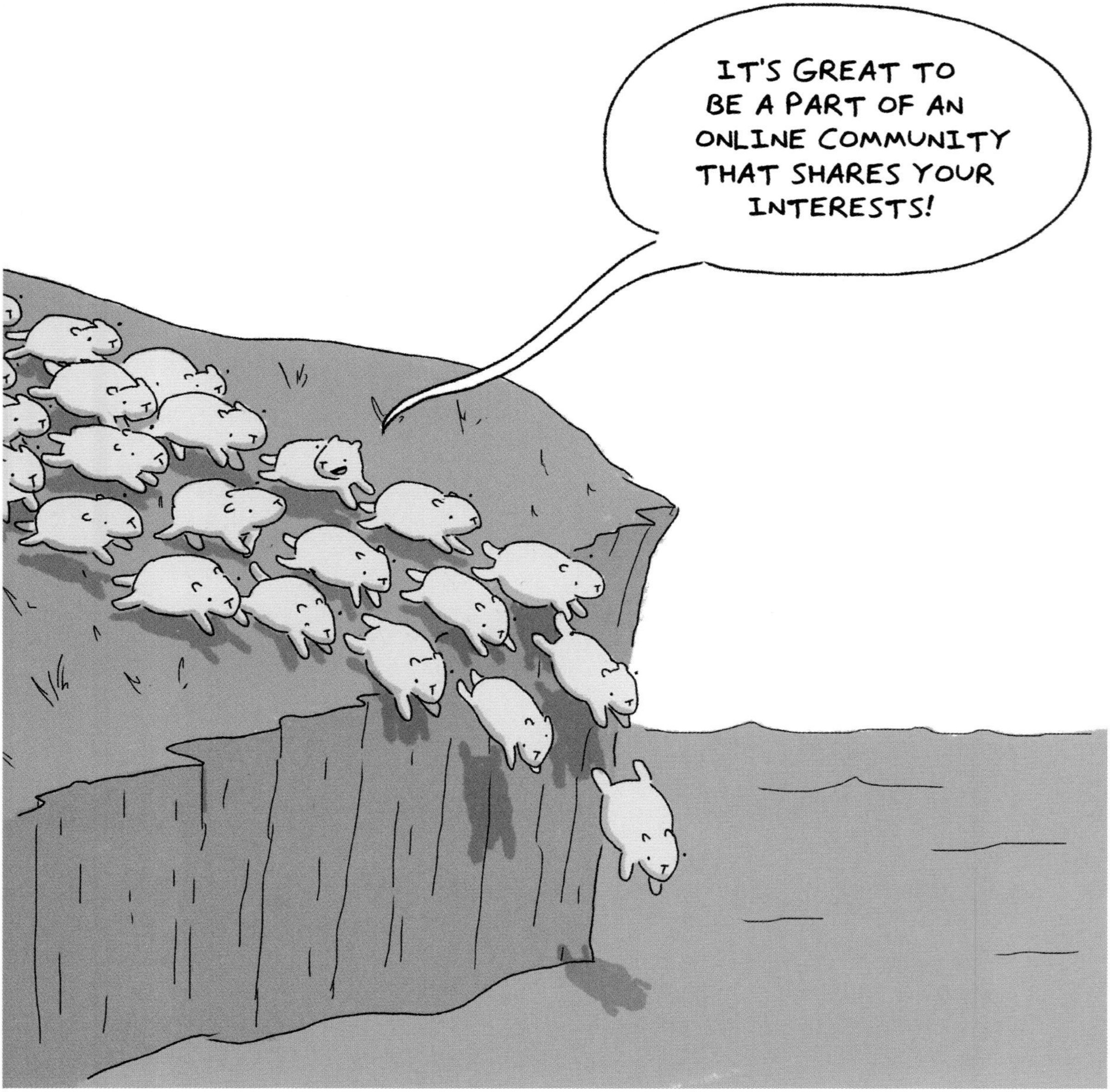
IT'S GREAT TO BE A PART OF AN ONLINE COMMUNITY THAT SHARES YOUR INTERESTS!

THINK THAT RELIGION IS RIDICULOUS? CHOOSE A LOGICAL MODERN REPLACEMENT!

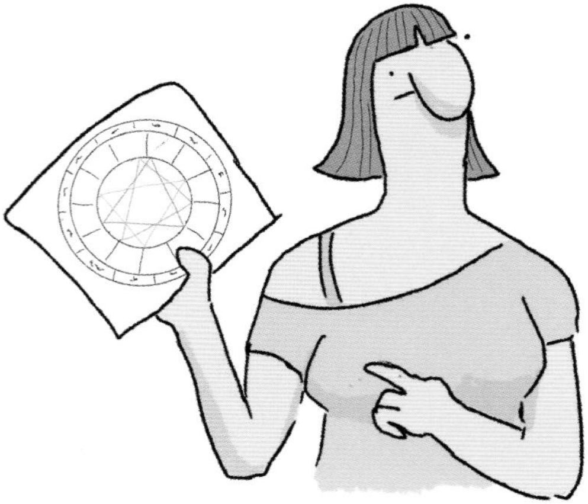

BELIEVE THAT ANIMAL SHAPES IN THE SKY DICTATE YOUR ENTIRE PERSONALITY

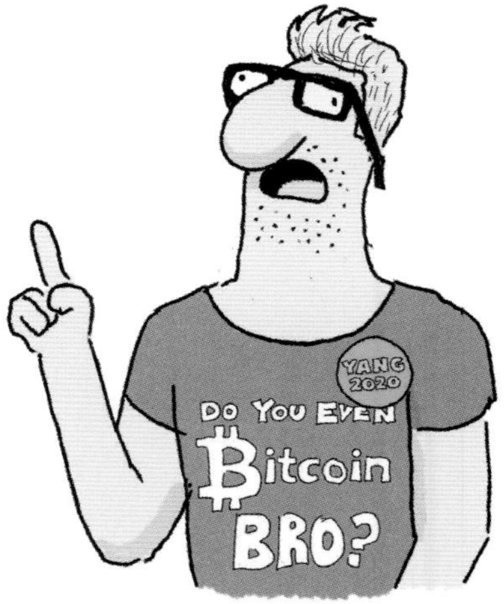
YANG 2020
DO YOU EVEN
Bitcoin
BRO?

BELIEVE THAT INVISIBLE, EASILY LAUNDERED INTERNET CURRENCY IS A GOOD IDEA

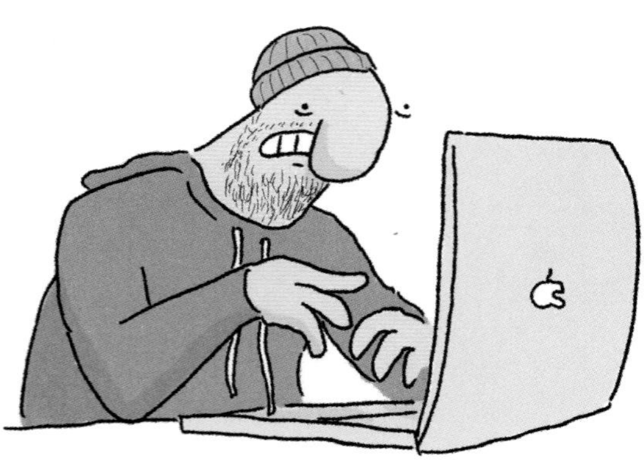

BELIEVE THAT EVERY MAJOR HISTORICAL EVENT WAS A FALSE FLAG EVENT

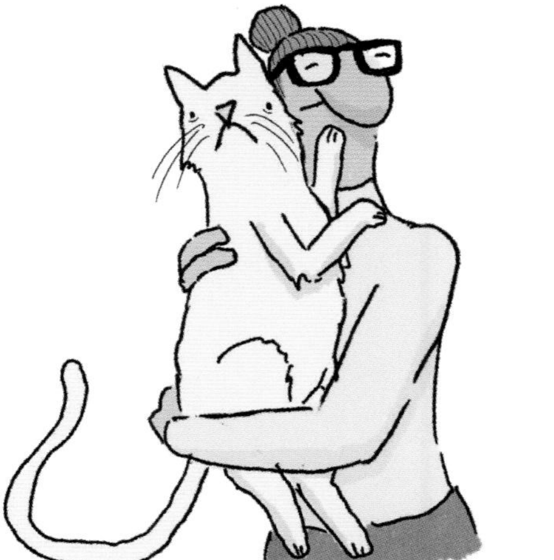

BELIEVE THAT YOUR CAT LOVES YOU BACK

RECENT DEMOGRAPHIC SHIFTS HAVE RESULTED IN 50% OF THE U.S. POPULATION LIVING IN NINE STATES: A HUGE PROBLEM FOR SENATE REPRESENTATION

18 SENATORS

82 SENATORS

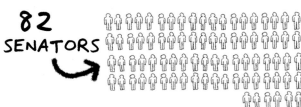

FOR 162 MILLION RESIDENTS

FOR 162 MILLION RESIDENTS

BUT DON'T WORRY: OUR FOUNDING FATHERS OUTLINED A SOLUTION FOR THIS SCENARIO!

WILL YOU HELP US AMEND THE CONSTITUTION TO MAKE THIS MORE FAIR?

NO.

(REMEMBERING THAT SOCIAL MEDIA'S FOUNDATIONAL STRUCTURE IS A LONG-CON SCHEME TO BENEFIT A NEW GENERATION OF MULTINATIONAL BILLIONAIRE VAMPIRES WHO HAVE FOUND A WAY TO SELL OUR DEEPEST FEARS AND INSECURITIES TO THE HIGHEST BIDDER, WITH ONLY PROFIT MOTIVE TO GUIDE THE ALGORITHMS THAT SHAPE THE WORLD WE SEE)

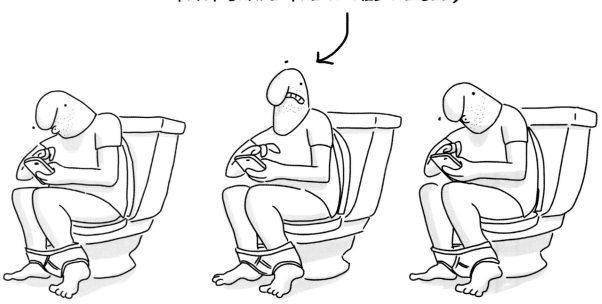

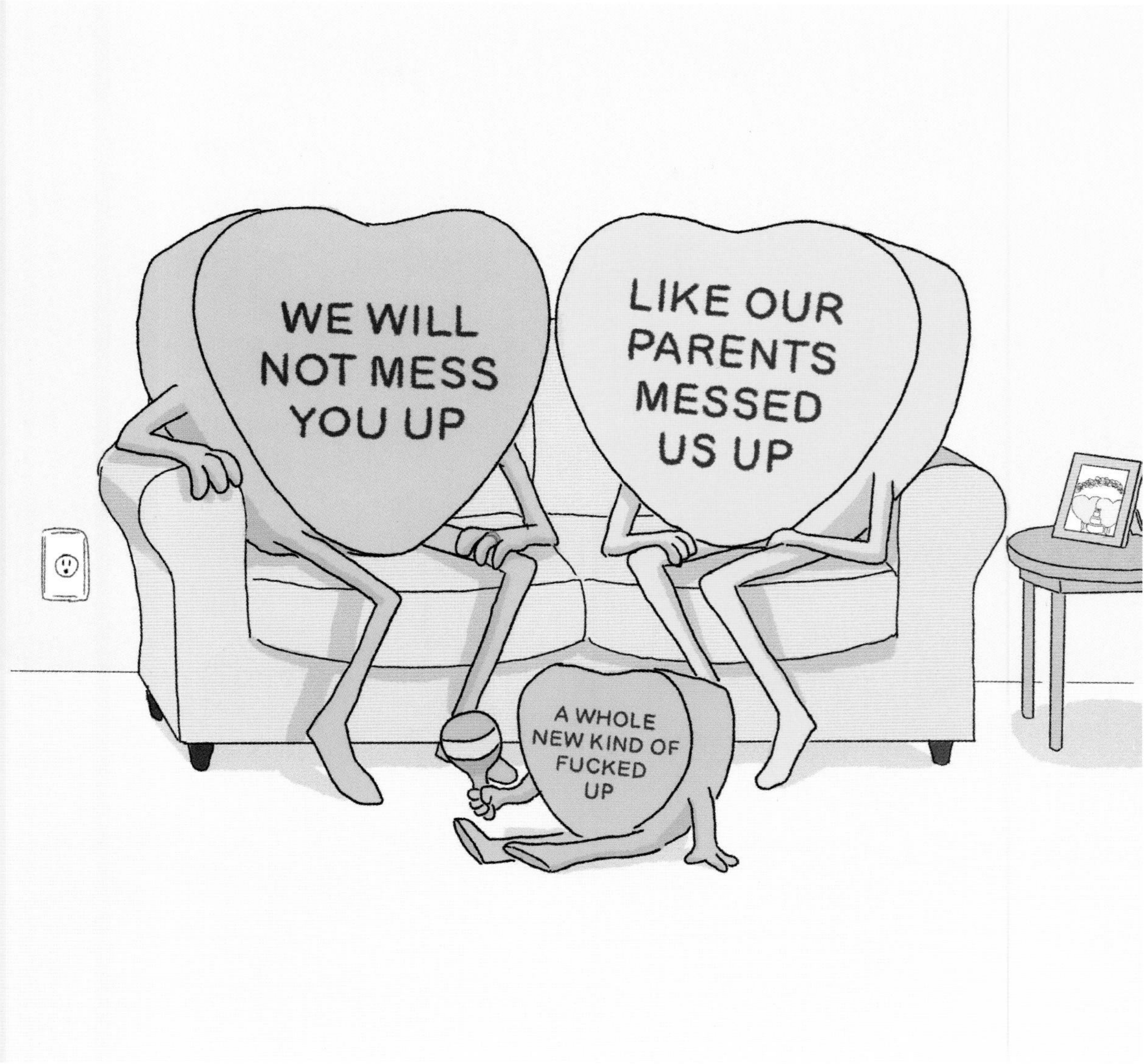
WE WILL NOT MESS YOU UP
LIKE OUR PARENTS MESSED US UP
A WHOLE NEW KIND OF FUCKED UP

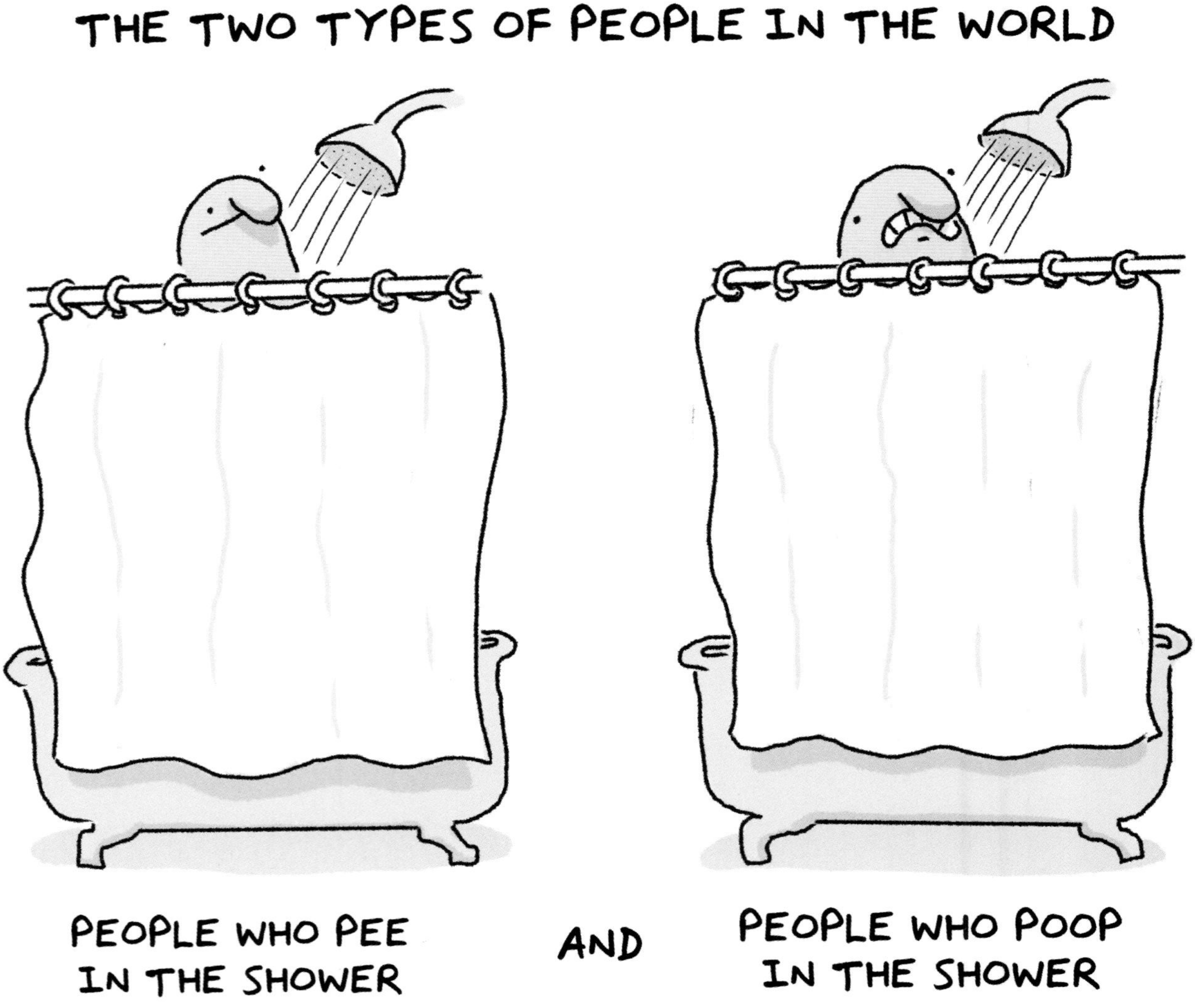
THE TWO TYPES OF PEOPLE IN THE WORLD
PEOPLE WHO PEE IN THE SHOWER
AND
PEOPLE WHO POOP IN THE SHOWER

Originally, I was toying with the classic joke about how there are two types of people in the world: people who pee in the shower and liars. My friend Dan challenged me to come up with something more surprising. The resulting comic printed on this page remains our mutual favorite collaboration, for reasons neither of us fully understand that probably date back to preschool.

WINTER HATS: A GUIDE

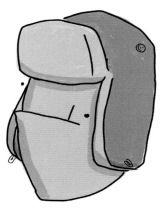

RABBIT HUNTER OR
STEALTHY PODCAST LISTENER

HAS CHECKED ESPN.COM
DURING A FUNERAL

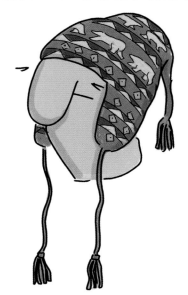

"EXCUSE ME, DO YOU HAVE
A MINUTE FOR THE ENVIRONMENT?"

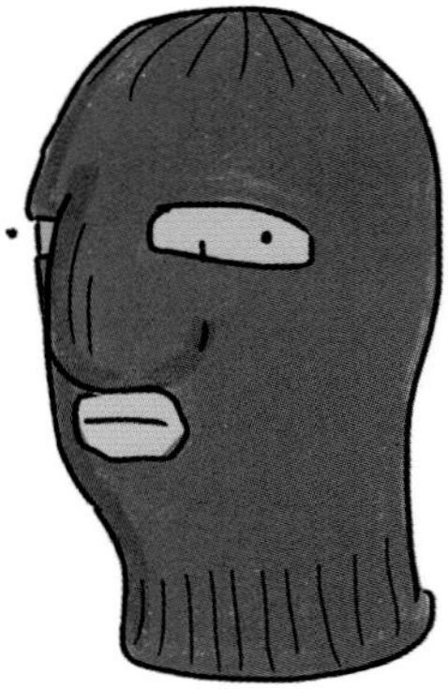

EITHER A HOSTAGE
SITUATION OR MANITOBA

PENMANSHIP:
AN EVOLUTIONARY STUDY

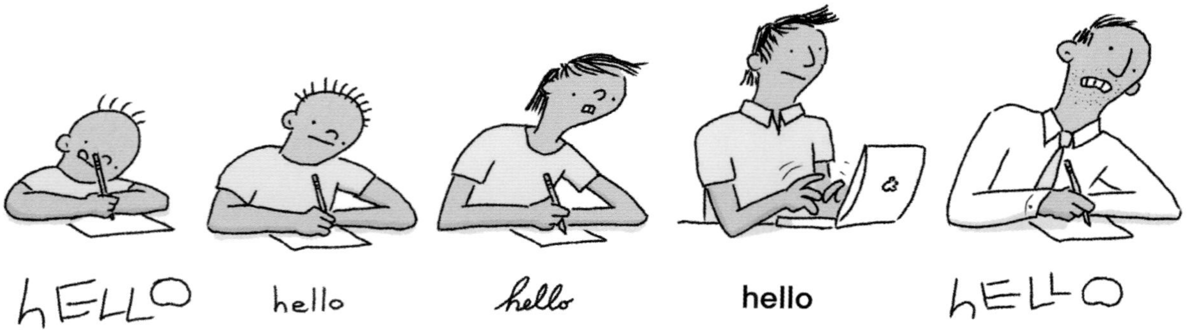
hELLO
hello
hello
hello
hELLO

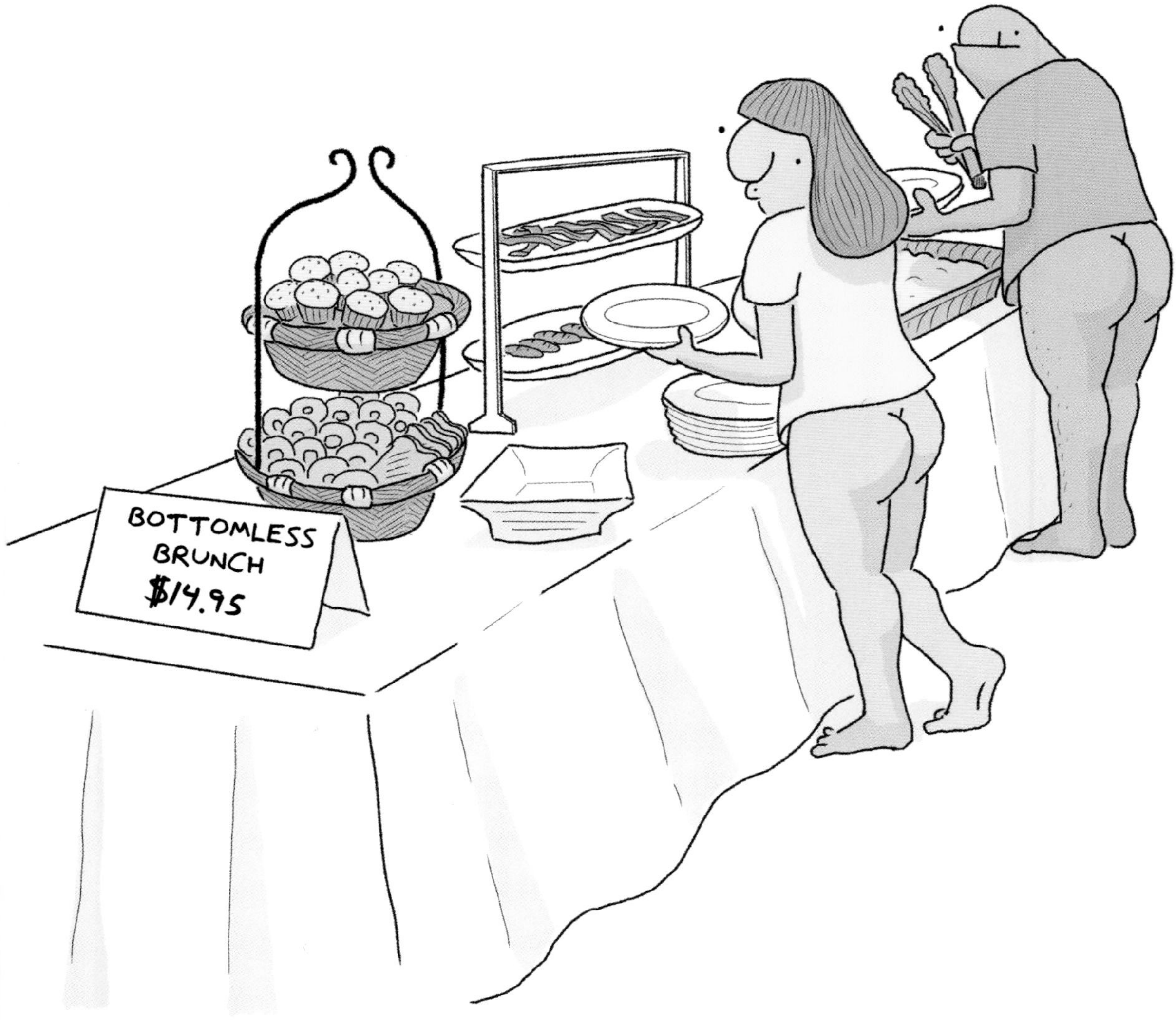
BOTTOMLESS
BRUNCH
$14.95

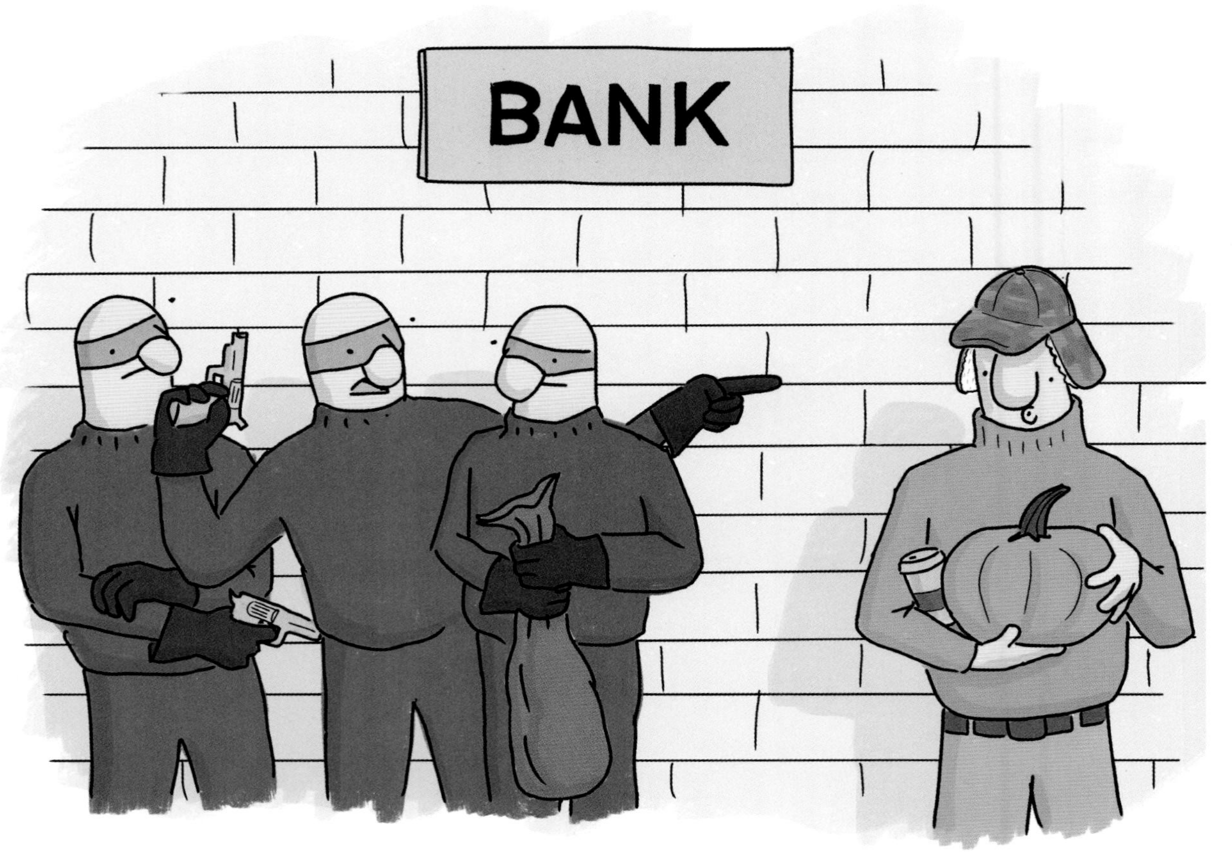
BANK

YOU BOTH TAKE THE EXITS,
I'LL TAKE THE FRONT ENTRANCE.
AND GARY... HE'S OUR FALL GUY.

A GUIDE TO SEASONS IN THE NORTHEAST

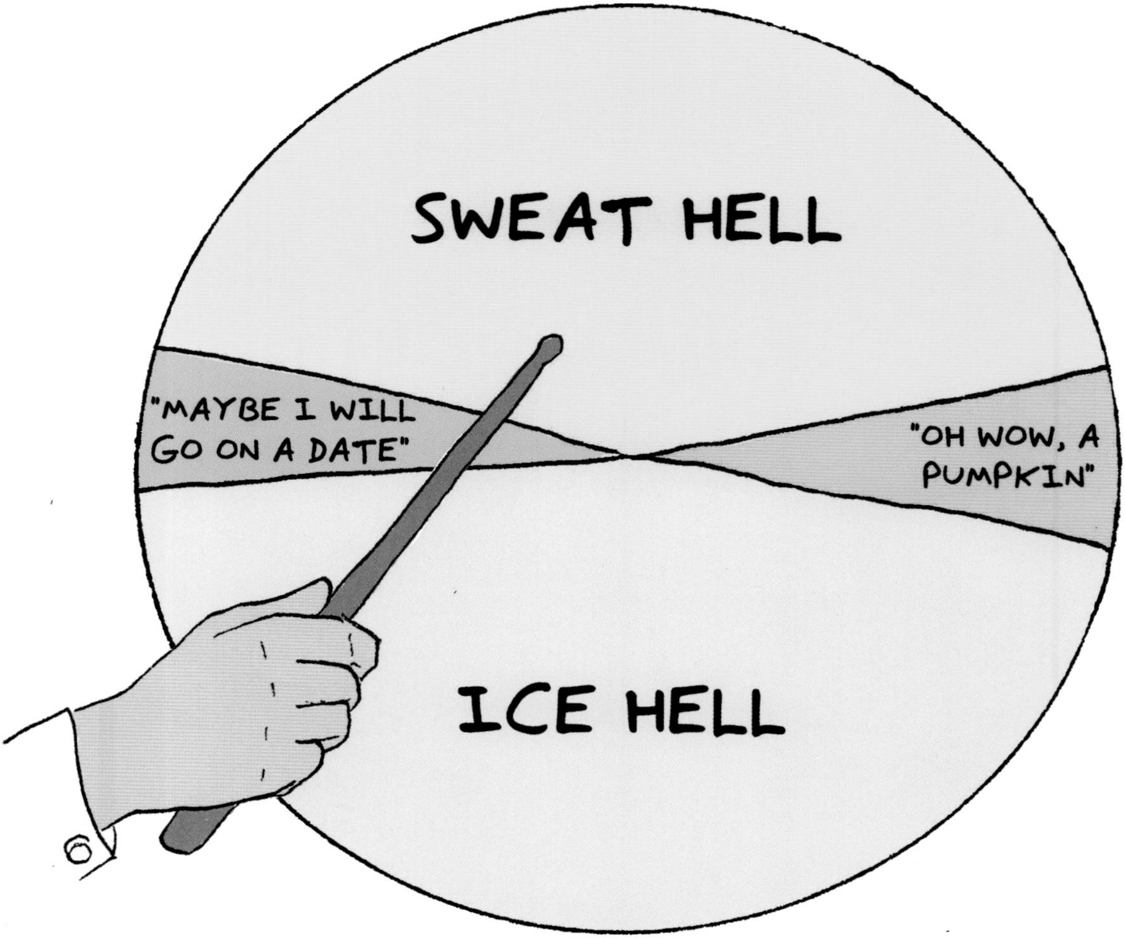

SWEAT HELL
"MAYBE I WILL GO ON A DATE"
"OH WOW, A PUMPKIN"
ICE HELL

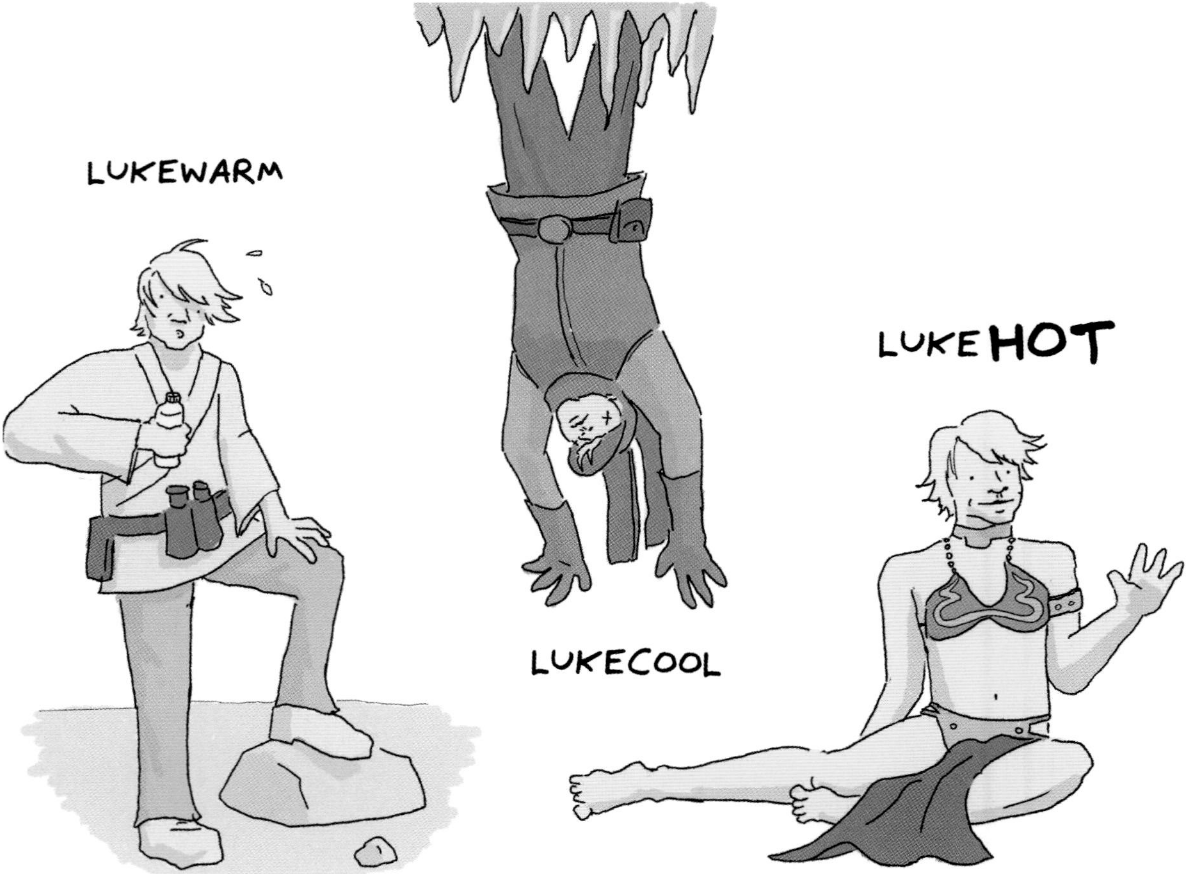
LUKEWARM
LUKECOOL
LUKEHOT

Mark Hamill favorited this one on Twitter, so I'm gonna take that to mean this is official Star Wars canon now.

LOOK AT CUTE
ANIMAL VIDEOS

READ THE
NEWS

WATCH
FOX NEWS

WHY SANTA MIGHT BE REPUBLICAN

- OLD WHITE GUY WHO LIVES IN THE MIDDLE OF NOWHERE
- WEARS RED HAT
- LECTURES OTHER PEOPLE'S CHILDREN AT THE MALL
- SAYS "MERRY CHRISTMAS" INSTEAD OF "HAPPY HOLIDAYS"
- TAKES MILK AND COOKIES EQUALLY FROM ALL CHILDREN BUT GIVES RICH KIDS MORE PRESENTS

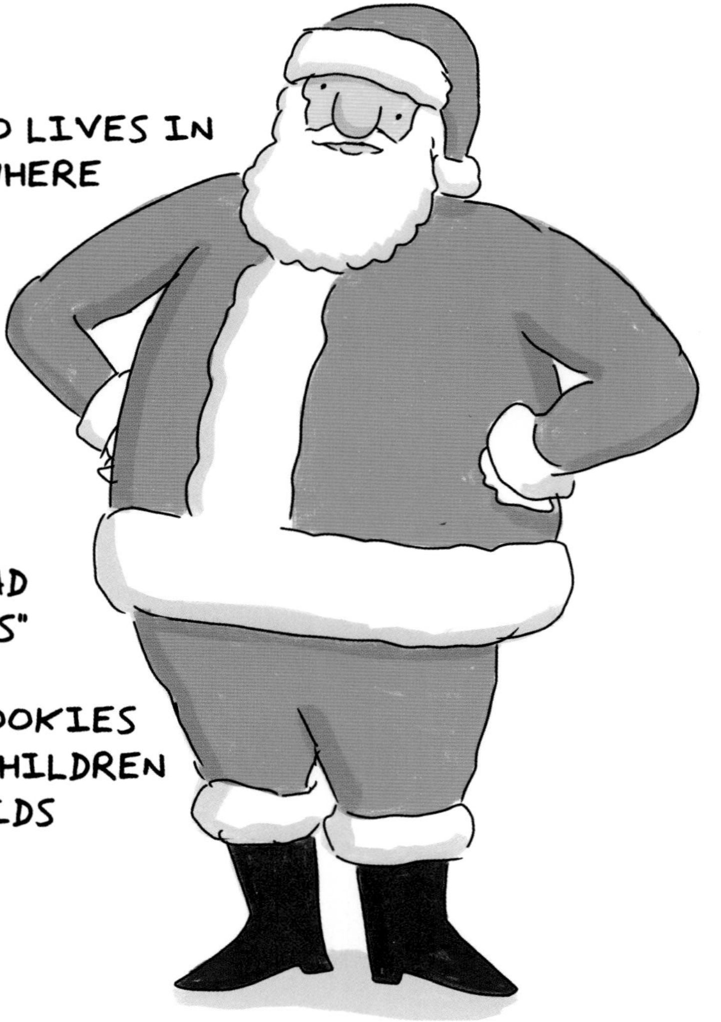

BANANA LIFE HACK!!!

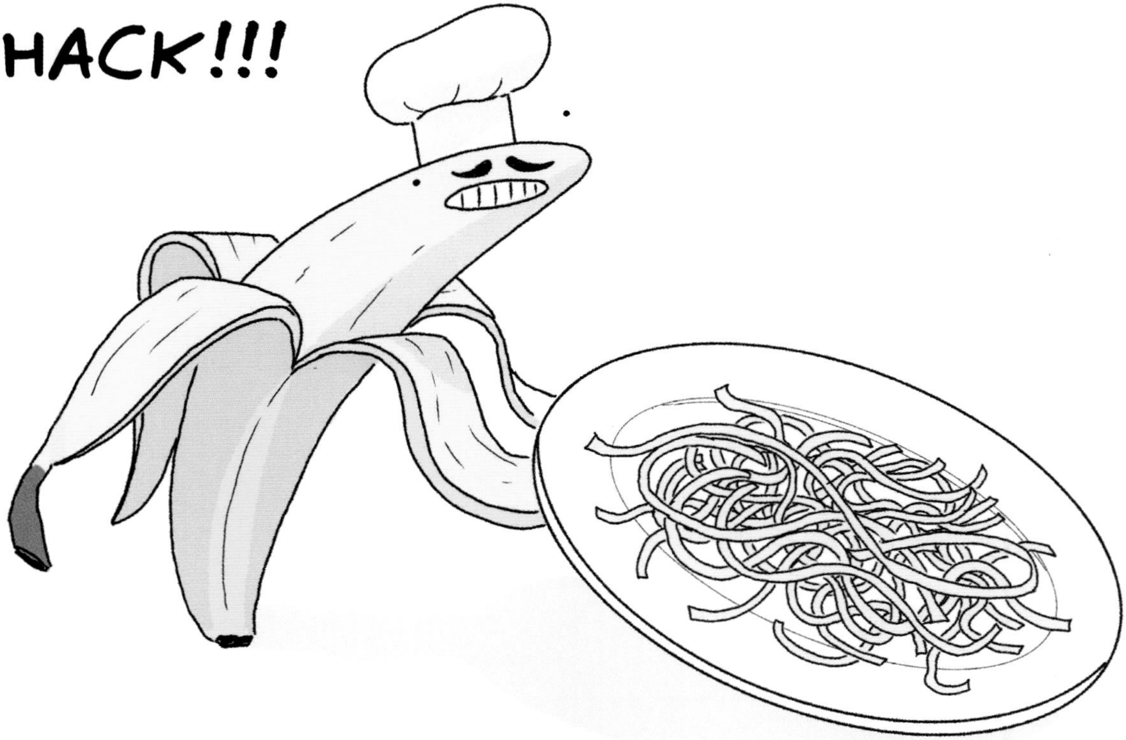

COLLECT ALL THE STRINGY BITS AND MAKE A BIG PLATE OF SWEET, GRAINY

BANOODLES!!

NEW TO PODCASTS? CHOOSE A GENRE!

LIBERTARIAN "BROPRAH" EVANGELIZES DMT AND INTERVIEWS RIGHT-WING YOUTUBE TROLLS

MAN WITH NO ACADEMIC CREDENTIALS YELLS ABOUT A HISTORY BOOK HE READ IN 9-HOUR INSTALLMENTS

SEEMINGLY NORMAL, NICE ADULTS PLAYFULLY CHITCHAT ABOUT GRUESOME MURDER

NERDS RECAP A SHOW YOU'VE ALREADY SEEN AND SOMEHOW IT'S LONGER THAN THE ACTUAL TV EPISODE

30 COMEDIANS YELLING OVER EACH OTHER

LIKE NPR'S FRESH AIR, BUT BY A DEPRESSED COMEDIAN WHO PROBABLY HAS CATS

...BUT ROCK BOTTOM IS MY COMFORT ZONE!

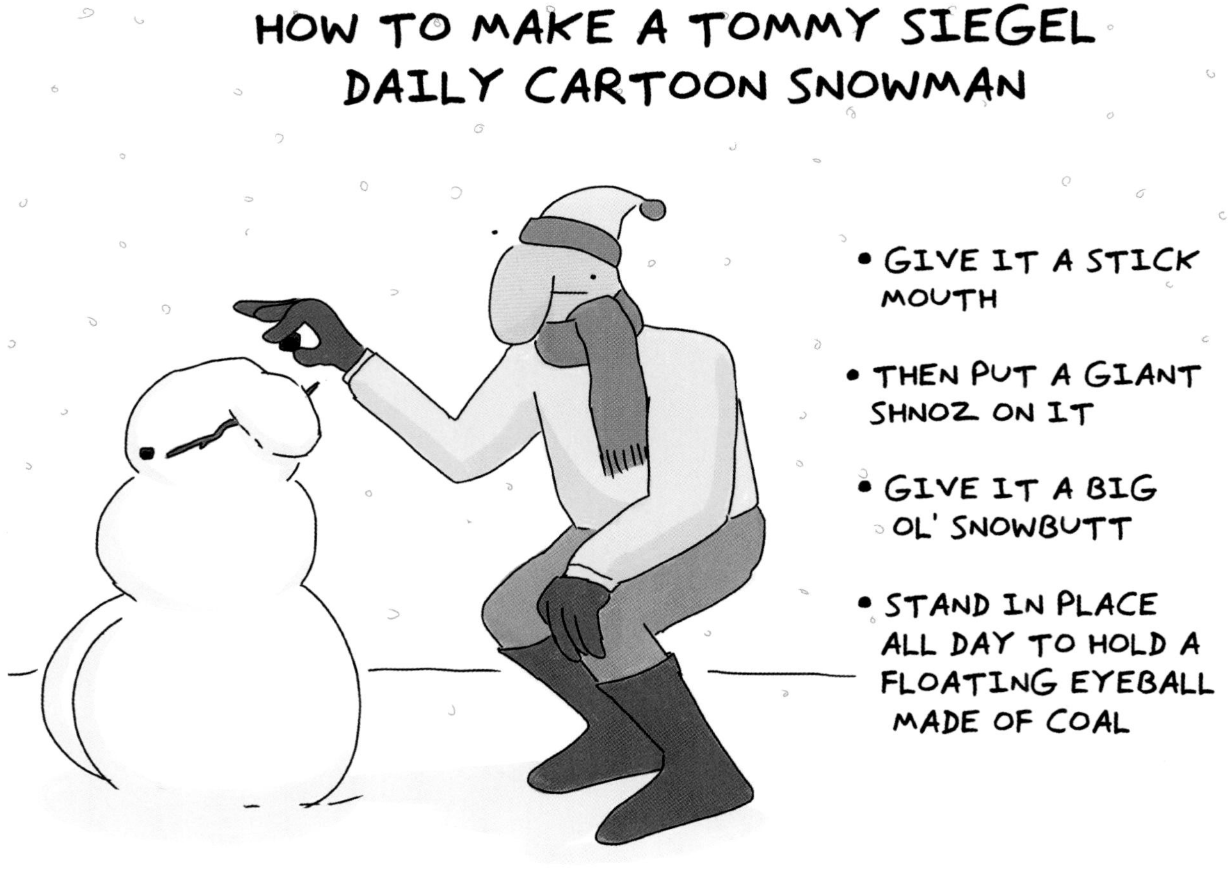
HOW TO MAKE A TOMMY SIEGEL DAILY CARTOON SNOWMAN
• GIVE IT A STICK MOUTH
• THEN PUT A GIANT SHNOZ ON IT
• GIVE IT A BIG OL' SNOWBUTT
• STAND IN PLACE ALL DAY TO HOLD A FLOATING EYEBALL MADE OF COAL

I just want it to be known that a handful of people actually made these in their yards and sent photos, which made my winter a lot brighter.

A FAREWELL TO BUTTS

Now that the dust has settled on my 500-day drawing challenge, it is much easier to see it for what it is. On one hand, butts. I got *really* good at drawing butts. On the other hand, it temporarily broke my brain.

Though it hurts to acknowledge, the attempt to conquer my social media addiction only made my addiction worse, now having my creative livelihood and identity forged inside its confines. As the project barreled on, even as I "won" inside the social media ecosystem and gained hundreds of thousands of followers, I couldn't help but wonder: Was I just another noodle in a soup of disconnected images that only served to create a larger picture of vague dread? Was I just another content creator turning everyone's brains into scrambled eggs? And why do I feel worse than I did when I started the project?

THE THREE TYPES OF SOCIAL MEDIA CONTENT: A GUIDE

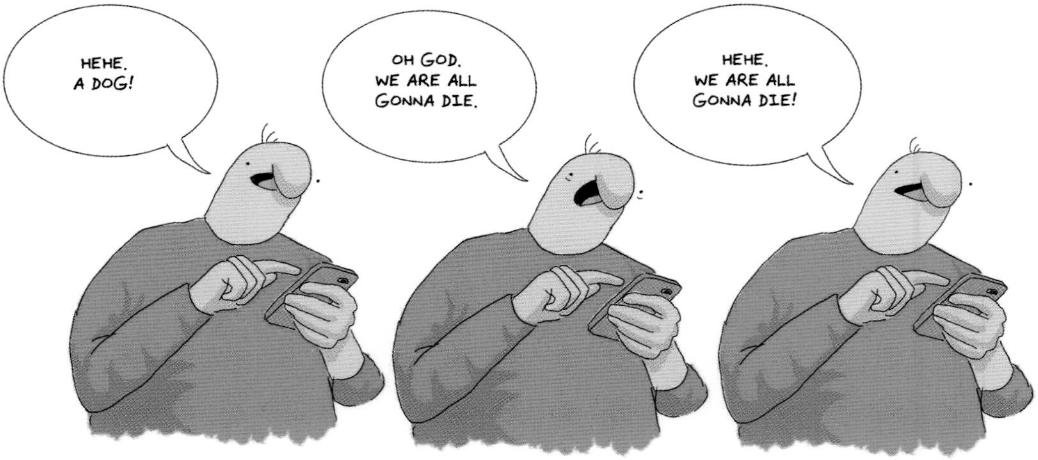
HEHE.
A DOG!
OH GOD.
WE ARE ALL
GONNA DIE.
HEHE.
WE ARE ALL
GONNA DIE!

At the end of the 500-day marathon, I concluded that it's impossible to meaningfully *win* social media. If you're playing the social media game, you're playing in Zuckerberg's casino with Zuckerberg's rules. And as long as you keep playing, the house always wins. Eventually.

But outside of the vessel of distribution, the plus sides of the project were enormous. Namely: I learned how to draw! It's honestly a little terrifying to look at my art from early in the project — it's as if some stranger drew it, without knowing the rules of my universe. Literally, *none* of their noses are stuck inside their mouths. And all of the feet are wrong.[1] I developed a voice as a cartoonist! I built an audience of hundreds of thousands of people! I got a book deal,

1. I continued drawing feet wrong until the last couple of months of the project, when someone messaged me to let me know that I draw feet wrong. And yes, this a foot footnote.

which is how you're reading this right now! It afforded me a new life, one that could provide me some semblance of control in a turbulent and unpredictable music landscape!

It was both the smartest and dumbest thing I've ever done in my life.

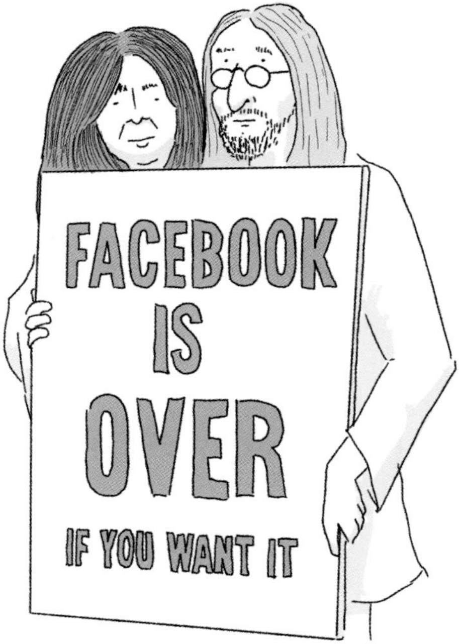
FACEBOOK IS OVER
IF YOU WANT IT

OK. So, yes, social media helped me achieve some of my wildest dreams. In some sense, I have to be grateful for the megaphone that made that possible. But on the other hand, touring bands don't go onstage every night to thank the oil conglomerates that provided diesel fuel for their tour bus to get from show to show.

With the project a few months behind in the rearview mirror, I remain dogged in my belief that if social media algorithms can be used to optimize stress, fear, and addiction in the pursuit of ad revenue, then they should also be able to encourage a sense of community. If it can encourage people to make art, then why couldn't it also foster sustainable ways to continue making it? If social media is capable of tapping into human social instincts, then don't the platforms that host it have some kind of responsibility to nudge it toward encouraging our better selves?

Sure, in some respects what we see on social media is just a reflection of human nature. But, it's important to remember that it's a mirror being warped for a specific outcome: maximum extraction of our time for ad revenue. The public library, I would note, is equally a reflection of who we are. It just has a different purpose than extracting data and selling advertising. So though I know I can be very negative about the current state of, well, everything . . . I mean it with a spirit of optimism. Despite it all, I do think we are capable of better. I *do* think technology can serve humanity. You hear that, Zuck?

For now, I'm leaving my phone at home whenever I can[2] and I'm working on finding some hobbies I can't optimize or maximize, like birdwatching. It took a few years of manic creative output and general anxiety for me to rediscover the simple pleasure of sitting in the park to do nothing at all but listen to whatever the hell it is that birds are saying to one another.[3]

I've also been getting more into the habit of finding ways to explore art that don't involve the internet. I've been going to a lot of live-figure drawing events in Brooklyn and getting increasingly better at drawing the human form without using myself as a model. The models, of course, have not been informed that I am drawing them as Chip People, and I do not plan to inform them.

---

2. Yes, this means I am lost at least once a day.
3. After a great deal of ornithological observation, I am fairly certain they are emotionally charged variants of "Hey!"

I suppose that my advice for anyone considering embarking on this batshit journey is the same as the advice I received: It's terrible, and if you want to do it, you should do it.

But be warned: You'll likely be a birdwatcher by the time it's over. Yikes.

HAROLD... THEY KNOW.

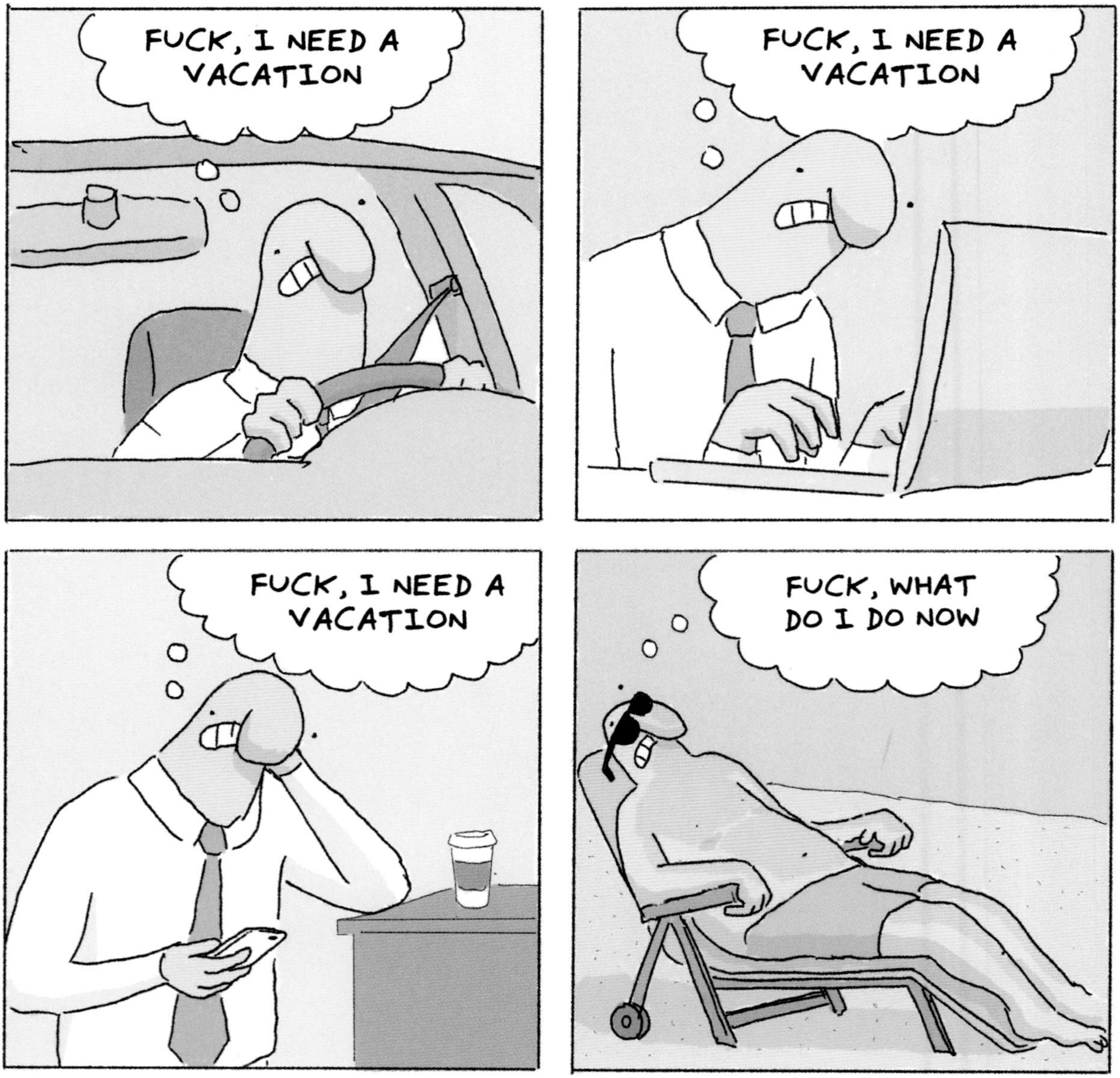
FUCK, I NEED A VACATION
FUCK, I NEED A VACATION
FUCK, I NEED A VACATION
FUCK, WHAT DO I DO NOW

And yes, this was my experience when I finished the 500-day challenge.

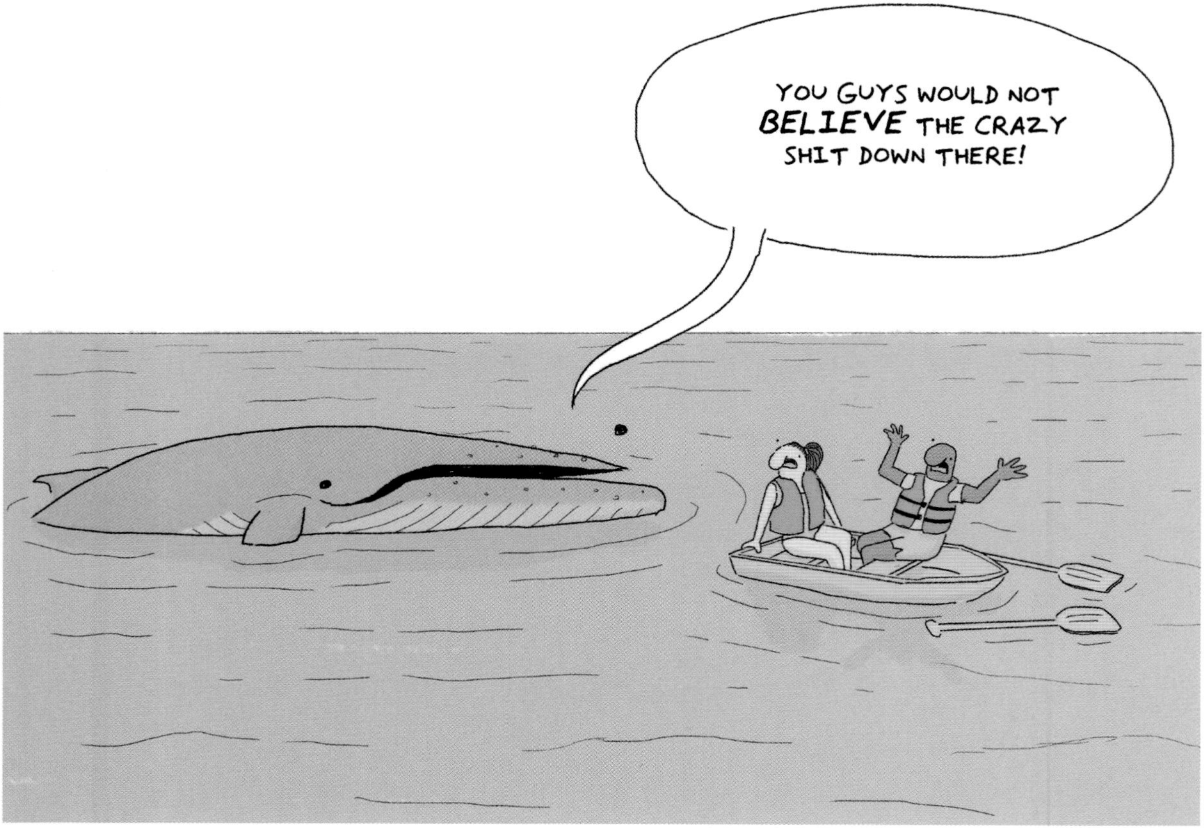
YOU GUYS WOULD NOT BELIEVE THE CRAZY SHIT DOWN THERE!

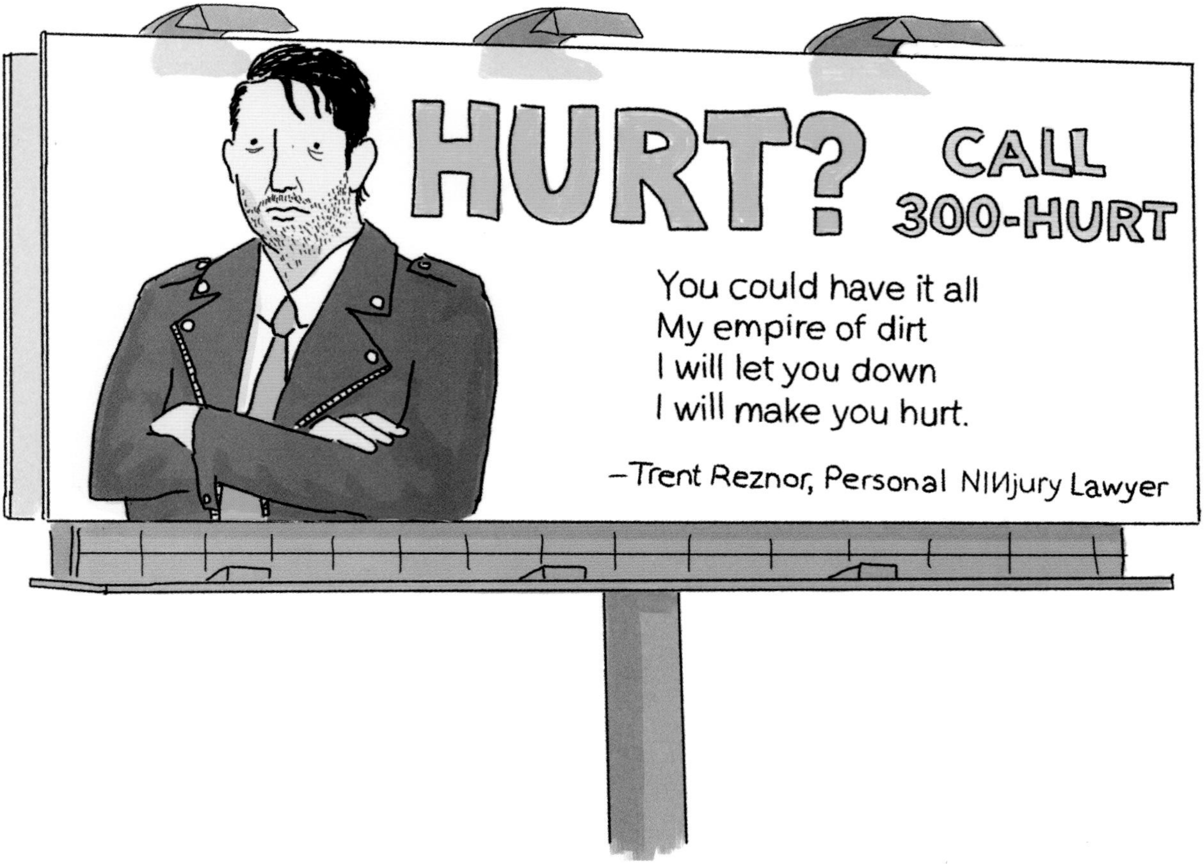
HURT? CALL 300-HURT
You could have it all
My empire of dirt
I will let you down
I will make you hurt.
–Trent Reznor, Personal NIИjury Lawyer

This one requires having some awareness of who Trent Reznor is. But I swear, if you know who he is, this is a good comic.

HOW CONSUMER CHOICE GUIDES OUR PRIVATE HEALTH CARE SYSTEM

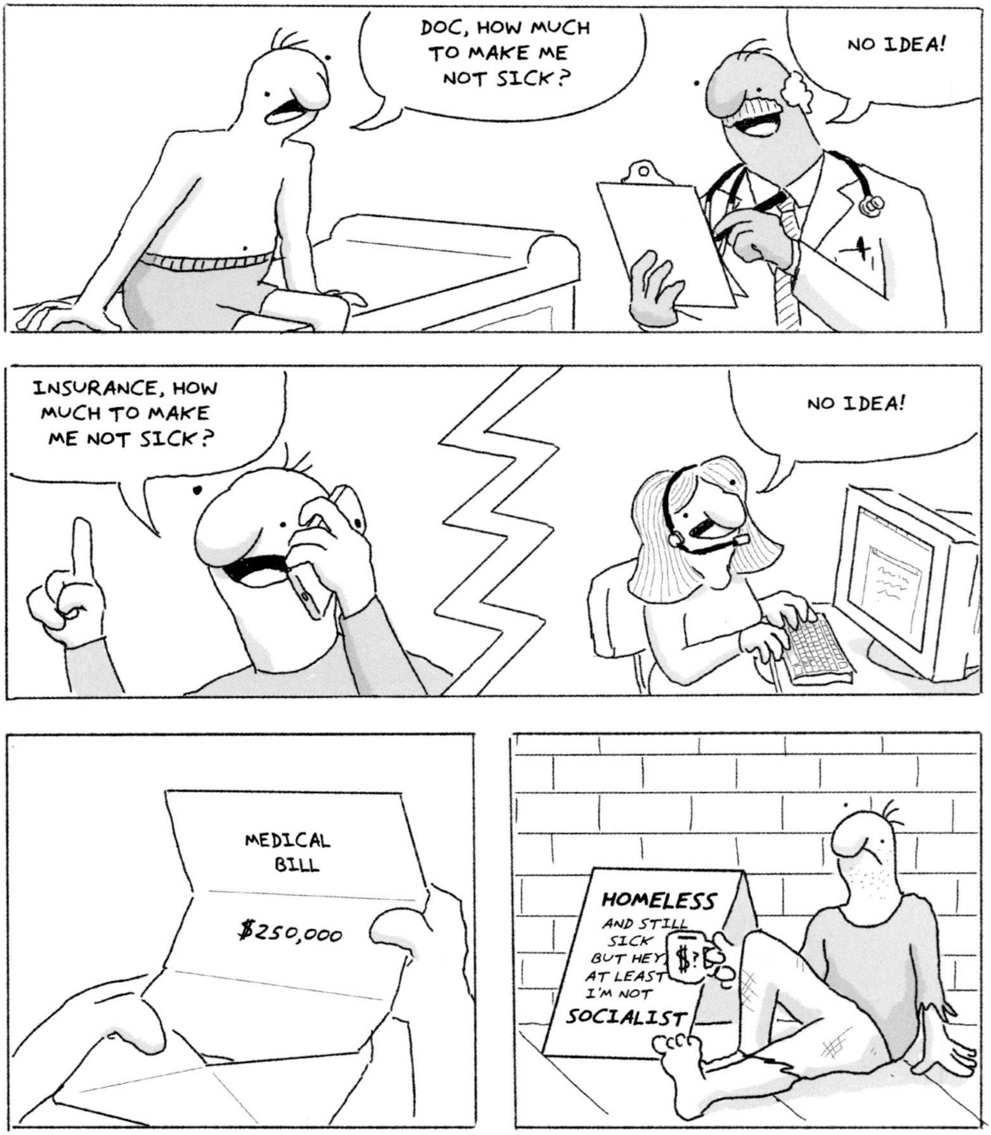
DOC, HOW MUCH TO MAKE ME NOT SICK?
NO IDEA!
INSURANCE, HOW MUCH TO MAKE ME NOT SICK?
NO IDEA!
MEDICAL BILL
$250,000
HOMELESS
AND STILL SICK BUT HEY, AT LEAST I'M NOT
SOCIALIST

HOW TO APPLY FOR A JOB, THEN

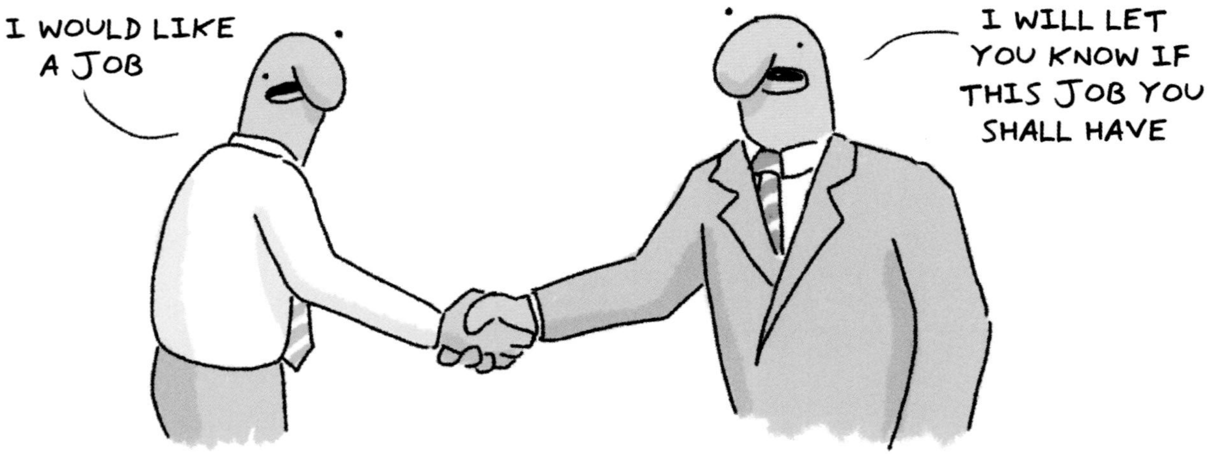
I WOULD LIKE A JOB
I WILL LET YOU KNOW IF THIS JOB YOU SHALL HAVE

HOW TO APPLY FOR A JOB, NOW

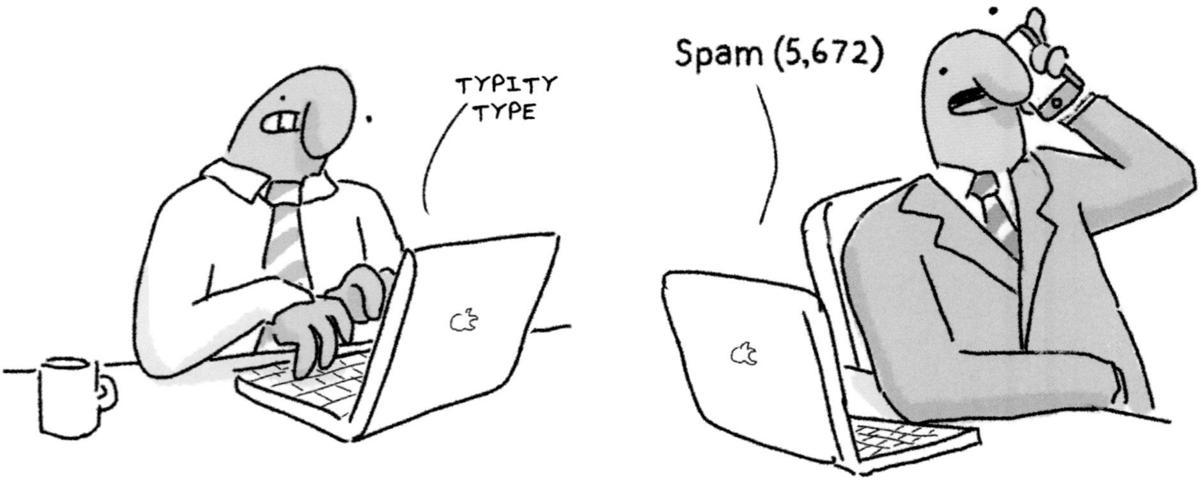
TYPITY TYPE
Spam (5,672)

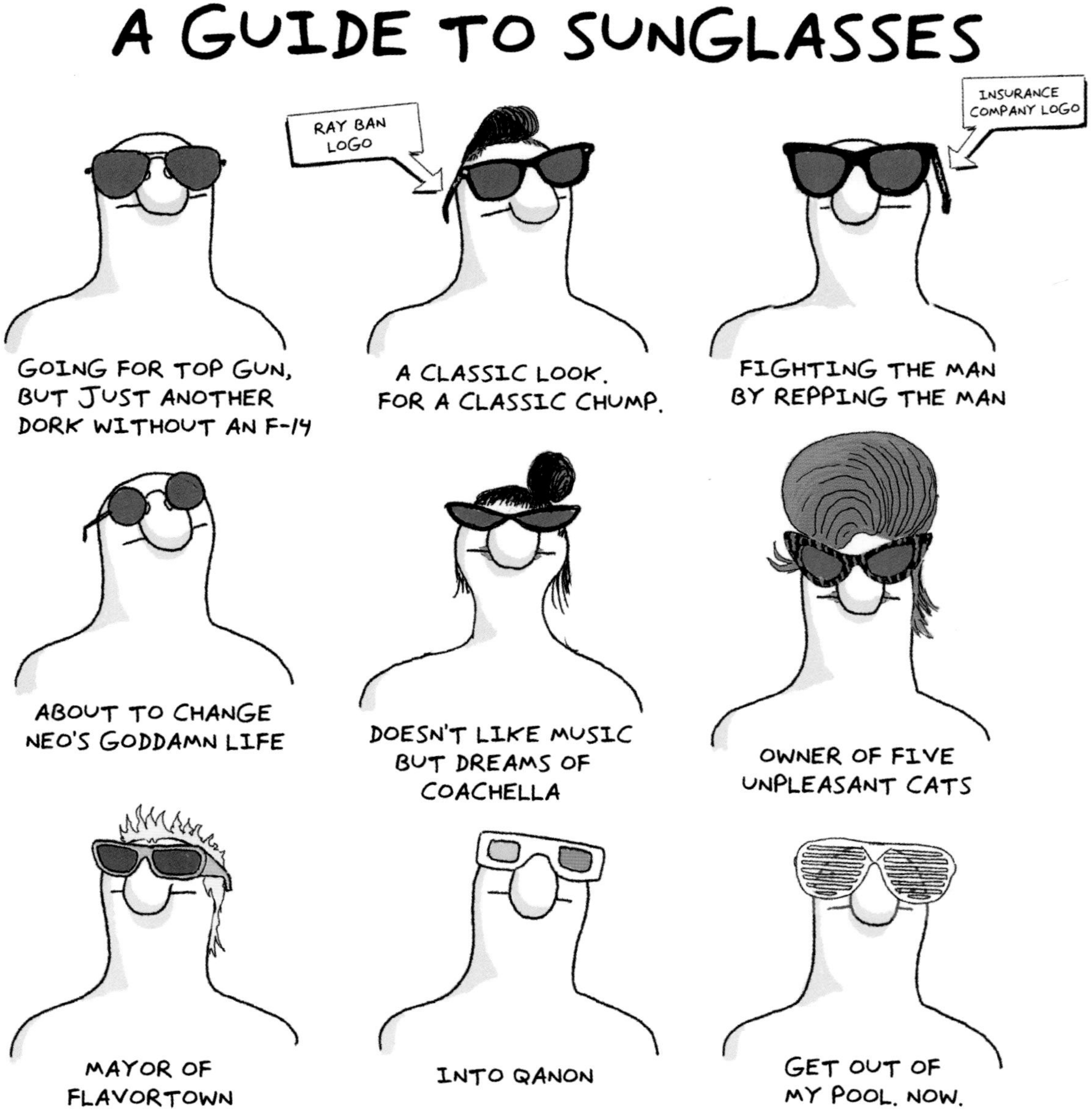
A GUIDE TO SUNGLASSES
RAY BAN LOGO
INSURANCE COMPANY LOGO
GOING FOR TOP GUN, BUT JUST ANOTHER DORK WITHOUT AN F-14
A CLASSIC LOOK. FOR A CLASSIC CHUMP.
FIGHTING THE MAN BY REPPING THE MAN
ABOUT TO CHANGE NEO'S GODDAMN LIFE
DOESN'T LIKE MUSIC BUT DREAMS OF COACHELLA
OWNER OF FIVE UNPLEASANT CATS
MAYOR OF FLAVORTOWN
INTO QANON
GET OUT OF MY POOL. NOW.

LEATHER DADDY LONG-LEGS

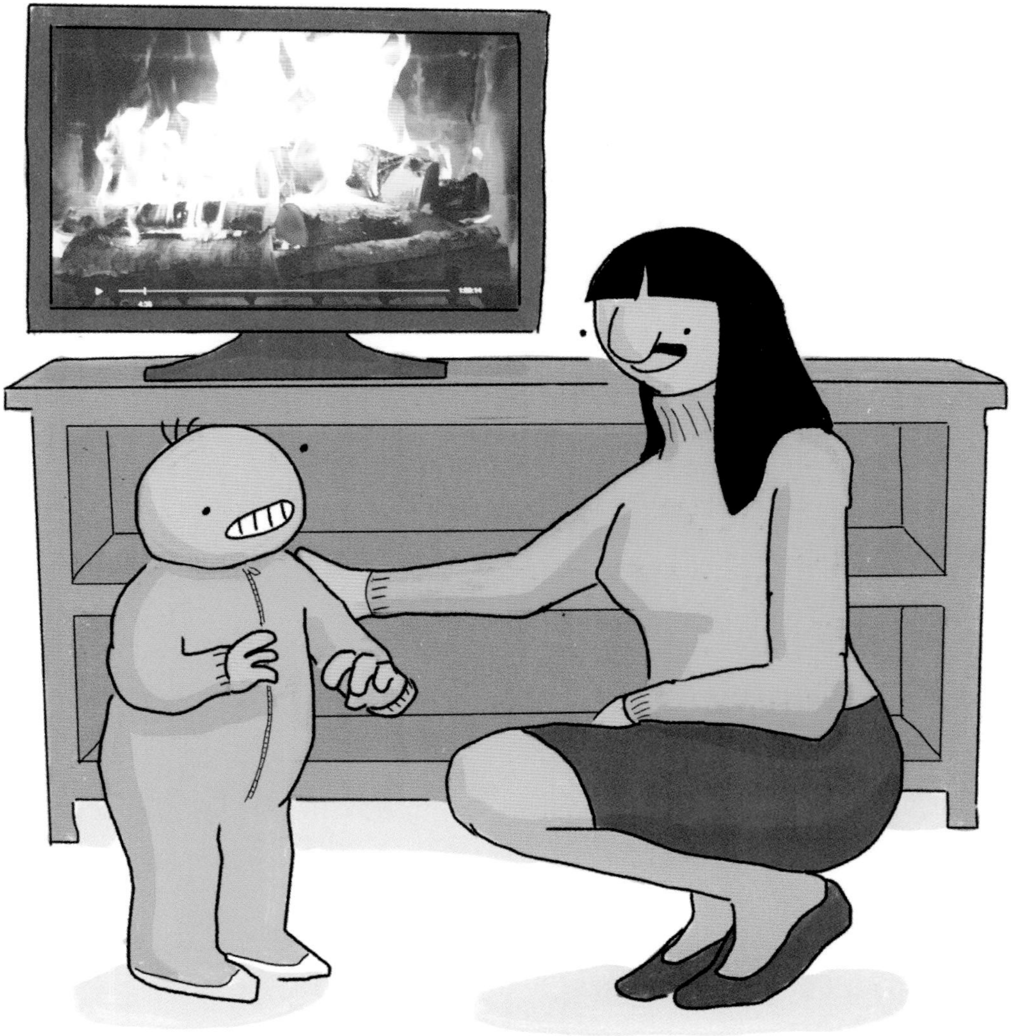

...AND THEN SANTA CLAUS COMES THROUGH THE "FIREPLACE 4K: CRACKLING BIRCHWOOD EDITION" TO BRING PRESENTS TO ALL THE GOOD BOYS AND GIRLS.

NEW YORK PIZZA

vs

CHICAGO PIZZA

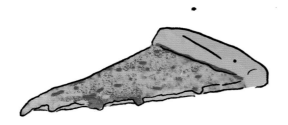 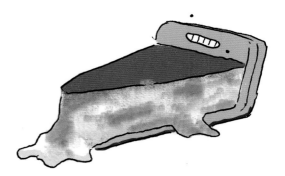

- HIGH VOLUME SALES = FRESH SLICES ALL DAY

- CONVENIENTLY FOLDABLE

- EAT IT WHILE SPEED-WALKING AND STRESSED

- WTF IS THIS

- IT'S A GODDANG CASSEROLE

- WAIT, AM I JUST SUPPOSED TO... SIT HERE AND EAT

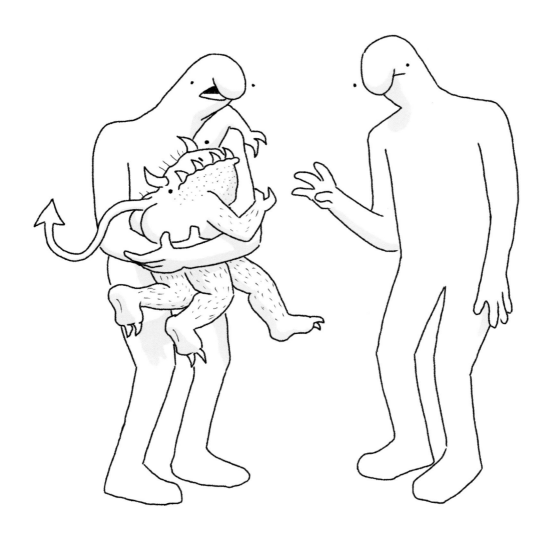

SURE, IT'S DISGUSTING, BUT IT'S NICE
TO HAVE SOMETHING THAT NEEDS ME.

(That's me on the right, every time I meet a friend's pug.)

A GUIDE TO BIRB WATCHING

LIL' BIRB

BIG BIRB

LONG BIRB

BUG BIRB

RAT BIRB

FUCK THIS
FUCKING
BIRB

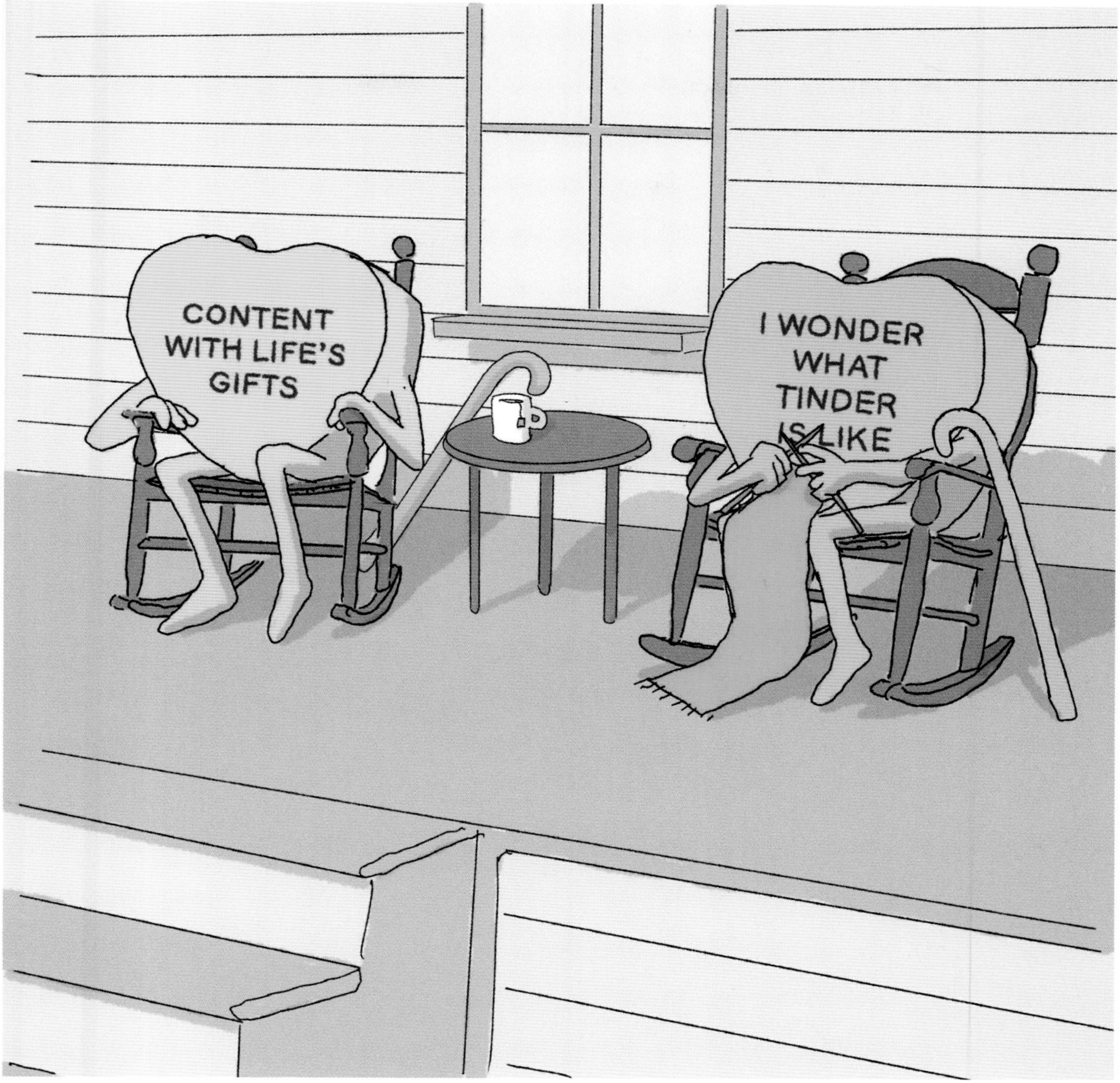
CONTENT
WITH LIFE'S
GIFTS
I WONDER
WHAT
TINDER
IS LIKE

PASTI
ANTIPASTI

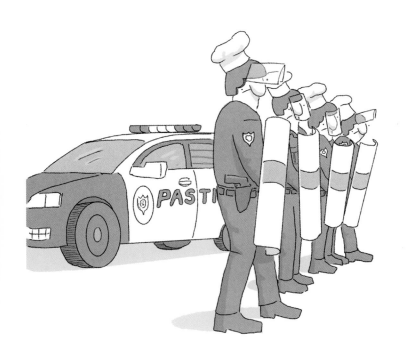

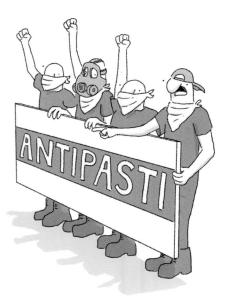

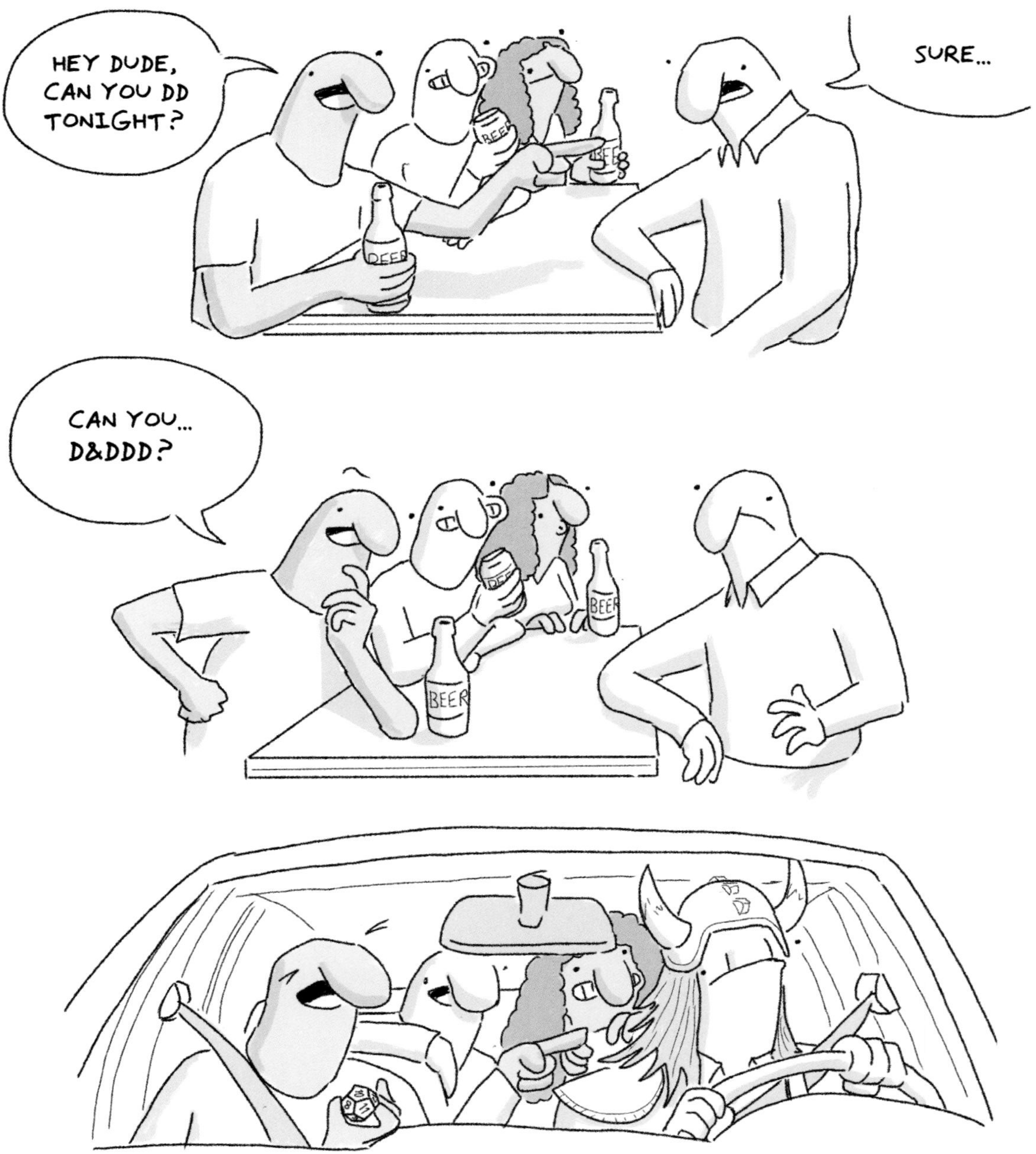
HEY DUDE, CAN YOU DD TONIGHT?
SURE...
CAN YOU... D&DDD?
BEER
BEER
BEER
BEER
BEER
BEER

"IT JUST DOESN'T CRACKLE LIKE
THE ONE ON NETFLIX"

A GUIDE TO MEN'S WINTER COATS

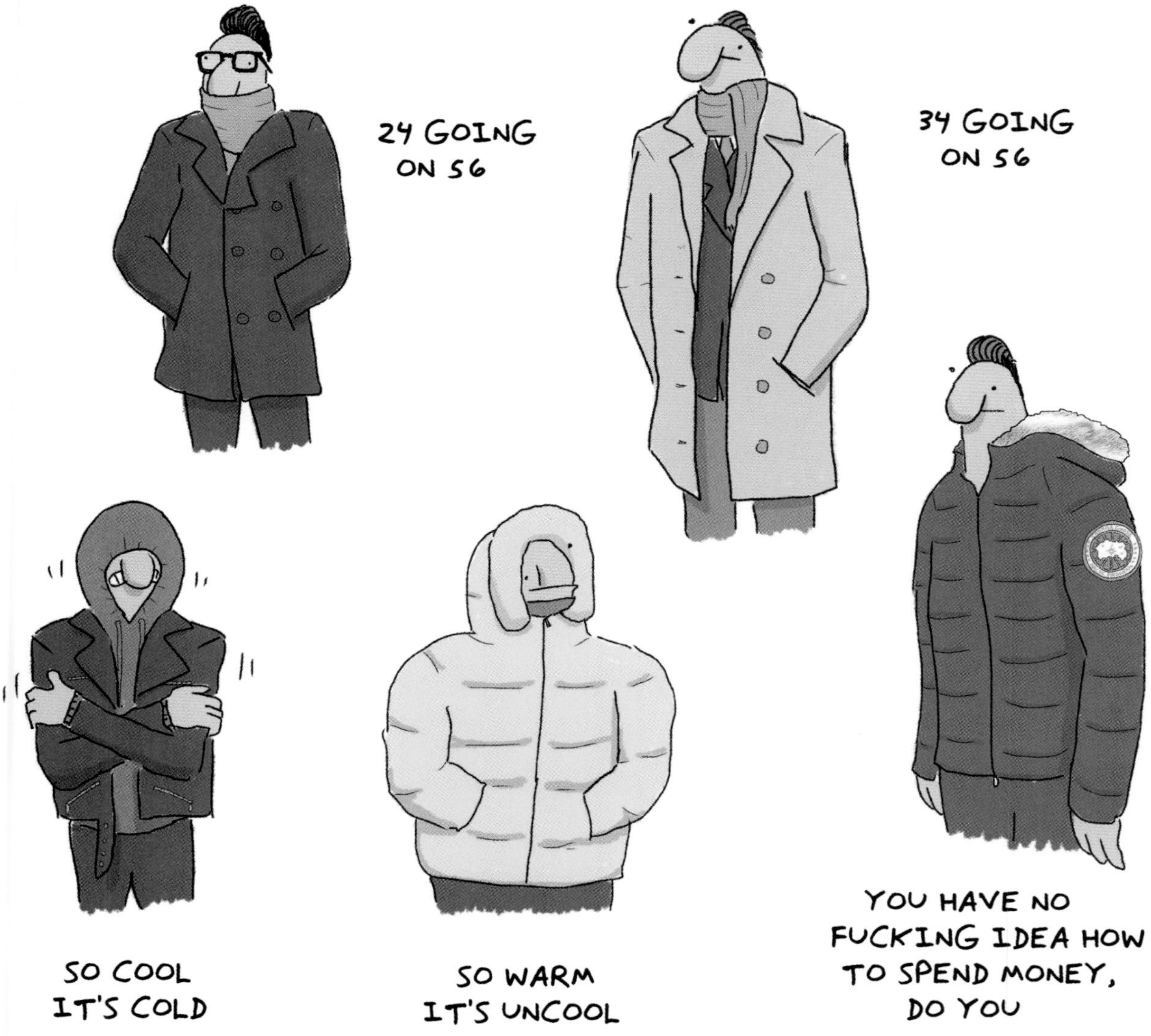
24 GOING ON 56
34 GOING ON 56
SO COOL IT'S COLD
SO WARM IT'S UNCOOL
YOU HAVE NO FUCKING IDEA HOW TO SPEND MONEY, DO YOU

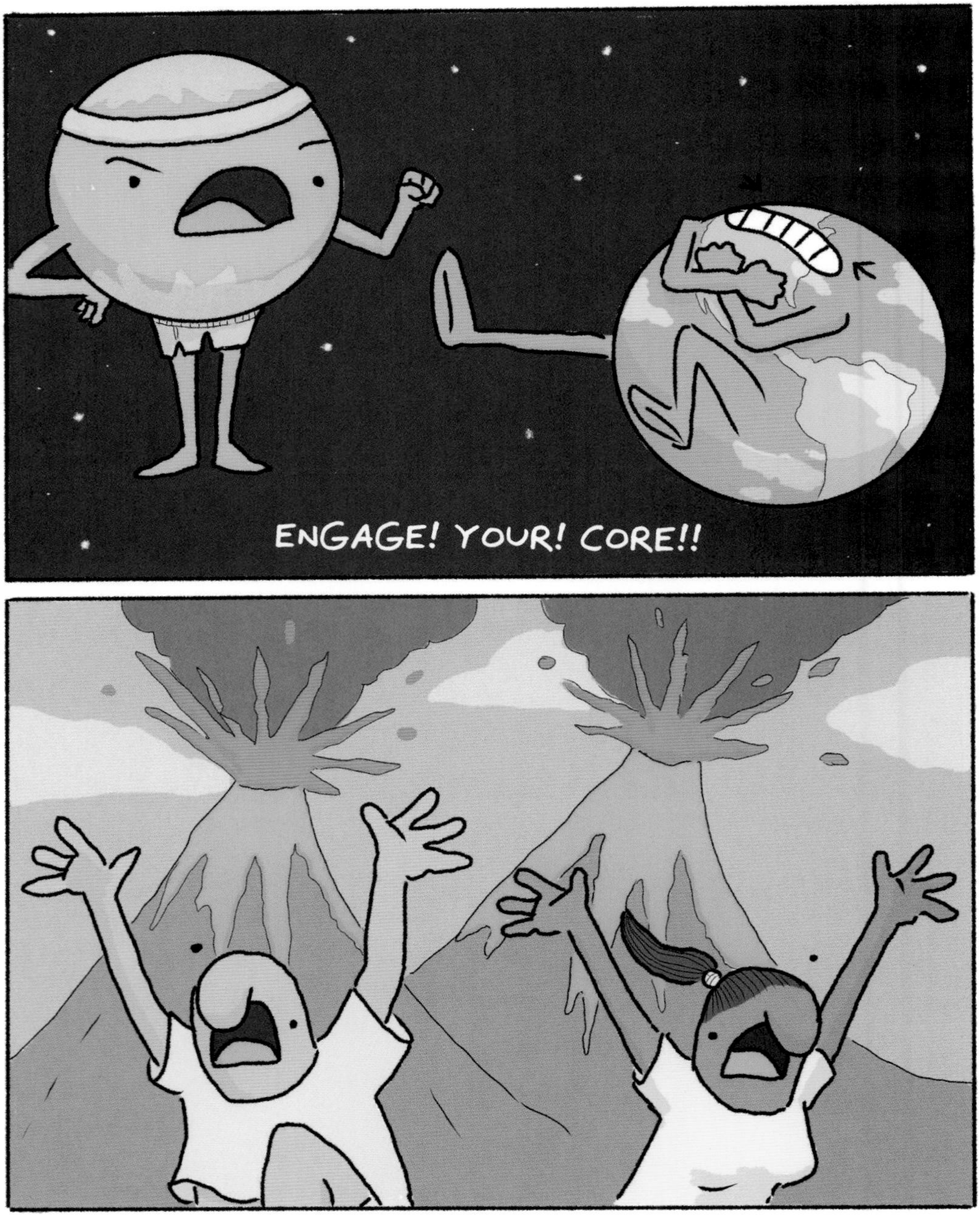
ENGAGE! YOUR! CORE!!

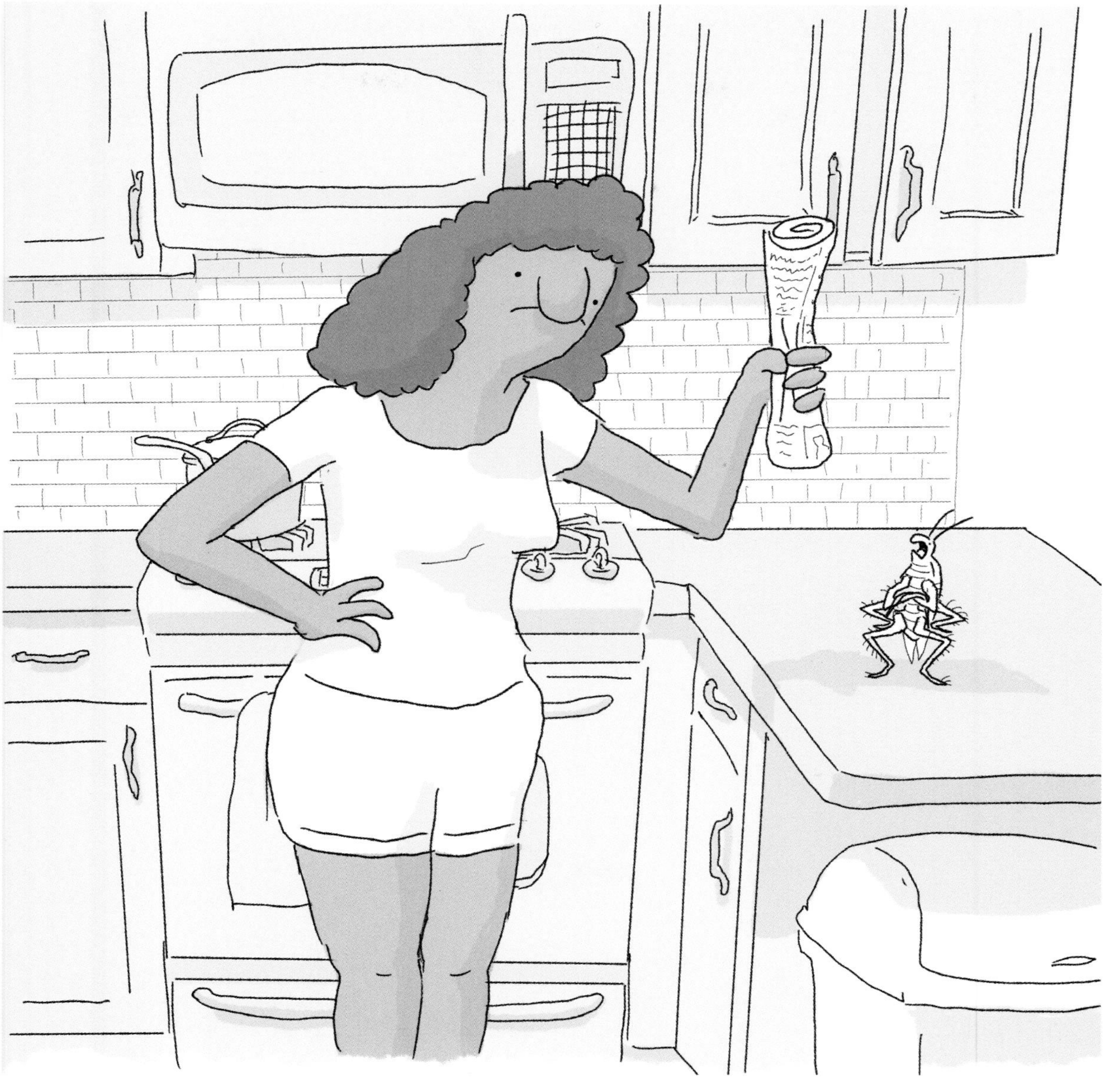

COWARD! YOU'RE JUST AFRAID
TO DEBATE ME ON MY YOUTUBE CHANNEL!

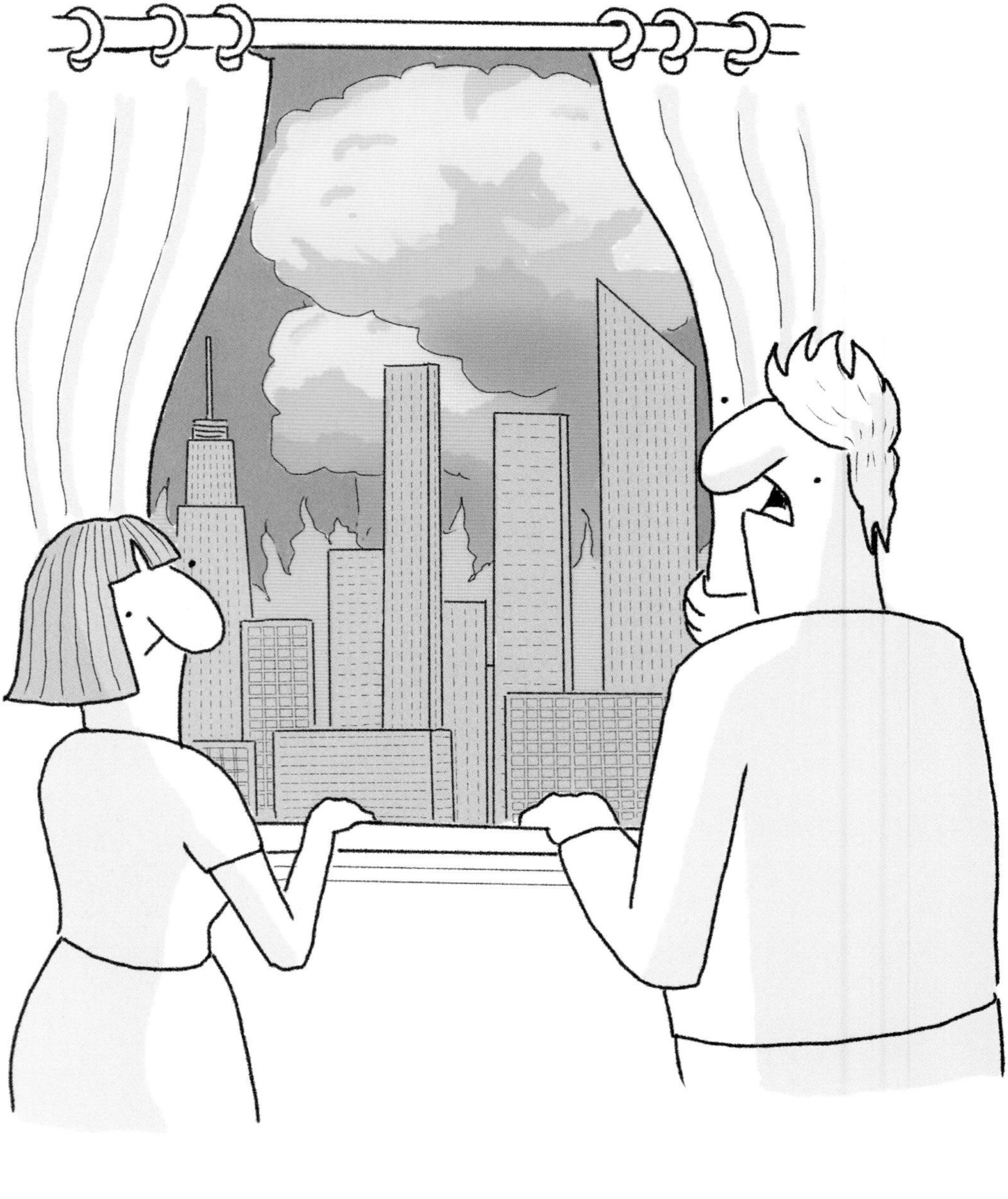

AT LEAST BLACK PANTHER WAS GOOD?

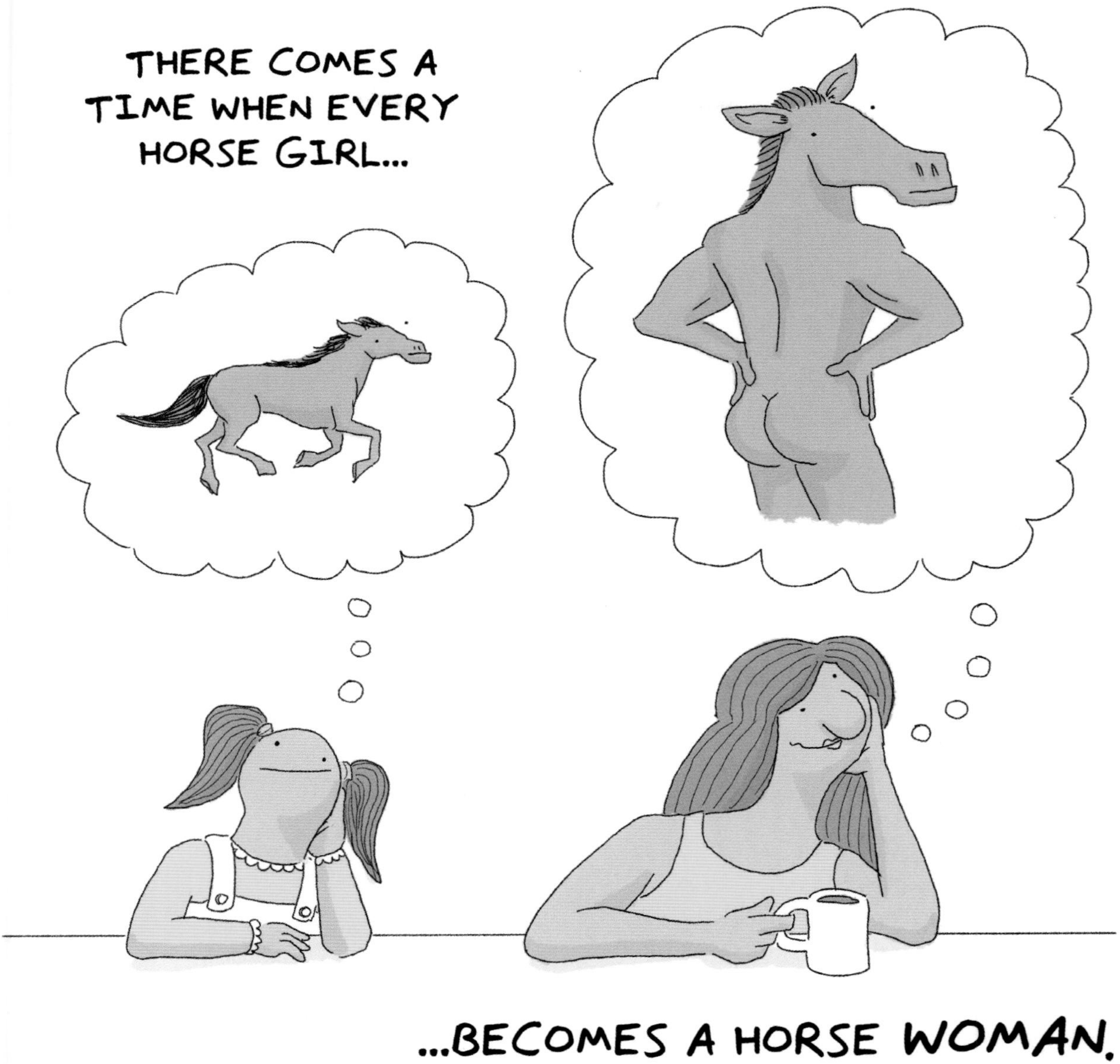
THERE COMES A TIME WHEN EVERY HORSE GIRL...
...BECOMES A HORSE WOMAN.

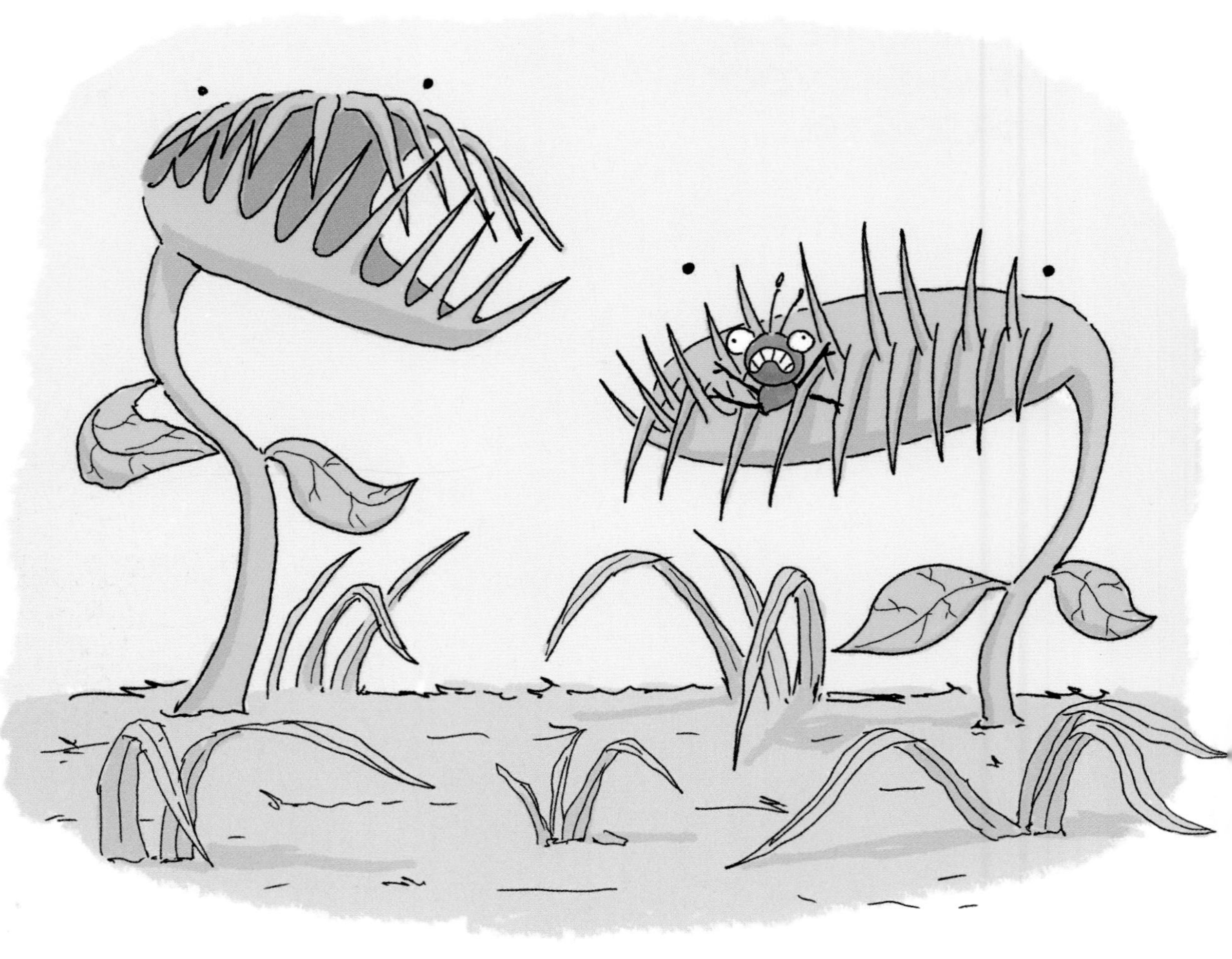

YOU KNOW, LENTILS HAVE TWICE AS MUCH PROTEIN PER SERVING.

A helpful tip from a vegan flytrap.

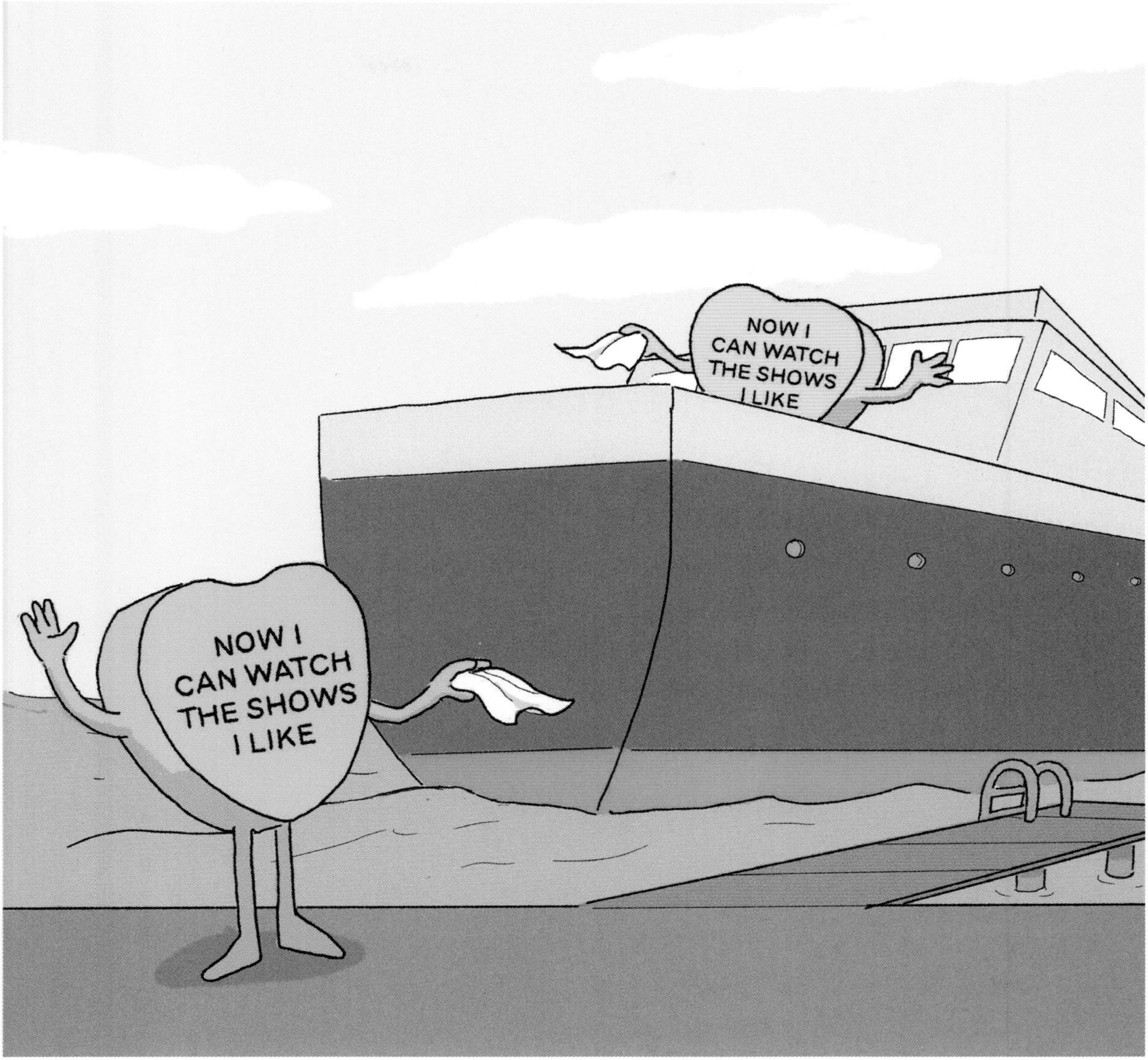
NOW I
CAN WATCH
THE SHOWS
I LIKE
NOW I
CAN WATCH
THE SHOWS
I LIKE

SEE YA LATER,
ALLIGATOR

AFTER WHILE,
CROCODILE

GO FUCK
YOURSELF,
IGUANA

HI, MY BOOK IS DUE TOMORROW

Right now, it is March 20, 2020. America is sliding into a multi-month pandemic lockdown, the stock market is falling apart, and millions of people became unemployed overnight with no clear end in sight. It's hard to imagine there's anyone on earth, let alone America, whose life hasn't been significantly upended over the course of the last week.

Social media is going just about as you'd expect during its first real global crisis. People are sharing panic-inducing, worst-case scenario articles that have left grocery store shelves

THE WORLD ISN'T GOING TO END

IT'S JUST GOING TO SUCK FOR A WHILE

empty, conspiracy theories about how the virus was manufactured by liberals to take down Trump, and fake cures that explain how to stop the global pandemic by gargling salt water and blasting a hair dryer up your nose. But on the other side of human potential: Musicians live-streaming music and conversation. More webcomics than anyone could ever want. FaceTime and Twitch hangouts with close friends and loved ones driven apart by social distancing. Nearly everyone has learned to adjust to the insurmountable awkwardness of FaceTime. It's all right in front of us: the simultaneous beauty and terror of connecting humans at light speed, in all of its color and complexity.

In a way, it's the first crisis where we've really *needed* social media. It's fitting that a pandemic requiring global isolation would happen just in time for all of us to be able to *kinda sorta* pull it off. I say *kinda sorta* because at this point, it does seem fairly unclear whether we are all about to have a nice time with friends on Zoom or lose our minds completely while live-streaming on Instagram, and it is still fairly unclear whether access to that technology will slow or accelerate our unraveling.

It was enough of a shock that I was driven out of semiretirement. Still bobbing around in the wake of the all-too-obvious burnout from doing 500 consecutive days of daily comics, I had become a sporadic comic artist. Now, I'm pushing them out daily. And with genuine enthusiasm! And with public health urgency! I guess I'm becoming a propagandist.

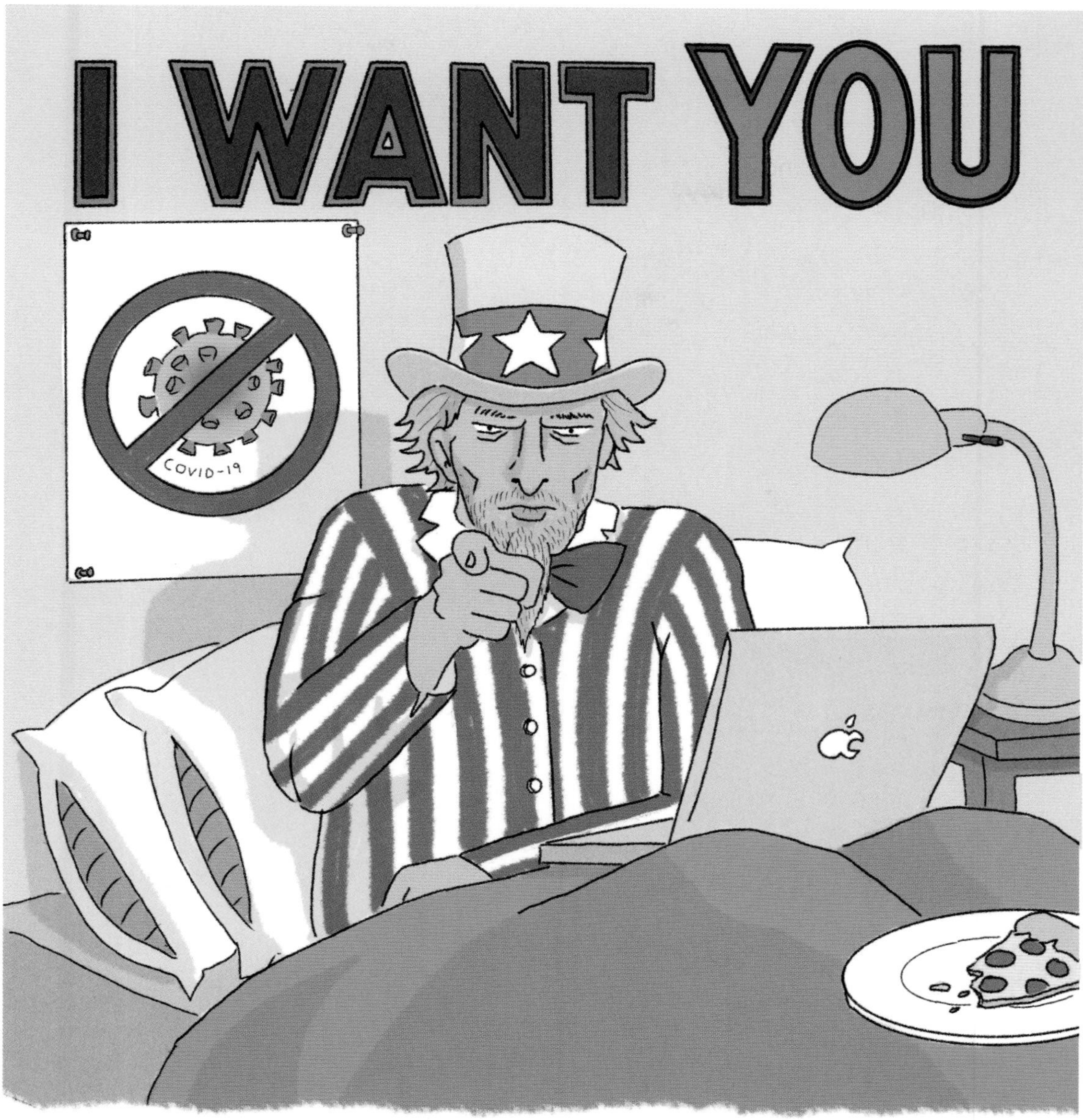
I WANT YOU
COVID-19

TO SIT YOUR ASS IN BED AND WATCH NETFLIX OR WHATEVER

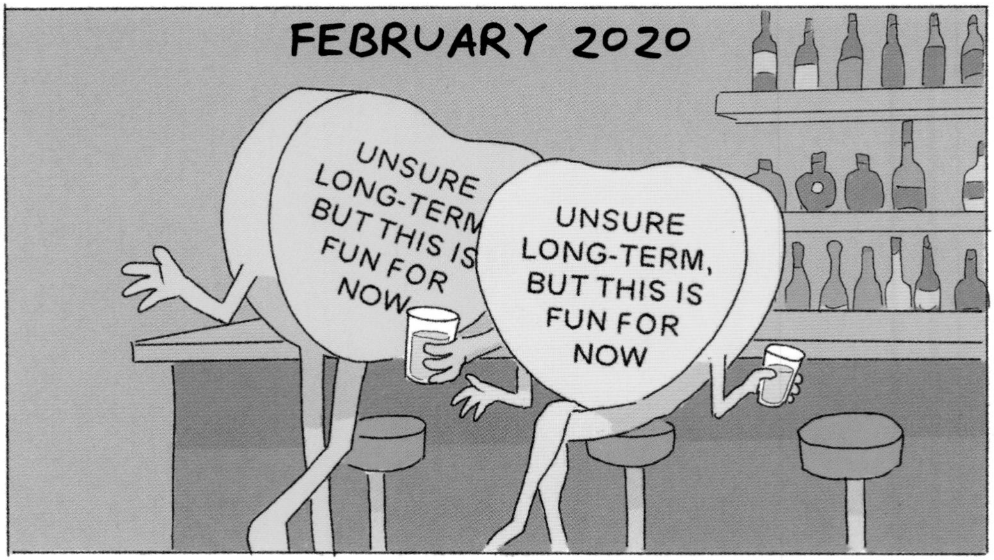
FEBRUARY 2020
UNSURE LONG-TERM BUT THIS IS FUN FOR NOW
UNSURE LONG-TERM, BUT THIS IS FUN FOR NOW

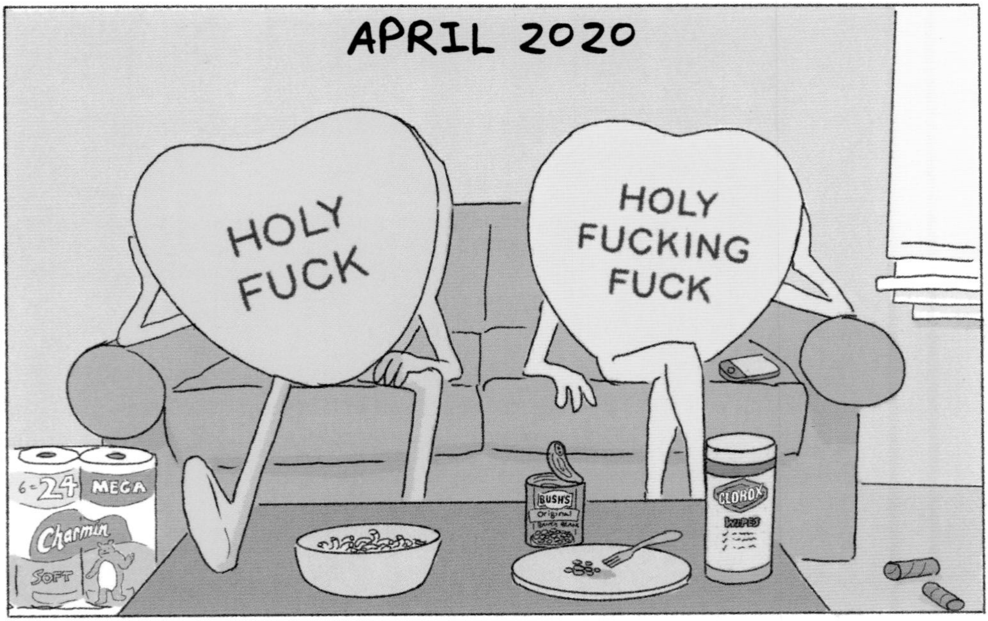
APRIL 2020
HOLY FUCK
HOLY FUCKING FUCK
6=24
MEGA
Charmin
SOFT
BUSH'S
Original
CLOROX
WIPES

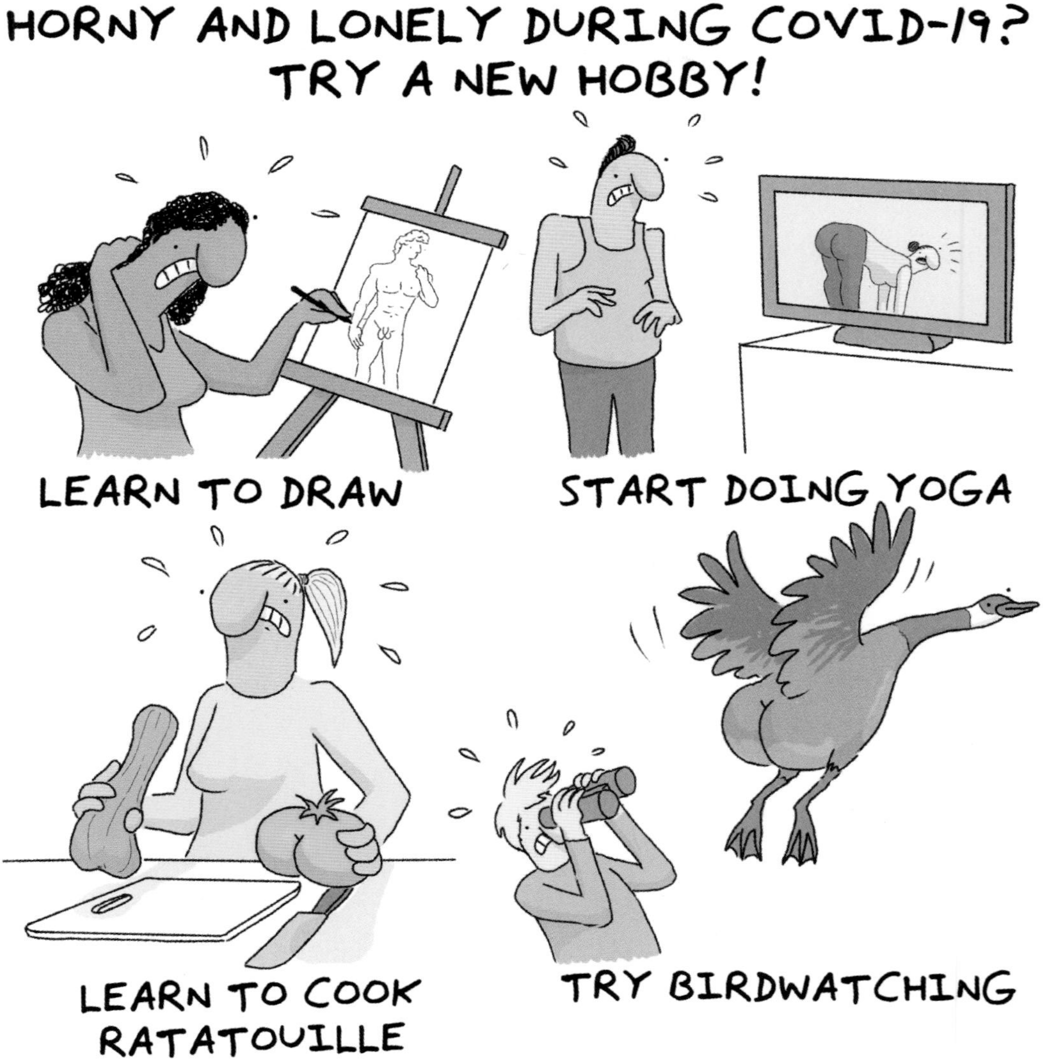

HORNY AND LONELY DURING COVID-19?
TRY A NEW HOBBY!
LEARN TO DRAW
START DOING YOGA
LEARN TO COOK RATATOUILLE
TRY BIRDWATCHING

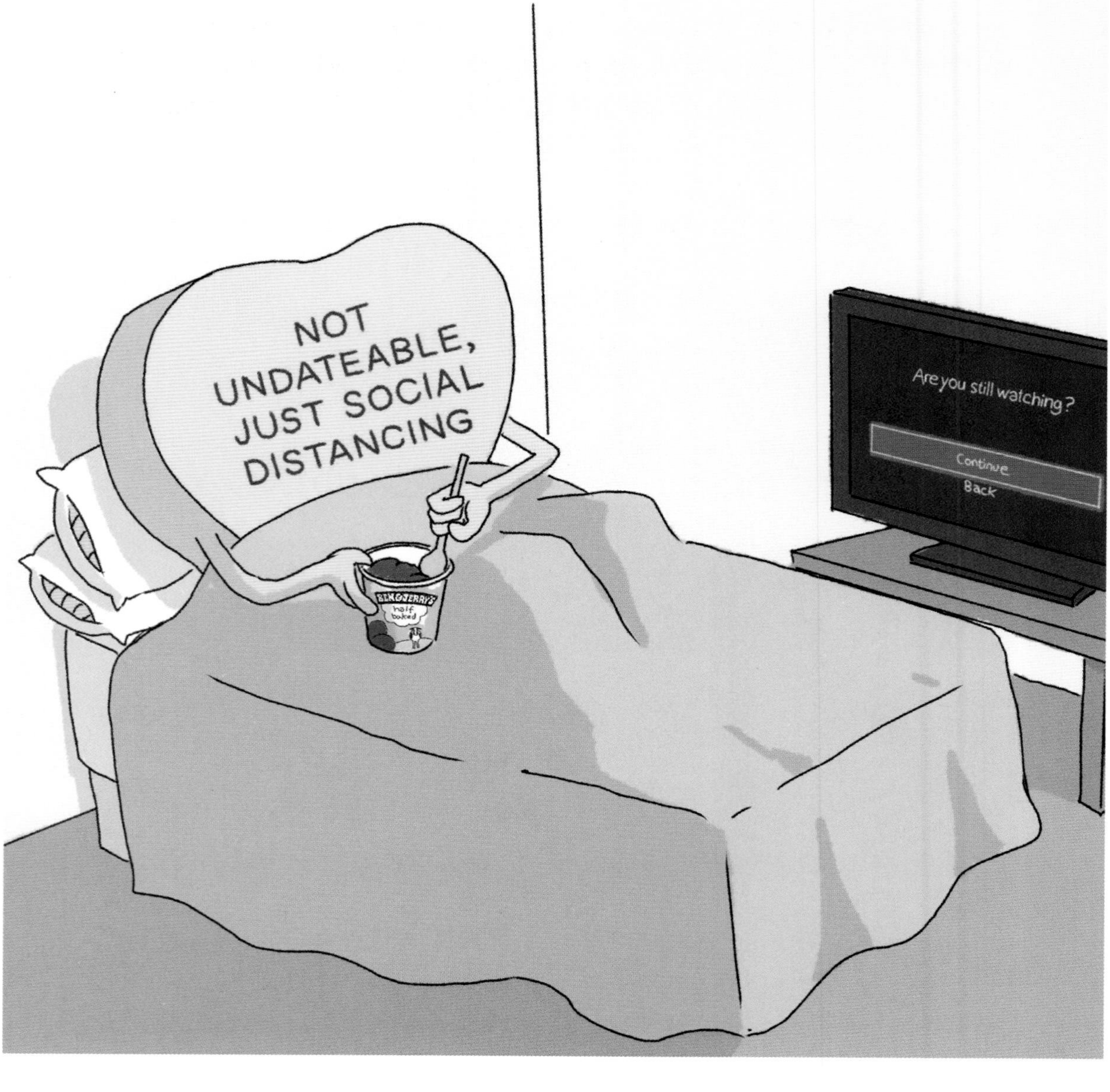
NOT UNDATEABLE, JUST SOCIAL DISTANCING
Are you still watching?
Continue
Back

My phone addiction, as you would expect . . . Well, after months of being under control, it is back with a vengeance, my friends. But my love of comics has returned with full force too. By the time you read this, a lot will have changed — but I know this is true:

I believe in the power of comics.

I believe there is a tiny, unblinking man who lives inside every can of potato chips.

And when the world is just too much? There are always birds to watch.

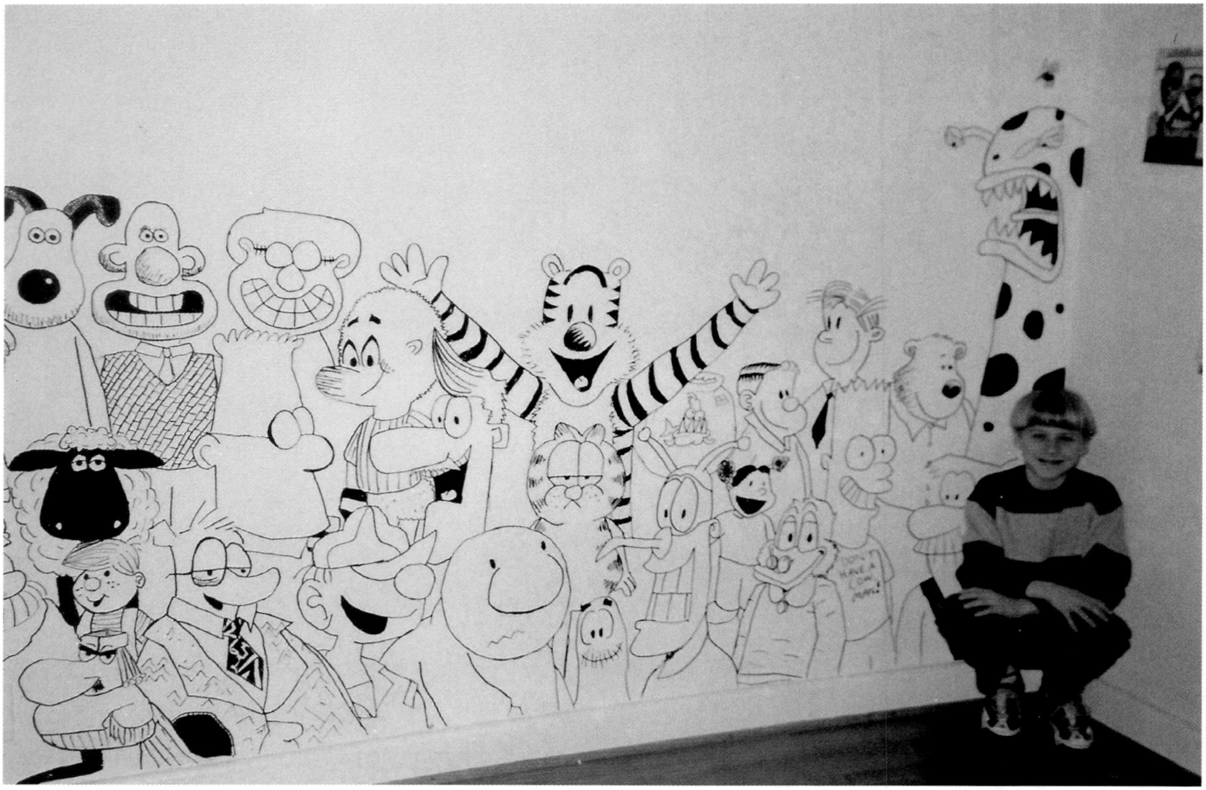
DON'T HAVE A COW MAN!

ACKNOWLEDGMENTS

First and foremost, an endless amount of gratitude to my parents, whose love and encouragement fanned the flames of my comics obsession as a kid. And here's the best proof: Against any responsible adult instinct, they let me draw all over my walls with a Sharpie pen in elementary school.[1] And even though they were convinced I was meant to be a cartoonist, they didn't question my judgment at all when I abandoned art completely to play rock music for a couple of decades.

To my best pal, Dan Kirkwood, who was the coauthor and editor for nearly all of the comics in this book. Living a few time zones away in Alaska, I can't imagine it was all that convenient to start every day with 10 different cartoon captions frantically texted from his caffeine-addled New York friend. I am pleased to report that he always chose the right caption.[2] Here's to another 500 comics, and maybe somewhere in there we'll finally get to make that desert-themed space Americana record we've been talking about.

---

1. Yes, I know you're squinting to figure it out, so I'll save you the effort: I can confirm the existence of a bowl cut in this photo. And it's best to not even imagine my previous haircut. Which was, in fact, a rattail.
2. And better yet, there's no way to ever know if he chose the wrong one.

To Ben Thornewill and Jesse Kristin, my bandmates and musical brothers, for putting up with me during this insane journey and contributing some excellent ideas along the way. "Doop Boop Drummy Drum Drum"[3] remains the funniest punchline in this book, and I didn't even think of it myself, a fact which fills me with blind rage.

To my sister, Julia, who has been a cheerleader for my creative efforts my entire life — and her husband, Andrew Breton, who loyally retweeted a terrifyingly large percentage of my 500 comics. To Siobhan Sanders, whom I owe a lifetime of gratitude. To Billy Libby and Jessie Willen, who made my comics funnier and who helped steer me out of the inevitable burnout. And to all of my family, friends, and loved ones who guided me through this bizarre experience, emotionally and creatively.

To my followers who cheered me on along the way, especially to those who supported my Patreon and gave me a glimmer of hope that it wasn't crazy to try to pursue comics as a career. And to whoever sent me this extremely good DM to the left.

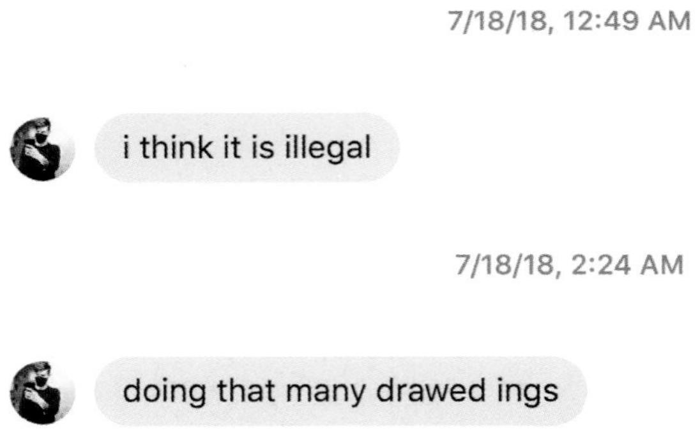
7/18/18, 12:49 AM
i think it is illegal
7/18/18, 2:24 AM
doing that many drawed ings

3. This is on page 42, for reference.

To my friend Deborah Copaken and to my agent Lisa Leshne (and Sam Morrice!) at the Leshne Agency, who believed in my ability to get a book published long before it was reasonable to think so. And to my editor, Lucas Wetzel, who was a total blast to work with and who continued vouching for my work in a professional setting even after I mailed him a Christmas-themed drawing of a naked Stacked-Potato-Chip-Man™ squatting over a chimney. And to production editor Amy Strassner and art director Diane Marsh: You killed it.

And lastly, a thank you to my loyal and hardworking coffee boys, who struggle every day to bring me to baseline functionality. I couldn't have done this without you.

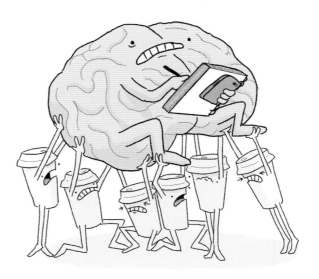

ABOUT THE AUTHOR

Tommy Siegel is a cartoonist and singer/
songwriter/guitarist in the band Jukebox
the Ghost, an internationally touring pop band
with a rabid cult following. In their 15-year
history as a band, they have played over 1,000
shows around the world, including appearances
on late night shows like Letterman and Conan
and festivals like Bonnaroo, Outside Lands,
Firefly, and Lollapalooza. Over years of touring,
Tommy began drawing cartoons by request for
fans of the band via social media during long
drives. In 2018, he started drawing a comic
every day for 500 days, which was eventually
whittled down into his debut comics collection, *I
Hope This Helps*. Born in Richmond, Virginia, he
currently lives in Brooklyn, New York.